MAN AND SOCIETY IN NINETEENTH-CENTURY REALISM

Determinism and Literature

MAURICE LARKIN

© Maurice Larkin 1977

First published 1977 by
THE MACMILLAN PRESS LTD
London and Basingstoke
Associated companies in Delhi
Dublin Hong Kong Johannesburg
Lagos Melbourne New York
Singapore Tokyo

ℓ ISBN 0 333 14155 5

Printed in Great Britain by
BILLING & SONS LTD
Guildford, Worcester and London

9/4/9.

Contents

Foreword
and Acknowledgements

> For twenty-five years he has been chewing over other people's ideas
> about realism, naturalism and all that sort of nonsense; for twenty-five
> years he has been lecturing and writing about things that intelligent
> people have known all the time...
>
> *Uncle Vanya*

Disraeli once remarked that if he wanted to read a book, he wrote one.
While for Disraeli this was perhaps a guarantee that the book would be
worth reading, necessity rather than conviction first prompted this
particular venture. As the non-academic knows from daily experience, life
is an interdisciplinary business. Yet when universities and colleges paid
tribute to the fact by launching a variety of interdisciplinary programmes,
it immediately became apparent that there was a serious shortage of
suitable books. As in the days before the printing-press, the lecturer
reverted to being the fountainhead of knowledge and wisdom; the spoken
word and the cyclostyled sheet acquired an oracular importance. And
although academics were initially flattered by the unaccustomed spectacle
of capacity audiences in their hard-benched lecture theatres, the education
columnists of the quality press were quick to assert a state of 'frustration
and disenchantment' among staff and students alike, especially in the
newer universities.

The paucity of suitable books still remains a problem, despite the
achievements of the last ten years. And the problem becomes especially
difficult when the subject covers several countries as well as disciplines.
The main currents of nineteenth-century literature and thought continue
to be unevenly served, despite the breadth of their appeal among the
general reading public, and despite their entrenched position in degree
syllabuses. It is especially surprising that such a well-trodden field as
Realist literature should have so few introductory surveys that treat it both
internationally and as the product of social and intellectual change. There
is no shortage of outline accounts of Realism, although most of these
confine themselves to the literature of one language. Nor is there a dearth
of social and intellectual histories of the nineteenth century. But few
histories are written with an eye to the requirements of the literature
reader; and of those that are, the majority are restricted to the writers of a
particular country.

Man and Society in Nineteenth-century Realism is unlikely to bring enchantment to the disenchanted, nor can it aspire to allay the suspicions of sceptics—particularly those who have misgivings about interdisciplinary activities. It is intended for the reader who requires an introduction to the determinist issues latent in Realism, and who wants an outline of the circumstances that engendered them. It examines the growing attention that thinkers of the eighteenth and early nineteenth centuries paid to environment and heredity as shaping forces; and it indicates how the social consequences of the French and Industrial Revolutions made writers aware that they were living in a rapidly shifting society that was moulding men in new and often disconcerting ways. The book compares the responses of the better known Realists to these developments: notably Stendhal, Balzac, Büchner, Mrs Gaskell, Flaubert, George Eliot, Turgenev, Tolstoy, Zola, Ibsen, Fontane and Chekhov. It considers their prescriptions for coming to terms with determinism; and it examines in particular the efforts of those who tried to find a foothold for morality and hope in a world where free will and autonomous choices no longer had an assured place, except on the level of subjectivity. Close attention is paid to the more ingenious of those endeavours, notably George Eliot's attempt to resolve the problem by taking a dichotomous view of life, distinguishing 'subjective' from 'objective' reality.

The final chapters look at the Realists' response to the economic changes of the later nineteenth century. They similarly outline the Realists' various reactions to evolutionary concepts of Man. From Balzac to Chekhov, *la bête humaine* had been a prime concern of Realism; and one of the continuing themes of the book is the literary legacy of evolutionary ideas, particularly those of Lamarck, Geoffroy Saint-Hilaire and Darwin.

Most introductions to Realism are concerned with it as a species of creative art, rather than as a response to changing concepts of Man and society. In reversing this emphasis, this book attempts to meet a need among readers for a survey where the focus is as much historical as literary.

The inherent shortcomings of such an undertaking are evident enough. The decision to restrict illustration to a handful of works that are familiar and easily accessible in cheap translation (the editions used are listed at the end of this Foreword) has resulted in some sad omissions. Italian *Verismo* is nowhere represented; and in the case of other literatures, a number of the points at issue could have been more cogently demonstrated by other works and authors, less readily available in English. It may seem odd, for instance, that figures such as Champfleury and Duranty make no appearance. But given the brevity of the book, it seemed advisable to confine it to the authors and works that are the staple fare of the general reader, and which feature widely in the multitude of degree-courses on nineteenth-century literature.

This undertaking owes a great deal to the University of Kent—particularly to the staff and students who participated in the interdisciplinary course on nineteenth-century Realism. Their knowledge and thoughts—and, above all, their scepticism—were a salutary sedative in times of unbuttoned enthusiasm; and if their subsequent warnings have been insufficiently heeded in these pages, it was not for want of trying on their part. On more specific issues, Mr. Edward Greenwood, Professor Maurice Crosland, Mr. John Gooding and Dr. Nicholas Phillipson have been a benevolent source of helpful comment and information. The book has also been very dependent on the patience, as well as the advice, of others. Mr T. M. Farmiloe of Messrs Macmillan has been generous with both, while Mrs Muriel Waring, Miss Beverley Spear and their colleagues completed the typing with remarkable cheerfulness, despite the tightest of schedules. As always, however, it is the writer's unhappy family which bears the burden of any book, and few families have endured so much as in this case. Even at his most dispiriting, the Reverend Edward Casaubon of *Middlemarch* never strained his wife's forebearance to quite the same degree; and if *Man and Society in Nineteenth-century Realism* has much in common with his *Key to all mythologies*, its open incitement to a Will Ladislaw to appear and complicate the marital scene is not the least of them.

September 1976   MAURICE LARKIN

Editions used

The editions mainly cited are Stendhal, *Scarlet and Black*, tr. Margaret R. B. Shaw (Penguin, 1953); Balzac, *Cousin Bette*, tr. Marion A. Crawford (Penguin, 1965); Balzac, *A Harlot High and Low (Splendeurs et misères des courtisanes)*, tr. Rayner Heppenstall (Penguin, 1970); Büchner, *Complete Plays and Prose*, tr. Carl R. Mueller (Hill and Wang, 1963); Mrs. Gaskell, *Mary Barton* (Everyman, 1965); Mrs. Gaskell, *North and South* (Penguin, 1970); Flaubert, *Sentimental Education*, tr. Anthony Goldsmith (Everyman, 1962); George Eliot, *Middlemarch* (Penguin, 1965); George Eliot, *Felix Holt, the Radical* (Panther, 1965); Turgenev, *Fathers and Sons*, tr. Barbara Makanowitzky (Bantam, 1959); Tolstoy, *Anna Karenin*, tr. Rosemary Edmonds (Penguin, 1954); Zola, *L'Assommoir*, tr. Atwood H. Townsend (Signet, 1962); Zola, *Germinal*, tr. L. W. Tancock (Penguin, 1954); Zola, *Earth*, tr. Ann Lindsay (Arrow, 1967); *Four Great Plays by Henrik Ibsen. A Doll's House. Ghosts. An Enemy of the People. The Wild Duck*, tr. R. Farquharson Sharp (Bantam, 1967); Fontane, *Effi Briest*, tr. Douglas Parmée (Penguin, 1967); *Plays by Anton Chehov*, tr. Elisaveta Fen (Penguin, 1964).

1 Beating the Bounds

Like the elephant encountered by the six blind Indians, Realism basks in a multiplicity of meanings. As a term it can be flexible or sharp-edged, depending on whether the scholar's roving hands have chanced upon the tail, the trunk or the tusks. The dozen or so writers whose work provides the focus of this short selective survey exemplify nineteenth-century Realism in the sharp, deterministic meaning of the term; and it is in this fairly assertive sense that 'Realism' is understood in the following outline. Whatever their viewpoint, these particular writers saw Man as the product of heredity and environment, even if they differed in the degee to which they followed the logic of this concept.

'Realism' was only one of their attributes. In several cases, their Realist work was confined to a fairly short-lived phase, preceded and superseded by various excursions into subjective territory. It was sometimes an austere period, suggestive perhaps of a young man's resolute but brief commitment to Temperance or regular exercise. Nor, as a rule, was Realism the most interesting feature of their work: imagination, symbolism and the various ingredients of what used to be called poetic vision were as often as not the qualities that gave it enduring appeal. Even so, their meticulous interest in material reality and their general concern for verisimilitude—the characteristics, in short, that the term 'Realist' most often suggests—were sustained by a firm belief that material factors played a predominant role in shaping men and making them what they were. This had been less true of the so-called 'realists' of the seventeenth and eighteenth centuries. Their interest in verisimilitude had not been so directly linked to their view of humanity. Like their nineteenth-century successors, they wished to enlist the belief of their readers in the characters and situations they describe, thereby increasing the reader's interest and involvement. In these earlier centuries, moreover, when reading was one of the few opportunities of being taken out of oneself, the writer who could enhance the credibility of his imaginary world through the judicious use of material detail was more likely to provide his readers with the escape they sought. If, furthermore, his ultimate aim was to make them return to their own world with more perceptive and more critical eyes, it was all the more important that his imaginary world should be persuasively 'real'. Such realism sprang from the same concerns that prompted many writers to present their narratives in the form of pseudo-authentic documents such as discovered diaries or collections of letters. The reader might not be expected to believe in their authenticity; but at a time when the omniscient narrator was less of an established convention, such devices helped the reader to forget the fictitious nature of the book and grant it a greater measure of sympathy and attention.

It is one of the more genial paradoxes of literature that this concern for realism should have important roots in the comic novel of the seventeenth century. Cervantes (1547–1616) was the most notable example of a number of writers who set about deflating the dramatic improbabilities and high-flown fancy of the traditional romance. Yet although their humour and irony invited the reader to suspend belief, their down-to-earth demonstrations of the limits of human nature gradually encouraged their more serious colleagues to devote more attention to the mundane details of day-to-day living.

The desire to enmesh the reader in the writer's imaginary world continued to be a prime motive of realism in the nineteenth century as earlier. But what was fairly new—and what in some measure gave nineteenth-century Realism its capital 'R'—was its greater concern for material reality as a shaper of Man: a concern which invested the detail of daily existence with an active creative role in the lives of the novelist's main characters, instead of being largely a back-cloth to their activities. Heredity and environment became major protagonists in the drama, until by the time of Zola they were usurping the stage.

'Determinism', 'heredity' and 'environment' are much-employed terms, meaning different things according to context. They are used here in a fairly conventional sense, but the reader in doubt may find Appendix A worth looking at (pp. 175–7). As explained in the appendix, 'heredity' is here understood to embrace the whole human bundle that is transmitted from parents to child by the fact of conception: body, brain and those peculiarities of personality that emanate from them. 'Environment' on the other hand includes everything with which the individual comes in contact between conception and death, including the whole realm of the unexpected, and all that is commonly if misleadingly described as 'chance'. Whereas Hippolyte Taine (1828–93, see pp. 128–30) distinguished *race, milieu* and *moment*, most determinists would regard *moment* as included in *milieu*. In short, 'environment' encompasses far more than it usually signifies when used by planners, social historians and the like. It subsumes every object the individual touches, every book he reads—every sight, sound and smell that may or may not affect his thoughts and feelings, consciously or unconsciously.

To prevent misunderstanding, it is perhaps also worth indicating at this point how 'determinism' was broadly understood in the context of nineteenth-century Realism. As explained in Appendix A, most determinists accepted that the individual had an identity that was separate from the influences acting upon him. They also accepted that the individual made active choices between alternative courses of action. He was not a mere forum in which two or more rival attractions fought for predominance; he had opinions and predilections that might in fact be stronger than the attractions of the alternatives before him. The bulk of determinists also recognised the reality of the choosing process; and they were aware that choices were often long and agonising precisely because of the absence of external constraint and because of the seeming 'freedom' open to the chooser. Yet in recognising the active identity of the chooser, they insisted that his identity and predilections were themselves the outcome of inherited traits, past experience and current needs. Similarly the alternatives that presented themselves to him were the product of circumstance: their nature and availability were ultimately determined by factors that lay outside the chooser's control. How he would react to them would depend not only on his tastes, but also on the circumstances and frame of mind he happened to be in.

An omniscient being, with all the data, would theoretically be able to predict the choice. But to posit determinism was not to posit prediction as a human possibility. Few nineteenth-century determinists envisaged a time when humanity could lay hands on all the data that would put prediction within its grasp. The odyssey and sources of merely one man's thoughts and inclinations would alone bankrupt the resources and ingenuity of any research team. However, these and other problems are looked at more specifically in Appendix A.

To translate determinism into fiction was an attractive if challenging task. The omniscient narrator had at his command all the causal factors that eluded the biographer. Only in fiction could determinism be demonstrated in all its plenitude, since the novelist was both manufacturer and manipulator of the complex of causal influences that made his characters what they were. There were, however, formidable difficulties. Heredity was not an easy subject for imaginative literature, especially in view of the rudimentary state of nineteenth-century knowledge on the matter (see pp. 126–31). There was in consequence a tendency for Realist authors merely to assert the hereditary factors, without making much effort to demonstrate them. Family resemblances might be brought out by similarities of conduct in certain situations; but that was about as far as it went. Whenever inherited characteristics were invoked, the reader usually had to take the author's assertions about his characters on trust, without having much opportunity for discerning them for himself. Environment, however, was a different matter. Its influence was visible and could be described in absorbing detail. The formative pressures of the family, school, work and marriage were all familiar ingredients of the Realist novel; the interrelation of developing characters, and the moulding influence they had on each other, were at the centre of its appeal.

Not that the nineteenth-century Realists invented 'the psychological novel', or the novel that portrays society. Daniel Defoe's *Moll Flanders*

(1722) was but one illustration that the early eighteenth century could produce a novel that not only presented a slice of life, however thin, but also made a significant attempt to show the individual as a product of society. Nothing could be more explicit than Moll's own explanation of her downfall: 'My mother was convicted of felony for a petty theft . . . and left me about half a year old, and in bad hands you may be sure.' Moll was now left, in her own words, a

> desolate girl without friends, without clothes, without help or helper, as was my fate; and by which, I was not only exposed to very great distresses, even before I was capable either of understanding my case or how to amend it, but brought into a course of life, scandalous in itself, and which in its ordinary course tended to the swift destruction both of soul and body.

And the opening chapters proceed to demonstrate this in detail. Indeed, when it came to the seamier side of life, a number of the eighteenth-century novelists were more forthright and explicit in their analysis than many of their nineteenth-century compeers, especially in England. Similarly there were eighteenth-century novels that pursued the theme of determinism with more relentlessness than all but a few of their Realist successors. The two best-known were significantly both humorous, Laurence Sterne's *The Life and Opinions of Tristram Shandy* (1759–67) and Denis Diderot's *Jacques le Fataliste*, written in 1772. For just as the seventeenth century had bred realistic description as a sardonic rejoinder to the high-flown improbabilities of the romance, so the eighteenth century, gingerly sampling Locke (1632–1704, see pp. 18–19) and his more ruthless successors, resorted to humour to demonstrate the implications of determinism for human self-respect. In this case, however, the laughter was not that of disbelief, but rather the laughter of recognition—recognition of the absurdity of the human condition, and recognition of the need to seize what comforts life had to offer. It was also, some might think, a laughter that was not unmixed with nervousness. Established beliefs and their consolations were clearly at risk—as indeed was any concept of Man that based his self-esteem on his supposed free will; the implications were too momentous to be accepted without a certain wariness. It was less upsetting to survey them through the protective bars of humour. The *frisson* experienced by the reader with traditionalist assumptions was initially a vicarious one; it was only on reflection that it took on a general significance with far-reaching personal implications. Not that the comic genius of Sterne and his colleagues was a mere cover for passing-off combustible goods; humour for them was also an end in itself. But the laughter was louder for having ambivalent undertones (see Appendix B, p. 178).

By the nineteenth century, however, especially in France, determinist ideas were too familiar a segment of the intellectual spectrum to warrant coyness on the novelist's part. Although such ideas might command the allegiance of only a small minority of the thinking public, the rest were less likely to be shocked by assumptions that had in fact been official government thinking in the 1790s (see pp. 26–9); indeed the curricula of the Revolutionary state secondary schools had briefly been based upon them (see pp. 26–8). Novelists themselves were readier to face up to the consequences of their own determinist leanings, even though in some cases they might still indulge in a certain ideological schizophrenia, balancing determinism on one hand with a utilitarian or emotional respect for traditional morality and religion on the other (see pp. 50–1).

Not only was the determinist novel of the nineteenth century a more confident affair, but the focus of its attention was markedly different. It became increasingly preoccupied with social change. Earlier writers, such as Defoe, (1660–1731), had portrayed the impact of society on the individual. And yet despite the freshness and clarity of Defoe's description of the thrusting mercantile world of late seventeenth-century London, his novels depict it in relatively static terms, in that there is little hint of major social change or movement. This is all the more significant when one considers Defoe's closeness to the pulse of politics and commercial life in Britain, and his awareness of the social dimension to the far-reaching political developments he had witnessed. His political and descriptive journalism, as well as his novels, reflects the slower pace of social change in Defoe's time. Although several decades separated the historical setting of *Moll Flanders* from its actual composition, Defoe had much less reason than Balzac or George Eliot to regard an interval of this length as setting him apart from the period he was describing. Admittedly the novel's first-person narrative form limits Defoe's opportunity for direct comment. Yet the reader is given virtually no dates, other than the concluding line 'written in the year 1683', and the story has no clear chronological span.

This was not the case with the nineteenth-century Realist novel. More often than not, time was pin-pointed with an uncompromising precision— as is immediately apparent from the opening sentences of a number of the novels examined in this survey. Balzac begins *La Cousine Bette* (1846): 'Towards the middle of July, in the year 1838, one of those vehicles called *milords*, then appearing in the Paris squares for the first time, was driving along the rue de l'Université'. In the same vein, Turgenev opens *Fathers and Sons* (1862): ' "Well, Piotr? Still nothing in sight?" asked a gentleman on the 20th of May, 1859, as he came out of the porch of the stage-coach inn'. If anything, Flaubert cuts it even sharper (*L'Education Sentimentale*, 1869): 'On the 15th September, 1840, about six o'clock in the morning, the *Ville-de-Montereau* was ready to sail from the quai Saint-Bernard, and clouds of smoke were pouring from its funnel.'

Nor was *le sans façon anglais* to be outdone; the first chapter of George Eliot's *Felix Holt* (1866) begins by telling the reader: 'On the 1st of September, in the memorable year 1832, some one was expected at Transome Court'. The indications of time in *Middlemarch* (1871–2) are admittedly much subtler, but are nonetheless there. By taking note of the political events to which the characters refer in their conversations, it is clear that the action of the novel takes place between 30 September 1829 and the end of May 1832.

Although this concern for chronological precision followed to some extent the current fashion of the historical novel, it also reflected the fact that society was changing rapidly. Even ten years either way could make a considerable difference to the mental image and expectations that the reader's imagination would create around a book's main characters. In novels that were increasingly concerned with the influence of society on the individual, it was particularly important that the writer should make it precisely clear when the action was taking place. Society in western Europe was changing at a speed which no previous generation had ever experienced. Britain, Belgium, France—and, later, Germany—were being visibly transformed by the momentous economic and political developments that had their roots in the last decade of the previous century. The Industrial Revolution was slowly spreading from Britain into western Europe, while the political and military disturbances that had earlier taken fire with the French Revolution, inaugurated a series of social changes that accelerated and diversified this transformation. The nineteenth century saw more visible change than the two previous centuries put together. Had Shakespeare visited England in the 1770s he would doubtless have noticed many changes—but far fewer than George Eliot saw in her own lifetime (1819–80). In 1812, when Dickens was born, the vast majority of people in western Europe earned their livelihood through agriculture (although in Britain this was true of only one in three); yet by 1870, the year of his death, only one in seven of the British population lived off the land, while even in France, the granary of western Europe, the proportion had sunk to a half.

Moreover, the economists of the time were aware of these changes, and their comments were increasingly echoed in contemporary literature. Not only was the nineteenth century recognised as very different from its predecessors but its perspective enabled both economists and novelists to discern clearly for the first time the changes that had been taking place before 1800. Eighteenth-century novels had shown remarkably little awareness of contemporary shifts in the pattern of rural and urban life in England. In a pre-railway age when communications were still rudimentary, it had been difficult for any individual to acquire an overall view of what was happening in the country as a whole. It was only in the nineteenth century that writers were given the geographical as well as the historical perspective to appreciate the extent of these changes. No previous generation of writers had felt so conscious of living in a shifting environment.

PART ONE

Stendhal, Balzac and Determinism

The social and intellectual context

2 The Shaping Forces of Society: Stendhal's Europe

Calendars, clocks and strong coffee were as essential to the art of Balzac as pen and paper; in a much subtler way, the same was almost as true of Stendhal. Both were men of their time in their concern for the detail and chronology of social change. If the indications in Stendhal's novels were often indirect—and occasionally coyly concealed—they were cheerfully overt with Balzac. This chapter attempts to provide a brief outline of the rapid and far-reaching social changes that made writers of their generation especially aware of society as a determining force.

Viewed as a whole, the greatest transformer of nineteenth-century society was the Industrial Revolution. Yet when the Realist novel emerged in France in the 1830s, the social change that encouraged it was not as yet primarily industrial. What impressed Stendhal (1783–1842) and Balzac (1799–1850) was not the factories and urban overcrowding that began to characterise certain very restricted areas of France, but the fact that power and esteem were shifting ground from one class of notables to another. This was a development which owed its shape and speed as much to political events as to the economic factors which underlay them and gave them meaning. What had been a long gradual process in Britain, unfolding since the seventeenth century, had in France taken the form of a series of rapid convulsions; a belated and therefore violent response to the failure of political change to keep pace with economic change.

Defoe (1660–1731) had portrayed an England where commercial interests were politically as well as economically important. And, as Henry Fielding (1707–54) and others had shown, it was a society where talent, money and lack of scruple could challenge noble birth and win. This advancement of the middle classes, however, was the product of a steady continuous adjustment of social and political attitudes to the facts of a changing economy, and in which the landmarks were of a subtler nature than in France. The upheavals of 1640–60 and 1688 meant much to a Defoe, yet they were less stridently assertive as socio-political turning-points than the 1790s were to be abroad. For one thing, the distinction between classes was much less marked than in France, and the man of wealth or talent crossed the frontiers more easily. And what he found on crossing them was not an Eldorado of exclusive privilege. The possibilities open to him still depended on his personal wealth and ability rather than on the perquisites of the class he had entered. The struggle between crown and parliament in seventeenth-century England was primarily a political struggle, in which the class issues were only partially explicit. It was mainly in retrospect that its influence on social evolution became fully apparent.

In such a society, a man's fortunes were largely the product of personal or family circumstance and his own activity. Employers, landlords and local magnates counted for more in his life than the state. The larger forces of the outside world impinged on him mainly in the shape of bad harvests and disease—'natural' phenomena which lay outside society's control and making. Wars and perhaps new taxes were the only major form of state-made event that might radically alter his life, and it was here that private lives and 'history' came into sharpest collision. 'Natural' disasters might shape 'history' but were not regarded as part of it—'history' being largely thought of as a record of human activity, in which human motivation and responsibility provided the main interest. As far as novelists were concerned, wars were the principal occasions on which 'history' intervened in their narrative. Otherwise the decisive events which befell their heroes were largely of a personal or circumstantial nature: encounters with other people, accidents, or strokes of good fortune. There was little need or inducement to place the novel in a precisely defined time span. If the hero was involved in some major 'natural' catastrophe, such as an epidemic or a famine, this did not require to be historically identified, since such happenings were seen as outside 'history', each being much like another, with no particular claim to belonging exclusively to a specific point in history. If wars were frequently left equally vague, they were often the only point of specific chronological reference in the book. Consequently, even a master of topographical and commercial precision such as Daniel Defoe, who traces the perambulations and finances of his characters with minutest care, even he gives his readers only rarely an indication of the year, or even the decade, when the action of his novel is taking place. (Novels that adopted an epistolary, diary or memoir form often contained a specific series of dates, corresponding to particular entries. But even in these cases, the year was often omitted.)

If the gradualism of change in England was reflected in the soft chronological focus of the English eighteenth-century novel, the violence and speed with which the pent-up forces of change eventually swept the Continent had its counterpart in the sharp precision of nineteenth-century Realism.

The establishment of revolutionary governments in France, the Low Countries and large parts of Italy and Germany had far-reaching effects on the lives of the population, even though these governments were short-lived. If the French Revolution created equality before the law, it made wealth and talent the criteria of power and influence. The last decades of the *ancien régime* had seen an aristocracy of birth tightening its grip on the offices of state. Whereas earlier monarchs had made use of able commoners by ennobling them, the aristocracy under Louis XVI (1774–92) became increasingly resentful of dilution from below, and insisted that the incumbents of military and judicial positions should be nobles of several generations' standing. It was therefore not surprising that the driving force behind the Revolution should be the professional bourgeoisie, whose aspirations were threatened by the increasingly aristocratic character of government service. Many of them were lawyers and civil servants, their legal training and administrative experience making them the most articulate spokesmen of the third estate. Their demands for the abolition of noble privileges and the creation of *la carrière ouverte aux talents* may have been largely the product of self-interest, but these aims were of equal interest to the mercantile and propertied bourgeoisie. The merchant, manufacturer and middle-class landowner likewise stood to gain enormously by a more equitable sharing of the tax burden among the three estates, while their sons and nephews would have the chance of attractive careers in the public service. Given this broad congruity of interest between the professional and commercial bourgeoisie, it is not surprising that the merchants, bankers and manufacturers should show little inclination to seek election to the various revolutionary assemblies, where their professional counterparts were so ably pulling the chestnuts out of the fire; their time was better spent nurturing the family business. There was as yet little divergence of interest between the two halves of the bourgeoisie. Common enemies united them, and nearly a century was to elapse before their respective roles of producer and consumer were to clash on such issues as protective tariffs and commodity prices. Even then, their common enemies were to keep them in constant touch, especially when socialists on the one hand or restive landlords on the other attempted to challenge their supremacy.

The Revolutionary reforms were largely initiated and steered by the professional bourgeoisie; yet it was the propertied and commercial bourgoisie who perhaps made most of them. With notable exceptions, the biggest prizes were still to be gained in economic enterprise, rather than professional practice; and when the Revolutionary and Napoleonic tides eventually receded, it was the propertied bourgeoisie, the owners of the means of production, who found themselves with the better part of the beach, financially speaking. It was they who had most to gain in a society where old restrictions were removed, and where the working classes had neither the protection of the old guild system nor as yet the right to strike or have unions. Such government restrictions as existed were mainly aimed at protecting French manufacturers against foreign competition, and, with memorable exceptions, they worked to the advantage of the producer rather than consumer—although protection of this kind also had the important social consequence of preserving a relatively high level of employment.

The professional bourgeoisie for their part could profit from *la carrière ouverte aux talents* and it was they who provided the administrative élite who governed western Europe during the years when revolution had the upper hand. Despite the set-backs of the Restoration period, their role in government was to continue expanding throughout the nineteenth century; and in countries like France the legal profession was to provide a large percentage of prime ministers and senior cabinet members in the later decades of the period. Even so, this was power and influence that was ostensibly exercised on the community's behalf; their activities were limited by others' mandates and confined to brief terms of office. The influence of the propertied bourgeoisie, on the other hand, lasted as long as their wealth—which could be a matter of generations.

There were also the massive indirect changes that the Revolution made in society. It thrust Europe into twenty-three years of semi-continuous war, with enormous consequences, not only for the millions who fought in Europe's first conscript armies, but for the countless others who made or lost money as a result of the economic repercussions of the war. Men of modest origins won rapid advancement in the army and in the expanding administration of the Napoleonic empire. There was also the wealth to be won through government contracts or through the acquisition of concessions in defeated countries, to say nothing of the elimination of commercial rivals at home and abroad. Conversely many businesses of long standing found their traditional patterns of trade disrupted, and lost ground to the opportunists whose fortunes were made by war. The same was true in the occupied and satellite countries, where indigenous merchants and manufacturers, who knew when to turn with the tide, were able to make considerable pickings at the expense of their less flexible neighbours.

Nor did the peace settlement of 1815 bring a return to the relative social stability of the *ancien régime*. The economic and political developments of the last thirty years had set in motion a process of social change which gathered momentum as peace-time conditions permitted the uninterrupted expansion of economic enterprise. Revolutionary activity was far from dead. 1830 and 1848 brought violent adjustments to the government of various states which forced them to take increased account of the shift of wealth and influence in nineteenth-century society. All this made for marked differences between one decade and another, and goes far to account for the Realist writers' concern for chronological precision.

Stendhal, society and politics

Stendhal admired genius. Yet for him, men like Danton and Napoleon were the product of their time rather than its architects—despite the lasting impact a Napoleon might make on society. For all Stendhal's cult of the will, he recognised that different times made different men.

Like Defoe, Stendhal knew the world at first hand, having played a variety of active roles during the Napoleonic Wars, until the Bourbon Restoration of 1814/15 drove him into embittered spectatorship. Son of a Grenoblois lawyer, the influence of distant relatives had brought him a staff-attachment to General Michaud in Italy in the early years of the Consulate. And then, after five years of ill-health in Paris, he had obtained a succession of government appointments and missions which took him to Austria, Prussia and eventually Moscow, where he witnessed the great fire and the French retreat. With a respected position and a respectable salary, he was able to sample the social life of the Empire at the height of its influence in Europe. When Napoleon's fall put an end to this glittering series of assignments, his life became largely a literary one. Restoration France had little to offer to an ex-Napoleonic official with liberal sympathies; and it was only with the revolution of 1830 that he entered government service once more.

Like Balzac, Stendhal recognised what the upheavals of 1789–1815 had unleashed, especially the expectations aroused by *la carrière ouverte aux talents*. Despite the attempts of the Bourbon Restoration to sit on this Pandora's box, these expectations could not easily be squashed into quiescence. If their reflection in Stendhal's fiction is less prolific than in Balzac's menagerie of social types, it is arguably more perceptive and persuasive. Balzac's fresco of early nineteenth-century France includes a host of boldly drawn examples of both the mercantile and professional bourgeoisie: men whose fortunes were tossed dramatically up and down by the successive changes of the Revolution, the Empire and the Restoration. Stendhal's spectrum, however, was less wide; and although *Lucien Leuwen* (written in 1834–5) was to give a pungent impression of the mercantile bourgeoisie in the 1830s, his most successful literary creation was arguably Julien Sorel, *paradigme exalté* of all those whose hopes essentially lay in *la carrière ouverte aux talents*. Son of a small sawmill proprietor of peasant stock, Sorel represents in particular the ambition of the *petit bourgeois* with talents and aspirations beyond his birth or fortune. It is his frustration under the Restoration—frustration above all with its attempt to restrict office once more to the old *notables* and their nominees—that makes *Le Rouge et le Noir* (1830) '*une chronique du XIX siècle*', as Stendhal claimed.

Stendhal had already observed in *Promenades dans Rome* (1829),

While the upper classes of Parisian society seem to have lost the faculty of strong and consistent feeling, the passions express themselves with a terrifying energy among the petty bourgeoisie, among young people who . . . have received a good education but whose lack of fortune obliges them to labour . . . Probably all the great men of the future will come of [this] class.

Symptomatically Sorel stands for social mobility rather than the creation of a juster society. When circumstance puts influence in Sorel's hands, he shows little inclination to use it in the interests of the less fortunate. And, for all his contempt for the upper echelons of Restoration society, he feels little affection for the class he has left behind him, other than for his few friends.

The novel has a double perspective. On the one hand it describes the impact of the Revolutionary and Napoleonic experience on the generation that lived after it. And, on the other, it demonstrates how the Bourbon Restoration (1815–30) shaped the outlook and attitudes of those it governed. On both scores it shows men as the product of the determining forces of society.

In his unflattering survey of Restoration France, Stendhal's motives were undoubtedly mixed: his ink was liberally laced with the juice of sour grapes. Yet although he could scarcely claim to be a dispassionate observer, his perspective was solidly based on a coherent concept of the nature of Man and on what his experience of successive regimes had taught him. His view of Man is examined in the following chapter (see pp. 21–6). But its implications for his political outlook were to put a premium on integrity (see pp. 24–5). He measured regimes by their readiness to allow their citizens to develop along their own chosen lines. This required honesty on the part of the regime—a sincere statement of its aims and expectations—and honesty on the part of the individual—especially in his analysis and recognition of his own motives and desires. He saw the Bourbon Restoration, with its self-interested alliance of throne and altar masquerading as piety, as an affront to both these criteria. Not only was it dishonest in what it professed to be; but it effectively encouraged its citizens to be likewise dishonest, since it only bestowed its favours on those who genuflected before its official beliefs and attitudes.

Julien Sorel is a case in point. Believing the Church to be the only career where a man of modest means can make his mark under the Restoration, he embarks on a profession for which he has no vocation other than ambition. He is obliged to be continually false to his nature and inclinations; and in the course of his various occupations, he observes that this is true of society in general. The young noblemen of the Faubourg St. Germain observe a polite ritual which allows no place for strength or sincerity of utterance, let alone action. And the provincial bourgeoisie, who are obsessed with material wealth and the outward signs of it, seek advancement through professing a conventional piety and loyalty to the throne. Stendhal had no illusions as to the nature of the provincial *notables*. They would be avaricious and philistine under any regime; as they had been under the Empire, and the Revolution, and the *ancien régime* before that. But the Restoration had implanted in them the added trait of hypocrisy. And for Stendhal, such a regime was the death of genius.

Stendhal had a fine nose for changes of ethos, even within the single span of individual governments. Although his personal fortunes had been closely geared to those of the Napoleonic regime, he had grown increasingly critical of the changing character of government during the Consulate (1799–1804). His liberalism was deep-rooted; and although his boyhood Jacobinism had begun as a reaction to the *bien pensant* royalism of his father's household (see p. 21), it had quickly acquired a momentum of its own. He regarded Napoleon's Concordat with the Papacy (1801) as an affront to the secular achievements of the Revolution, just as the creation of the Empire itself (1804) and an Imperial nobility (1808) struck him as a betrayal of democratic ideals. Moreover this return to a semi-established religion and hierarchical ideals encouraged, in Stendhal's view, a barren and insincere conformism in society at large. In the later years of the Empire, he sensed a growing moralistic pretence in Imperial society, which, though less marked than that of the Restoration, was nevertheless at variance with the opportunistic self-seeking that had characterised the ascendancy of many of its noted figures (e.g. *Journal*).

It was therefore not enough for writers to speak of regimes as simple entities; they had to indicate the years in question. If Stendhal in his own case often chose to do this indirectly, the allusions were clear enough to the contemporary reader.

By the same token, the panaceas of one period could be the poison of the next. For all his admiration of the young Bonaparte, Stendhal was later to recognise the pernicious irrelevance of the Napoleonic legend to contemporary needs, especially to those of the young men of the 1830s.

> France has been deceived by the glory of Napoleon and tormented by absurd desires. Instead of *inventing* its destiny, it wishes to *copy* it; it wants to see, starting again in 1837, the century that began in 1792 (*Mémoires d'un touriste*, 1838).

He was also not uncritical of the regime that restored him to favour in 1830. From the comfort of his consul's office in Civitavecchia, he passed harsh judgements on the reign of Louis Philippe 'this most crooked of kings', while his private correspondence is explicit in its condemnation of such episodes as the repression of the Lyon silkworkers in 1834. Yet, like many middle-aged liberals, his perception of the injustices of the time was blinkered by the limited perspective of a bourgeois *mondain* with a comfortable salary. In cautioning the younger generation against Napoleonic dreams, he asserted

> the voice of philosophy cries out . . . : 'But all the odious abuses are now abolished in France; if the Almighty himself put a pen in your hand to correct such abuses, you would be at a loss; you wouldn't know what to write; there are no more radical reforms needed in France, no great upheavals *to hope for or fear*' (*ibid*).

For all that, his view of society and politics remained coherent and consistent, reflecting a concept of Man that was the product of vigorous reading and thought. How he arrived at it, and where it stands in the context of determinist ideas, is examined in the next chapter.

3 Determinist Thought: Stendhal and the Eighteenth-century Inheritance

Tracing influences is regarded in many quarters as a disreputable game, and, like many disreputable games, it can rapidly become a pleasurable addiction. The hazards of disentangling the many factors that make a novelist what he is are obvious enough. While a number of the major Realists claimed to be directly indebted to various of the thinkers mentioned below, others had read none of them. Yet they all moved in a society where the intellectual climate, that much maligned term, had been conditioned by them. Like huge savanna trees, their contribution to the atmosphere was diffusive and hard to quantify, but nonetheless far-reaching.

Precursors

The genealogy of determinism is a deep-rooted many-tendrilled plant, not easily unearthed. But the ideas that are most relevant to Realism began to bloom in significant number in the mid-eighteenth century. Prior to this, traditional Christian thinking on the one hand, and the bulk of rationalist thought on the other, had shown only a limited awareness of the dependence of the mind on external influences and pressures. In a somewhat crude intuitive way, the various churches had recognised these factors in their emphasis on the careful upbringing of children in the matter of morals. Indeed, character building was to continue to be a central part of Christian private education, long after the secular state secondary schools of the nineteenth century had abandoned their ballast and staked their gowns on academic attainment. But Christians had fundamentally thought of the individual as a creature endowed by God with the ability to distinguish good from evil, a faculty that was supposedly *in situ* by the time the child was seven, the so-called age of reason. This concept assumed that Man was provided with a certain basic moral equipment that was largely independent of outside influences. A similar assumption was implicit in the idea of Natural Law: the idea that there were certain basic moral truths that were self-evident to all men, no matter how and where they had been brought up. It was also an axiom of non-Calvinist Christianity that God would never allow the individual to be tempted beyond his powers of resistance—a sobering and bracing thought for the believer in times of sore temptation, be he a captured Christian, tortured by proselytising heathens, or a hungry traveller confronted by an unattended loaf. If he succumbed, he was morally guilty, unless his powers of judgement were demonstrably impaired, through no fault of his own.

If concepts of this kind came sharply under attack from determinists, it was also true that some of the more optimistic eighteenth-century rationalists were similarly vulnerable. The faith they expressed in Man's basic virtue was no less problematical than the Christian concept of Original Sin—and arguably more dangerous in its clean-limbed assumptions as to what untutored human nature could achieve. Rather like the Christians, they regarded the child as endowed with autonomous powers of understanding, which only required to be developed and exercised to come into effective operation.

The challenge to these positions came from two interrelated but distinct sources: materialist determinism of the one hand, and empirical ideas on the nature of knowledge on the other. The Graeco-Roman world had had its share of grim determinists; but the Middle Ages had largely relegated them to the shelf of pagan museum pieces, despite the profound respect they received in certain quarters. The seventeenth century, however, saw the emergence of a new school of materialist determinism, which notably included Thomas Hobbes (1588–1679). Calvinism had already made many minds receptive to a predestined view of the human condition; but it was a determinism that was part of a divine plan, sanctioned and observed by a living God. For Hobbes, by contrast, destiny was encapsuled in material reality, whose motions determined all things and whose force unmasked free will as no more than a subjective illusion, a chimera like the immortal soul. Both strands in fact were to leave their mark on the period, notably on the determinism of Defoe—the fortunes of characters like Moll Flanders and Captain Jack reflecting a curious amalgam of fragments of his family Calvinism on the one hand, and an attentive reading of Hobbes on the other.

The most repercussive book of these years, however, was John Locke's deceptively mild-mannered *Essay concerning Human Understanding* (1690), which was to be the cornerstone of the empiricists' theory of knowledge. Infecting Condillac (1714–80) and the 'sensualist school' of a century later (see pp. 19–20), it likewise helped to launch Laurence Sterne into his quizzical voyages around the implications of determinism, and through him, Diderot (see p. 178). Yet Locke claimed not to be a materialist. His essay, as its title states, was a study of how the mind acquires knowledge and understanding. And the determinism that its conclusions suggested to his later disciples was not regarded as implicit by the bulk of his contemporaries, nor indeed by Locke himself. Even so, his insistence that all knowledge was acquired through the senses—and that none of it was innate—gave determinists a formidable weapon. They could claim that what a man thought and did depended on what his senses encountered, and that different milieux made different men. Locke himself, however, chose not to go so far. He reserved the power of reflection to Man's innate being. Although he saw the mind as a *tabula rasa*, he claimed that it could nevertheless comprehend and reflect on what the senses wrote there. In this way the protagonists of the soul and free will were seemingly left with some sort of handhold to which their convictions could cling, and Locke counted himself among their number.

The materialist determinism, of which Hobbes was an exemplar, was far from dead, however; and in Julien Offray de La Mettrie (1709–51), it was shortly to find a hard-hitting mischievous proponent (see pp. 31–2). On the concept of knowledge, however, La Mettrie was less interesting. And paradoxically it was the cautious Abbé Etienne de Condillac who set the cat among the pigeons in this quarter, even if both cat and pigeons were slow in taking stock of the situation. It was his views in particular that initiated Stendhal's boyhood thoughts on determinism.

Condillac is described, somewhat epigrammatically, by most French encyclopaedias as 'le maître de l'école sensualiste'. His life was somewhat more prosaic than this title might suggest, his fame resting on a number of treatises that were to have a far-reaching influence on French thought during the later part of the eighteenth century. Using John Locke as his point of departure, he maintained that all functions of the conscious mind—acts of concentration, making judgments, remembering, etc.—were achieved by the same mental process: by comparing information received through the senses. Condillac's novelty lay in his dispensing with Locke's autonomous realm of reflection (see above). Locke had separated Man's innate capacity for reflection from the rest of his mind, thereby elevating it above the general forum of received impressions that constituted the greater part of his consciousness. Although Condillac had initially accepted this distinction, his subsequent *Traité des sensations* (1754) argued that reflection was no more than a developed form of comparison: a mental juxtaposition of received impressions, past and present. Analogous views had been expressed by David Hume in his *Treatise* (1739) and more fully by David Hartley in his *Observations on Man* (1749), but Condillac appears to have arrived at these opinions independently, and with much more impact on succeeding generations in Europe as a whole.

Condillac's more percipient readers saw that if judgement was completely reliant on sense impressions, a man brought up in one milieu might have entirely different intellectual and moral standards from someone raised elsewhere. It potentially brought into question the whole concept of

Natural Law, since it was now much more difficult to assert that there were certain moral truths, self-evident to all men, irrespective of upbringing. Furthermore, as La Mettrie had already indicated (see pp. 31–2), it was now open to doubt whether a man's motives could be described as morally 'good' or 'bad' in the traditional sense, since his mind was merely responding to the impressions which his senses brought to him. One could not say, with the same simplicity, that his mind had made a responsible choice between yielding to sin on the one hand or following the promptings of divine grace on the other, since the mind was equally vulnerable to whatever the senses encountered and communicated to it.

For all his prestige, however, Condillac had two major faults in the eyes of his later disciples. On the one hand his concept of the mind left little room for the inconvenient facts of immanent needs and desires. In legitimately ridding the mind of Locke's autonomous powers of reflection, he had also cleared it of the innate inclinations that caused the newborn creature to feel around for sustenance and warmth, or shrink from uncomfortable objects. In short, his view of the mind was too passive: a result, perhaps, of his celibate remoteness from the wriggling realities of the nursery. The second criticism was that despite the enormous implications of his thought, Condillac himself was only prepared to pursue them part way. Although he was not one of these new-fangled churchmen who allowed his calling to intrude into his private life or interfere with the pleasures of the table, he had professional proprieties to observe; and he was anxious that his concepts should not lay him open to the charge of materialism. He therefore made a point of specifically aserting that the soul exists, and of claiming moreover that the soul would indeed be capable of direct knowledge, without the mediation of the senses, if it had not been condemned to total dependence on the body through the Fall. This declaration, however, remained no more than an assertion, which he made no attempt to integrate convincingly with the substance and logic of his work; and it was here that he and his agnostic and atheist disciples parted company.

Helvétius and Stendhal

With Claude-Adrien Helvétius (1715–71), the amalgam of ideas that was to inspire Realism becomes much clearer. It was he who brought together the materialist determinism of La Mettrie (see pp. 31–2) and the *sensualisme* pioneered by Condillac. Like many determinists, he had medical connections, his father, grandfather and great grandfather all having had distinguished careers as physicians to various royal figures. His father's influence at court, however, spared Claude-Adrien himself the necessity of earning a hard professional living; and as a farmer-general of taxes, his wealth, charm and good looks enabled him to indulge his intellectual curiosity to an enviable degree. Among many adventures, he once disguised himself as a celebrated dancer at the Opéra to enjoy the plaudits of the audience as he pirouetted, masked, in front of them. Indeed it was his *flânerie*, as well as his philosophy, that was to appeal to Stendhal at the turn of the century.

This indulged child of fortune, however, dramatically imperilled his favour at court by shocking orthodox opinion with his *De L'Esprit* (1758), a minor bombshell of a book, which was publicly burnt by the hangman for challenging the existence of the non-corporeal soul. Its main interest for determinists was the particular stress it laid on social forces in forming the mind. Aided by its *succès de scandale*, it rapidly covered Europe in a succession of translations; and Helvétius was later to become an acknowledged inspiration of English Utilitarianism. In James Mill's view, 'Helvétius alone is an entire army. Bentham himself was but a disciple of Helvétius'. Yet his emphatic belief in the influence of *milieu*, to the virtual exclusion of heredity, was to find critics among the later generation of determinists: notably the Idéologues of the 1790s, whose more sustained medical knowledge was to make them aware of the physiological factor of inherited characteristics. Helvétius by contrast believed that the mental potential of most men was approximately equal at birth, and that subsequent differences were the outcome of upbringing and education. Even so, Helvétius's trenchant aphorisms were to reverberate through generations of Realist literature: 'the inequality of minds is the effect of . . . the difference of education'; 'the man of genius is only the product of the circumstances in which he has found himself' and a host of other incisive assertions. It was this stress on environment that made such a deep impression on Stendhal when he encountered *De l'Esprit* and *De l'homme, de ses facultés intellectuelles et de son éducation* (1772) in 1803.

A disciple of the Idéologues as well as of Helvétius, Stendhal was to bring to the novel a determinist standpoint that was the direct product of the intellectual activity of his time. His early atheism was initially a revulsion against the traditional religiosity of his family. His mother, to whom he was deeply attached, had died when he was seven, leaving Stendhal to the mercies of a conventionally pious father and a maiden aunt whom he detested. Accused by his aunt on the one hand of not having shown enough grief at his mother's funeral, and assured by a priest on the other that his mother's death was the will of God, his dislike of the *bien pensant* ambience of the household was accentuated by the *maladresses* of a clerical tutor.

School under the Revolution brought him his first contact with the ideas of the Idéologues (see pp. 23 and 26–8), which made him aware of the determining influence of hereditary factors, as well as environmental ones. This was an important encounter which was to keep in check his later enthusiasm for Helvétius, making him sceptical, in particular, of Helvétius's belief in the approximate equality of men at birth. Yet the continual stress that Stendhal's novels were to put on environment owed much to Helvétius. For Stendhal, the particularly striking feature of

Helvétius's theories was their claim to account for the extraordinary being, the man of genius, as well as the ordinary run of humanity; this was a major consideration for Stendhal, who was fascinated by the phenomenon of exceptional men like Danton and Napoleon. Helvétius believed that 'it is emulation which produces geniuses, and the desire to shine that creates talents . . . the science of education is perhaps no more than the technique of arousing emulation.' All of which was to confirm Stendhal's preference for the thrusting ethos of Revolutionary and Napoleonic France, rather than the static would-be caste structure of the Restoration. Moreover, for Helvétius, 'the most decisive characters are often the product of an infinitude of petty unforeseen events . . . There is no change that an unexpected happening cannot bring about in a man's character.' Stendhal, for his part, affirmed that 'genius of all kinds is nothing other than an extra strong dose of commonsense, and commonsense is obtained through . . . observation and reflection. Success lies in the single-minded pursuit of an objective.'

It was also from Helvétius that Stendhal acquired other major items of his intellectual furniture. Like the Utilitarians, he was strongly attracted by the simple dictum that the avoidance of pain and the search for pleasure are the motivating forces behind all human action; and he was likewise disposed to agree that morality is founded exclusively on self-interest (while conceding that making others happy could itself be a source of happiness).

Le Rouge et le Noir (1830) is a treasury of Helvétiana (see especially pp. 24−5), not least in Julien Sorel's last thoughts on the nature of life. 'There is no such thing as *natural law* . . . there is nothing *natural* except a lion's strength, or the needs of the creature who suffers from hunger, from cold'; 'when it's a question of securing or losing a ministerial portfolio, my honest drawing-room folk fall into crimes precisely the same as those the need for a meal has inspired'. His conclusions, moreover, on the significance of existence echo a vibrant strand of determinist thought that stretches from La Mettrie (see pp. 31−2), through Cabanis, to Positivism. '[A hunter's] boot strikes an ant-hill . . . The most philosophical among the ants will never be able to understand . . . So it is with life, death and eternity'.

Stendhal and the Idéologues
The determinism of Helvétius found both an affirmation and a critique in the work of the Idéologues. Brought into political prominence by the events of the French Revolution, the Idéologues maintained a spiritual connection with the long-dead maestro through his widow, Madame Helvétius, whose salon at Auteuil provided them with a regular meeting place. Indeed their encounters in the 1790s around the chair of the ageing madonna of French determinism gave them a certain cohesion and identity.

Like Helvétius, the Idéologues saw no place for the soul in their understanding of human motivation. What Condillac considered as a function of the soul, the Idéologues regarded as a question of transformed nerve messages—their aim being to reduce the activities of the mind to precise physiological terms. Their leader in this bold design was Pierre Cabanis (1757–1808), Mirabeau's personal doctor. In a famous analogy, he declared that the brain secretes thought as the liver secretes bile, and that to think was to use one's neural system. Cabanis maintained that mental growth and the evolution of personality were closely linked with the body's development, and, unlike Condillac, he attached a great deal of importance to innate behaviour, which he saw as pre-existing the influence of external pressures felt through the senses. In his opinion the feeding habits of newborn chicks were but one of many examples that indicated the existence of inherited as well as acquired behaviour. He therefore rejected Helvétius's belief that men were born approximately equal. Even so, he was convinced that the development of many characteristics—especially mental—was strongly affected, perhaps largely determined, by personal relationships and group pressures in early emotional life.

There were times, notably after Napoleon's *rapprochement* with the Church, when Cabanis found it expedient to point out that his views were perfectly compatible with the concept of a divine first cause. Yet, when he was freest to speak his mind, he took what might be called a Positivist stand on such matters. In his *Histoire physiologique des sensations* (l'an VIII), he observed

> The inscription on one of the ancient temples . . . has the first cause of the universe speak in a truly great and philosophical manner: 'I am what is, and what has been, and what will be; and no-one has known my nature.' Another inscription said: 'Know thyself.' The first is the confession of an inevitable ignorance. The second is the formal and precise indication of the goal which rational philosophy and moral philosophy should follow.

Stendhal was later to claim that Cabanis's *Rapports du physique et du moral* (1802) had been 'my bible when I was sixteen'. Although chronology divests this remark of literal truth, Cabanis was undoubtedly one of the high priests of the new orthodoxy taught in the Revolutionary *écoles centrales*, such as that at Grenoble which Stendhal attended as an adolescent from 1796 to 1799. Certainly in 1805, when Stendhal's material and amorous fortunes were at a low ebb, he sought solace in Cabanis, as indeed he did again, when in happier circumstances, in 1811. It was Cabanis who opened his eyes to the importance of instinct and inherited characteristics—thereby counterweighting the exclusive environmentalism of his other principal mentor, Helvétius (see pp. 21–2). Cabanis claimed moreover that already at birth most individuals belonged to certain broad categories of temperament, categories which Stendhal proceeded to apply to his biographical studies of painters and musicians.

Stendhal characteristically saw his own temperament as fundamentally '*mélancolique*', a category he came increasingly to equate with *l'homme supérieur*.

Cabanis also believed that regional differences of climate and ways of life had a strong environmental influence on the inhabitants: 'the air, the food, drink, waking, sleeping and the various types of work have a very far-reaching influence on the ideas, passions and habits, in short the moral state', a conviction that Stendhal sought to embody in his own work, not always happily.

For Stendhal, however, perhaps the most interesting aspect of Cabanis's theories was the importance he attached to subconscious inclinations—more particularly those that would seem to defy the rational arguments of self-interest. He suggested, for instance, that the individual may contain several partial selves, each at variance with the other. It was here that Cabanis both complemented and qualified what Stendhal had learned from Helvétius. Helvétius had claimed, more simplistically, that thought and great deeds are instigated by the passions. It is a recurring issue in *Le Rouge et le Noir*, and is arguably a partial key to Julien Sorel's puzzling nature: the curious combination that he represents of emotional drive on the one hand and cool-headed calculation on the other. Stendhal took particular note of Helvétius's remark, 'The passions can do everything. There is no stupid girl who does not become quick-witted through love. It inspires in her all sorts of schemes for outwitting the vigilance of her parents'. And the lesson was to bear obvious literary fruit in the stratagems of Madame de Renal and Mathilde de la Mole.

Cabanis's concept of conflicting selves brought depth and diversity to Helvétius's single-minded view. He claimed notably that emotional inclinations and rational self-interest could be at odds with each other, on a subconscious as well as a conscious level. And it is tempting to see Julien Sorel's shooting of Madame de Renal as a case in point. Counter to Julien's interests and ambitions, the episode might seem to be superficially inconsistent with his scheming disposition. But this is to ignore the emotional side to Julien's nature. To seek a simple explanation of a complex response obviously runs the risk of doing violence to the subtlety of Stendhal's psychological awareness. Yet Julien's attack has often been persuasively interpreted as an emotional response to Madame de Renal's accusation that he has used seduction as a means of social advancement. By destroying his career, as well as his mistress, he would arguably be asserting the falseness of the claim, albeit subconsciously. Whether this owes anything specifically to Cabanis can only remain a matter for conjecture; but the similarities of approach are at least interesting.

Stendhal's ideas on happiness, on the other hand, owed most to Helvétius. Helvétius's emphasis on the emotions encouraged in Stendhal the belief that happiness depended on acknowledging the importance and claims of the emotions—and it also underlay his conviction that sincerity and spontaneity are the key to self-fulfilment. This might seem superficially at variance with Stendhal's insistence on the need to discipline the emotions; a precept he tried to follow in his own life, and which is reflected in Julien Sorel's (albeit clumsy) attempts to seduce Madame de Renal and Mathilde de la Mole. The two goals are in fact complementary, in that self-discipline is dependent on self-awareness, and self-awareness can only come through sincerity. Self-discipline is not a denial of the emotions; it is, on the contrary, a guarantee that they can be indulged to the full when the time is ripe. Moreover, for Stendhal, sincerity is sincerity with oneself: the recognition and acceptance of one's fundamental desires. To enjoy them fully, their fulfilment may have to be postponed or tempered, according to circumstance; they may similarly have to be concealed from people who might otherwise oppose them.

Yet for Stendhal it remained axiomatic that self-discipline and tactical concealment were questions of method, which must not obscure sincerity with oneself nor, fundamentally, sincerity with other people. His childhood had given him a hatred of pretence and false piety; and his experience of Restoration society was to give him a particular hatred of the institutionalising of these attitudes on a national level. Indeed it is these features of Restoration life that induce Julien Sorel to adopt the hypocrisy and deceits of the milieux he enters. Despite the tactical advantages that they initially afford, they too often stand in the way of his true happiness. The joy that should have come from his passionate encounters with Madame de Renal and Mathilde de la Mole is constantly obstructed by the particular role he feels obliged to play to consolidate his conquest. Yet it is his fundamental qualities of feeling and determination that attract these women—just as they also attract the loyalty of the men who stand by him in his subsequent difficulties. Although his deceits and stratagems have assisted him to gain entry into society, they are merely the lubricant which enable his qualities to come to the notice of his patrons, his qualities being the main reason for his social advancement. When finally self-confrontation in the condemned cell enables him to take stock of himself, without calculating for a future he will never see, it is sincerity that triumphs. Sincerity in the shape of Madame de Renal and their love for each other; sincerity in his ability to utter his thoughts, without weighing their effect on the future fortunes that now no longer exist.

Another significant influence on Stendhal was Cabanis's contemporary and friend, Antoine Destutt de Tracy (1754–1836). It was Tracy who brought home to Stendhal how determinism could be reconciled with a satisfying concept of the individual will. Like the other Idéologues, Tracy recognised that what the mind 'willed' was no more than the outcome of needs and received impressions. But he also affirmed, and here the focus of emphasis was different, that the mind was not a mere passive recipient of messages and demands from the rest of the body. It could itself galvanise the body into the relentless pursuit of specific objectives, despite the discomfort and deprivation that it might have to endure to achieve them. This was not a departure from determinism: single-mindedness of this sort merely reflected the dominance of one desire over others in a disciplined mind; the dominant desire itself was still the outcome of needs and received impressions. Even so, this was a change of emphasis that was particularly congenial to a temperament like Stendhal's, which admired determination and energy, and their embodiment in figures like Danton and Napoleon. It encouraged him to create characters with thrust and indi-viduality—characters which would satisfy the reader's criteria of what constituted a hero, but which were still consistent with a determinist view of the world.

Stendhal had embarked on Tracy's *Idéologie* in December 1804. But from 1805, Stendhal's reading leaned increasingly towards contemporary Romanticism, and towards those literary figures of the past, such as Corneille, who exalted the heroic, spontaneous aspects of human nature. These excursions were the subjective counterpart of what he had learnt on the level of 'objective' reality (see pp. 20–5) from Helvétius, Cabanis and Destutt de Tracy; they complemented rather than superseded his respect for the Idéologues, and confirmed his interest in spontaneity and the exceptional being.

The Idéologues and education
Like many of his contemporaries, Stendhal's early encounter with the main currents of the Idéologues' thought was a direct outcome of the extraordinary ferment of the 1790s and the educational system it produced. The influence of the Idéologues spread much more rapidly than that of their intellectual forbears, and owed a great deal to the political circumstances of the time. Whereas under the *ancien régime* Helvétius had found it expedient to make a public denial of his atheism, the Idéologues under the Revolutionary government were entrusted with important reforms, notably that of secondary education. Among much else they were commissioned to draw up proposals for the remarkable *écoles centrales*, the state secondary schools that were established in 1795—only to be shortly replaced by Napoleon's *lycées* in 1802. Indeed the law of October 1795, which brought them into being, was the work of P. C. Daunou (1761–1840), a close associate of Cabanis and Tracy. The *écoles centrales* were arguably the most ambitious experiment in schools to be made before the twentieth century; and their abolition by Napoleon was a major tragedy for the development of educational method. They were an attempt to set up a new educational concept, based directly on the theories of Condillac and the Idéologues. There was to be a minimum of one in each department, and by 1798 ninety-seven had come into existence.

In their blueprint for them, the Idéologues stipulated that they should use a basic French, from which all elements of ambiguity had been removed, and which would correspond as closely as possible with the objects and phenomena that they were describing. This would not only make for clarity and understanding, but it would remove many opportunities for duplicity and evasiveness, thereby helping to develop character and personal integrity. The idea was of the pure essence of Condillac: a basic French of this kind would provide a more direct link between sense impressions and mental concepts, thereby making the two correspond more closely.

As for subjects and teaching methods, the accent throughout was on practical work and relevance to the business of living. Science played a much fuller part in them than it had done either in the colleges of the *ancien régime* or in the *lycées* that Napoleon was to introduce. Science teaching moreover was to be done as far as possible by practical example—each school ideally to have chemistry and physics laboratories, a botanical garden and natural history museum. Once again, this emphasis on direct experience was in part yet another act of homage to the Idéologues' belief that sense impressions were the basis of all knowledge and understanding. It may also have owed something to the influence of Rousseau (1712–78). At the same time the syllabus was carefully geared to what were seen as the stages of mental growth. It was recognised that when boys are relatively young, their strong points are memory work and basic skills, and that their ability to understand the issues that underlie history and literature are fairly limited. Consequently the syllabus for this age group, twelve to fourteen, was restricted to modern and ancient languages, drawing and natural history. Between the ages of fourteen and sixteen, when their understanding was sufficiently developed to grasp the simpler laws of science, the syllabus comprised mathematics, physics and chemistry. Literature and history, however, were kept for the final years, from sixteen to eighteen, when they also studied legislation and what was rather confusingly called 'general grammar', but which in effect was a philosophy course.

Not only were the Idéologues intimately concerned with the foundation of the *écoles centrales*, but they were also closely involved in their subsequent development. In 1799 Destutt de Tracy became responsible on a national level for supervising the courses of 'general grammar' and legislation. True to the Idéologues' principles, he reminded teachers that they should put particular emphasis on the theories of Locke and Condillac; his own *Projet d'éléments d'idéologie* (1800) was composed especially for these schools. Cabanis, for his part, became the schools' director of hygiene.

From a pedagogic point of view, it must be admitted that the *écoles centrales* made the serious mistake of regarding their pupils too much as university students rather than boys. The two-year courses in each subject were chosen and taken as self-contained units, without any subsequent 'post-experience' classes, which might have kept the subject alive in the boys' minds and facilitated its integration with other subjects. And the somewhat adult character of the schools was indirectly and somewhat incongruously reinforced by the law of 17 November 1797, which required government officials to be products of the state-school system. The bizarre result was an influx of middle-aged *fonctionnaires* into the *écoles centrales*, where they could be seen fiercely jostling their adolescent fellow scholars in the corridors and undergoing a host of other mild indignities, in order to obtain the necessary certificate of attendance. Only married men were spared this brief return to their happiest days.

In practice, moreover, the *écoles centrales* fell far short of fulfilling the Idéologues' recommendations. Paucity of money in a period of war hamstrung the schemes for providing laboratories, while the fact that the only readily available supply of teachers was from the old colleges meant that the aims of the Idéologues were often only partially understood or were sometimes deliberately ignored. Nevertheless the clergy who had taught in the colleges of the *ancien régime* contained a number of able men who had been Christians in nothing but outward conformity, and who were now able to profess their real opinions under the Revolution. Stendhal, who never suffered fools gladly, always felt a certain grudging gratitude to the *école centrale* of Grenoble for laying the basis of his later appreciation of the *Idéologues*.

Despite their limitations and their brief existence, the French state system of *écoles centrales* produced several successive crops of young men, many of whom were to move into positions of administrative and social importance. With *la carrière ouverte aux talents*, Napoleonic France chose its personnel from among the educated; and despite Napoleon's distrust of the Idéologues and the *écoles centrales*, a considerable proportion of the new generation of young officials had passed through the philosophy classes of these schools before they were abolished in 1802. Even then, the new *lycées* that replaced them were obliged in practice to employ the staff of the old *écoles centrales*. Although the syllabuses reverted to a more traditional pattern (with no philosophy), many of the men teaching them had been permanently affected by contact with experimental methods and *laïcité*. Despite the fact that Napoleon brought back religious teaching into the *lycées*, he could not change attitudes overnight.

The same was true to a lesser extent of the other secondary schools that came into existence under Napoleon, and which took some of their staff from the *écoles centrales*. Balzac as a boy attended the Collège de Vendôme (1807–13), which had been an Oratorian school under the *ancien régime*, but, as a result of secular metamorphosis, became an *école centrale* between 1795 and 1802. Changing with the times it then reverted to being a college which took younger boys; and in Balzac's time was run by two ex-Oratorians, one of whom, Jean Dessaignes, was an enthusiastic disciple of the Idéologues. Although both men had married, they retained their Catholic faith; but their methods were very much in the spirit of the *écoles centrales*, with the senior boys occasionally getting up at four in the morning to set off on a ten-mile hike to visit an observatory or an iron foundry. A man of active intellect, Dessaignes wrote a physiology text-book for his philosophy class, and was also engaged on a *magnum opus* demonstrating the connection between bodily processes and the emotions. At thirteen years of age, Balzac left the school too young to have participated in the senior classes; but he accompanied Dessaignes on his botany expeditions while convalescing at the headmaster's rural retreat. Whatever they may have discussed, however, it has to be recognised that Balzac's enthusiasm for physiological thought really came later, through the influence of his father's friend, Dr. Nacquart (see pp. 32 and 38).

The Idéologues and politics

Like other intellectual groups during the Revolution, the fortunes of the Idéologues varied with political circumstance. They throve best in the optimistic years of liberal domestic reform, and least well in periods of crisis and suspicion. When, with other intellectuals, Condorcet was hounded by the Montagnards, it was Cabanis's gift of a phial of poison that enabled him to forestall the guillotine.

It may seem strange, in retrospect, that Cabanis, Destutt de Tracy and their friends should have greeted Bonaparte's coup d'état of 1799 with some enthusiasm. In their eyes the young general was still the saviour of Republican France; the man who had defeated the foreign forces of reactionary rulers, and who would now bring order and light to the murky intrigues of the Directoire. Bonaparte was also the patron of science—the enlightened visionary who had taken scholars to Egypt, including Geoffroy Saint-Hilaire (see pp. 33—5), and who had tried (albeit unsuccessfully) to persuade Destutt de Tracy to accompany him. Indeed his respect for the Idéologues was demonstrated on his return to Paris, when he made a point of visiting Cabanis at Auteuil, the shrine of Madame Helvétius, to whom he asked to pay his respects.

This mutual esteem, however, was short-lived. When Bonaparte's autocratic nature and illiberal intentions became all too clear, the Idéologues rapidly became the spearhead of the liberal opposition to him. He referred to them as 'vermin', 'fit to be drowned', and removed them from the Tribunat as soon as a constitutional loophole gave him the opportunity. They were, however, essentially intellectuals, rather than politicians, and they made little effective attempt to oppose the successive stages that brought into being the Imperial dictatorship. They helplessly watched the resumption of a utilitarian alliance between church and state, and could do little to prevent the secular ideals and adventurous curricula of the *écoles centrales* being replaced by the intellectual conformism of the new *lycées*.

Their revenge, moreover, when it came in 1814, was short-lived, and at the mercy of the victorious Allies. It was Destutt de Tracy, appropriately enough, who formally proposed Napoleon's deposition in the Senate; but the circumstances were scarcely what he and his colleagues would have wished. Furthermore, the Bourbon Restoration of the following year was to find the Idéologues once again a distrusted sect, with no role to play in an increasingly clericalised state. It was not until 1830, when the Bourbon monarchy was overthrown, that they came back into their own—those who were still alive. And although the new Orleanist monarchy was secular in spirit, they were never to enjoy the prestige and personal influence that they had had in the 1790s. Their principal monument in fact was the incoming generation of ministers and senior civil servants, many of whom had received their secondary school education in the short-lived *écoles centrales* of the Directoire. Junior administrators under the Empire, they had been driven into the political wilderness by the Restoration, only to emerge triumphant in the distribution of prizes after the 1830 Revolution.

4 Man and Beast: the Balzacian Jungle

Although Balzac, like Stendhal, admired the Idéologues (see pp. 22–30), his determinism had other sources. It was the roaming prophets of the Muséum National d'Histoire Naturelle, rather than the urbane sages of Auteuil, who provided his main intellectual sustenance. As he lost no opportunity in pointing out, *La Comédie Humaine* had its particular inspiration in the evolutionary ideas of Etienne Geoffroy Saint-Hilaire (see pp.33–7), whose work attempted to demonstrate determinism in action, as well as assert it as a fact of life.

As a gloss on Balzac's carnival of human animals, the following pages indicate the main trend of evolutionary thought in Balzac's time, and illustrate how Balzac sought to apply it to his vision of Man and society.

Evolutionary theory and 'La Comédie Humaine'

'*La bête humaine*' is a concept that long predates Zola. If it was Zola and his dourer Naturalist contemporaries who made it the focal point of their vision of mankind, the ebullient eclecticism of Balzac had been perennially fascinated by the similarities between society and the animal world— similarities that for Balzac came near to reflecting an underlying identity.

From the time of Anaximander (?610–?547 B.C.), if not earlier, there had been successive attempts to try to discern a unity linking living things. Julien Offray de La Mettrie and others had claimed a close affinity between Man and the higher apes. A physician by training, La Mettrie's deterministic view of Man had appeared in unabashed abrasive form in a book with the uncompromising title of *L'homme machine* (1748), in which he exhorted his startled readers to 'conclude boldly that man is a machine, and that in the whole universe there is but a single substance differently modified'. Indeed, he believed that the different species of animal, including Man, were the result of a long series of permutations of matter. For him the main criterion which differentiated the various echelons of the animal world was the complexity of their neural systems, while the principal feature that distinguished Man from the higher apes was the power of speech, which gave him the key to more complex forms of thought as well as communication. An ape taught to talk 'would be a perfect man, *un petit Homme de Ville* . . . able to think and profit from his education.'

Like the nineteenth-century Positivists, La Mettrie believed that 'it does not matter for our peace of mind whether matter be eternal or created, whether there be a God or not. How foolish to torment ourselves so much about things we cannot know'. But, for him personally, there was no soul in the Christian sense—no ghost in the machine.

One of the bolder inferences of his belief in the physical basis of mind was his hope that science would one day be able to improve Man ethically. He believed many criminals to be 'sick' not 'evil', requiring diagnosis by doctors rather than punitive treatment. Indeed the terms 'vice' and 'virtue' he considered to be meaningless, except in the utilitarian sense of being conducive or otherwise to the wellbeing of society.

Few other eighteenth-century evolutionists were quite so forthright in their public statements. Leading zoologists, such as Georges de Buffon (1707–88) had lent the weight of their respectability to tentative ideas on the mutation of species; but it was essentially in the Revolutionary and Napoleonic period that the principle of evolution became a major issue for scientific debate, when Jean-Baptiste de Lamarck (1744–1829), Etienne Geoffroy Saint-Hilaire (1772–1844), and Georges Cuvier (1769–1832) engaged in prolonged and semi-public skirmishings which were to culminate much later in the famous confrontation of 1830.

The omnivorous imagination of Balzac responded with enthusiasm to these discussions. As a child at the Collège de Vendôme, the monstrous tot had periodically tried to perceive a principle of unity in the world—although his speculations on the nature of this principle were later to oscillate uncertainly between regarding it as mere matter, or alternatively as an intangible force. There was always to remain a latent conflict in his mind between the rival attractions of materialism and vitalism. From boyhood he had been obsessed with the exercise of will; conceiving it initially as a force like electricity. 'Before long I shall possess the secret of that mysterious power. I shall compel all men to obey me and all women to love me' (1820). His mother, for all her conventional piety, had been interested in Mesmerism; and the vitalistic side to his thoughts may have owed something to her, despite her remoteness from her children. His father by contrast was a freethinker and Freemason who had nevertheless retained a knowledgeable respect for religion—a combination which was to be reflected in the complex, and at times ambivalent, attitude of his son to the Church.

The materialist and physiological side to Balzac's thought, however, perhaps owed most to the friendship and influence of the Balzacs' family doctor, Jean-Baptiste Nacquart. Nacquart had written a number of books, including a substantial study of the brain, in which he emphasised the physical basis of thought and enunciated a utilitarian philosophy. For him morality was 'a matter of convention between men living together', 'an outlook shaped by the wellbeing of society'.

The evolutionary ideas that were later to prove so fundamental to *La Comédie Humaine* were initially the outcome of Balzac's dispersed energies and interests while a law student in Paris. In 1816–17 he found time to attend a number of science lectures including Geoffroy Saint-Hilaire's lectures at the Muséum d'Histoire Naturelle. As he afterwards acknowledged, it was these that initiated the train of thought that later shaped the underlying theories of *La Comédie Humaine*; already he was wondering whether Geoffroy's principle of the Unity of Composition (see pp. 34–5) could be applied to human society. And when he took to writing fiction in the 1820s, the possibility of giving the concept literary form increasingly excited him. Rival enthusiasms, however, and a disastrous excursion into the business world (see p. 47) postponed further pursuit of the project until the 1830s—by which time France had witnessed the *grande bagarre* between Geoffroy and Cuvier (see below).

Like so many concepts concerning Man and the nature of life, Geoffroy's speculations were deeply indebted to the intellectual ferment of the 1790s when public discussion of these issues was no longer inhibited by the official attitudes of a throne-and-altar establishment. These turbulent and invigorating years found Geoffroy, Lamarck and Cuvier colleagues together at the Muséum d'Histoire Naturelle. They learnt a great deal from each other, Cuvier sharing and stimulating his compeers' inquisitive investigation into the 'chain of being' idea, which lay at the basis of the evolutionary concepts that were later to divide him from his two colleagues.

Their diverging paths were a partial reflection of their temperaments and attitude to authority. Geoffroy and Cuvier were invited to accompany Bonaparte's expedition to Egypt in 1798, an opportunity which the adventurous Geoffroy characteristically accepted and the cautious Cuvier declined. Geoffroy devoted his energies to comparing the mummified animals and birds he found in the various tombs with living specimens of the same species which he caught or shot in the Nile delta. Refusing, with customary tenacity, to hand over his collection to the invading British army, when General Hutchinson occupied Egypt in 1801, Geoffroy returned to France with tangible evidence that these species had scarcely changed in thousands of years. Yet he and Lamarck interpreted the fact in a radically different way from Cuvier. Cuvier claimed that the findings conclusively demonstrated the fixity of species, each species being a separate creation by God; whereas Geoffroy and Lamarck merely concluded that much longer time sequences were needed to produce significant changes.

Cuvier's retreat into traditional orthodoxy was perhaps not entirely unconnected with the change in official attitudes. The intellectual adventurousness of the mid-1790s had given way to the conformism of the Consulate and Empire, where conventional assumptions were a surer passport to official honours and advancement. When the conformism of the Empire eventually gave way to the bleak reaction of the Restoration, Cuvier's conservatism grew more intransigent, causing Stendhal to comment, 'What servility and baseness has not been shown towards those in power by Monsieur Cuvier'. At the same time his hostility to the evolutionary theories of his former colleagues became steadily more virulent, until the two sides met in public combat in 1830, when he accused Geoffroy of pantheism—a serious accusation in the claustrophobic climate of Charles X.

Lamarck in fact had died in the previous year, leaving Geoffory to take the lead in this affair. Among much else, Lamarck had sought to account for the genesis of living things without recourse to a divine creator. In a manner superficially reminiscent of Anaximander, he attributed the appearance of primitive forms of life to the effect of heat, sunlight and electricity on moist matter: these organisms thereafter evolving into more complex forms, as internal and environmental factors furthered their development. What particularly intrigued his readers was his inclusion of Man in the process; not unlike La Mettrie half a century earlier (see pp. 31–2), he attributed the complexity and sophistication of the human mind to the advanced development of Man's neural system. And, like Cabanis (see pp. 23–4), he saw a close connection between moral attitudes and physical factors.

Lamarck believed that in the case of most vertebrates the pursuit of food and other objectives had caused them to develop particular muscles in particular ways, which, when constantly repeated, had resulted in the development of new physical characteristics. Unlike the later disciples of Darwin (see pp. 124–6), Lamarck assumed that new attributes could be 'occupationally' acquired by one generation and then transmitted biologically to the next, an assumption that was to characterise most evolutionary theories of the first half of the nineteenth century.

Geoffroy broadly accepted the general corpus of Lamarck's beliefs, and was himself to give the system the portmanteau title of 'evolution' in 1831. His own personal contribution to its development was to put particular emphasis on environmental factors in determining change; and he later extended the system to include invertebrates—a move which helped to ignite the great dispute with Cuvier in 1830. At the same time, running parallel to these developments, was his expansion of Buffon's principle of 'the unity of composition' (1753), a concept which had a lineage stretching back to Aristotle. Like previous exponents of this principle, he stressed the basic structural identity of vertebrate animals—fish, reptiles, birds and mammals—an identity which seemed to suggest a common ancestry. An important corollary to this was the emphasis he put on the principle of balance, according to which the development of one physical feature was accompanied by a corresponding reduction in another: the business of living in a particular environment leading to the development of certain muscles and the atrophy of others. It was this in particular that had fired Balzac's imagination when he attended Geoffroy's lectures in 1816—17.

Balzac's intention to apply these principles to human society, and to give them literary shape, was indirectly coloured by his reading of Scott's Waverley novels. Scott's success in presenting characters in a historical setting made Balzac realise that an equal success might be achieved in presenting characters in a contemporary setting where the interrelation of social types and the milieu in which they worked could be more easily documented and convincingly demonstrated. Although such a demonstration had been no part of Scott's brief, his popularity convinced Balzac that the exercise he had in mind could be attractively packaged and make money. And so, Balzac's fictional forays into history were shortly to be followed by his novels on contemporary society.

The concept of *La Comédie Humaine* reached fruition in his mind in 1833—4, when he envisaged supplementing his existing novels with further works that would illustrate all the major aspects of contemporary life in France. When the enterprise acquired its formal shape and title in 1841, his foreword to the series was at pains to emphasise its debt to Geoffroy Saint-Hilaire, especially to his 'impressive law of each for himself, on which rests *the unity of composition.* There is but one animal . . . The animal . . . acquires the peculiarities of its form from the environment in which it develops. Zoological species are the outcome of these differences.' 'I saw that in this respect, society resembled Nature. Does not society make from Man as many different men as there are zoological varieties, according to the environment where his activity takes place?'

Balzac recognised, however, the dangers of pushing the concept too far. There was the the growing fact of social mobility and the movement that took place between occupations. Not only might a merchant's son become a lawyer, but the merchant himself might change occupations, thereby making it hard to postulate the development of occupational types in the same way as animal species. Even so, these objections were less serious in Balzac's day than later. Despite the far-reaching changes of the early nineteenth century, social mobility was still modest in its proportions. Sons generally followed their fathers' occupations, and often developed the attitudes of mind and behavioural habits that they had daily observed in their fathers. Not only did it require considerable effort to rise to a superior occupation, when entry was dependent on education and wealth, but skills and aptitudes learnt from parents were often a strong inducement to pursue the same kind of occupation. And, if it was a family-run concern, there was generally a guaranteed place for a son of the house. In this way aptitudes and opportunities tended to complement each other, thereby intensifying the peculiar characteristics of the occupation as well as the specialised aptitudes of the families that pursued them.

The factors here at work, however, were largely environmental, though not exclusively. Inherited mental or physical attributes might well determine in the first instance the occupational niche filled by a family—and might solidify it thereafter. Conversely, the child who inherited a certain physical or mental attribute that was less apparent in his parents or grandparents might be drawn or pushed into a different occupation. Even so, occupational 'evolution' in human society was clearly much more flexible and swift-moving than anything Geoffroy envisaged for the animal kingdom in general. And Balzac was aware of this: his scheme was sufficiently elastic to envisage individuals whose aptitudes and inclinations lay in other fields—and who might in consequence be drawn into a different occupation. This, for Balzac, was but another instance of the complementary role of aptitudes and occupations in forming social types: the exceptions and misfits would be drawn off into other occupations that suited them. He also saw that any argument for the hereditary transmission of acquired skills was complicated by the fact that men often marry women of different aptitudes and backgrounds.

When Buffon described the lion, he polished off the lioness in a few sentences; while in society the woman is not always just the female counterpart of the male. A marriage may contain two utterly different people.

Although Balzac saw the need for caveats, his imagination and capacity for seeing affinities between disparate phenomena were often stronger than his sense of logic or experience of scientific probability. He continually overstates his case, not least in *Splendeurs et Misères des Courtisanes*, one of the component novels of 'Scènes de la vie parisienne'. Written and published in fragments between 1837 and 1847, it focuses attention on the professions of law, crime and prostitution, occupations which Balzac saw as particularly illustrative of his theories. 'Theft and the traffic in public prostitutes have much in common with the theatre, the police, the priesthood and the military. In these six conditions of life, the individual takes on an indelible character. He can no longer be other than he is.' The book abounds in statements such as 'The magistrate smiled in a manner exclusive to magistrates, just as a dancer's smile is like nobody else's.' A police agent, complimenting another on his being well-informed, significantly remarks 'You fellows are well-trained, what ears you've got! . . . Social Nature equips all its species with the apparatus they will need! . . . Society is another kind of Nature!' Even so Balzac points out that the similar skills required of the police and the criminal permit individual movement from the one occupation into the other; the arch-villain, Vautrin, symptomatically concludes a life of crime by becoming head of the Sûreté.

A concept that finds notable illustration in *Splendeurs et Misères des*

Courtisanes is Geoffroy Saint-Hilaire's theory of 'the unity of composition', with its principle of compensation (see pp. 34−5).

> A banker is accustomed to weigh and balance different pieces of business . . . Conversational wit should no more be demanded of [him] than poetic images of the understanding of a mathematician. . . . The same law governs the body: perfect beauty is almost invariably coupled with coldness or silliness.

Baron Nucingen's infatuation for the Jewish courtesan, Esther Gobseck, is symptomatically seen in occupational terms.

> Such a flowering of sudden youth in the heart of a lynx, an old man, is one of those social phenomena which physiology can best explain. Weighed down by business cares, constricted by ceaseless calculations . . . adolescence and its sublime illusions reappear . . . like a buried seed whose . . . magnificent flowering obeys the chance of a sun which unexpectedly shines late.

Balzac admittedly often outdoes Sherlock Holmes in picking up improbable clues to states of being: Esther's hands 'were soft, transparent and white, like those of a woman brought to bed of her second child'.

Balzac pursues these explorations on several levels. If he remains primarily concerned with occupation, he is also much interested in racial characteristics. Although environmental in origin, he sees them as transmitted biologically. 'The instincts are living facts whose cause resides in some necessity endured. Animal species result from the exercise of these instincts.' And in describing the oriental characteristics of Esther Gobseck, he instances the respective grazing habits of mountain and lowland sheep, which remain unaltered, even when their habitats are reversed. Balzac later claimed, with a certain self-congratulation, that the composition of this passage 'necessitated the reading of several volumes'.

It was not only in the subject matter of his novels that Balzac paid homage to Geoffroy Saint-Hilaire. His imagery, though prolific, is remarkably consistent in its evocation of the competitive nature of the animal world. When businessmen and criminals are likened to lynxes and tigers, the labels, once given, remain, and are not used in the promiscuous fashion that characterises the work of most writers of imagery, including Shakespeare. Baron Nucingen remains a lynx, and Vautrin's criminal associates remain tigers in the various novels in which they successively appear; and, in keeping with the consistency, the virtuous characters are rarely allowed to 'step stealthily like a lynx' or 'fight like a tiger', even in the best of causes. A less predatory animal has to be found, since Balzac's similes are not merely adverbial, they are adjectival as well.

A striking feature of his work is the close connection between personality, profession and physical appearance. Vautrin's aunt has 'eyes . . . as those of a tiger . . . The general expression of this animal physiognomy was one of treacherous sloth.' To some extent this is Romantic exuberance; but it also reflects Balzac's interest in physiognomy and phrenology. It is admittedly often hard to disentangle this interest from the more commonplace demands of dramatic presentation, as in his description in *La Cousine Bette* (1846) of the wealthy Brazilian, Baron Henri Montès de Montejanos. 'His forehead, projecting like a satyr's, a sign of obstinate tenacity in passion . . . below which a pair of clear eyes glittered . . . tawny and untamed'. The emphasis is as much on the subjective response of the beholder, as on the facts of Montès's appearance; yet, as always, the description is in strict keeping with the subsequent role that the character plays: in this case, the executant of a terrible revenge. This sort of description was to be a commonplace of nineteenth-century fiction—later perpetuated in the *Boy's Own Paper* and its attendant *genre*—without its practitioners having much conscious debt to the pseudo-science of phrenology and physiognomy. But with Balzac, it was a carefully cultivated debt, continually acknowledged in his frequent references to Lavater and Gall, whose names re-occur in over a dozen of his novels, as well as in the foreword to *La Comédie Humaine*.

Like so much else, Balzac owed his initial acquaintance with their work to the family friend and doctor, Jean-Baptiste Nacquart (see p. 32).

Physiognomy and Phrenology

Johann Kaspar Lavater (1741–1801) would probably have been astonished and dismayed at the role his work played in the canon of determinist thought after his death. A Swiss pastor, with a considerable reputation as a spiritual adviser, his *Physiognomische Fragmente zur Beförderung der Menschenkenntniss und Menschenliebe* (1775–8) did little more than attempt to establish certain tentative links between face and character. But when published in France in 1820, in a handsomely illustrated edition, it made a great impact on the reading public, including Balzac, and quickly became ammunition in causes which Lavater would have been the first to repudiate. This was scarcely the case with Franz Joseph Gall (1758–1828). Although intended by his parents for the priesthood, the Catholicism of his adult life was a mere membership ticket, a gesture in the direction of authority and society, which, for all that, did not prevent his books being placed on the Index and his body consigned to unconsecrated ground. *Bon vivant* and society light, his medical practice in Imperial and Restoration Paris included such illustrious patients as Stendhal, Metternich and Saint-Simon. Paradoxically, his major contributions to neuroanatomy—which are the basis of his present reputation—were not the cause of his celebrity during his lifetime.

His pioneer work on the brain and nervous system is now seen as crucial in emancipating scientific opinion from the kind of humoral theories that were still entertained by luminaries such as Cabanis (see pp. 23–4). Whereas Cabanis and Bichat (see p. 67) believed that the passions were based on the thorax and abdomen, Gall asserted that the brain was the organ of all mental functions. He claimed, moreover, that the various functions of the mind were performed by different components of the brain, thereby challenging the Cartesian belief in the indivisibility of mind, and effectively putting psychology on a firmer physiological basis. Many of the details of his work—and several of his major conclusions—were wrong, yet his studies of the nervous system were later recognised as axiomatic to any understanding of its development.

Nor was he a man to restrict his activities to the dissecting table. He made numerous visits to mental asylums, prisons and schools, where he gathered a long series of case histories, and alarmed some of the more susceptible inmates by taking plaster casts of their heads. The serried ranks of white somnolent faces that lined his laboratories reflected his boyhood conviction that mental characteristics could be inferred from visible characteristics; he believed, for example, that prominent eyes invariably indicated a strong memory. In his later work on the brain, he came to the significant if overcategorical conclusion that each compartment corresponded to a particular mental function; but he also assumed, somewhat simplistically, that the activity of each compartment varied with its size. Since the protruding surfaces of these compartments impinged upon the bony surface of the cranium, he went on to infer that the contours of the skull would reveal which compartments of the brain were most active; and in this way a man's mental propensities could be gauged by the shape of his head. This in fact was the foundation of nineteenth-century phrenology, which was to continue attracting disciples well into the twentieth century. It was an indirect if unflattering tribute to Gall that in Nazi Germany the heads of primary school children were to be systematically examined, not only for lice, but for the size and configuration of the skull.

If Balzac's respect for Lavater and Gall is reflected in his meticulous attention to facial detail, he saw the human face as something more than a physiognomist's map. Environment too is present in the ravages of hard experience; and it is no accident that his most arresting creations are arguably his mature characters whom time and tribulation have scoured into rugged individual shapes—his younger characters seeming insipid by comparison. He was equally attentive to speech. Pronunciation and delivery were the vocal consequence and counterpart of the facial conformation that revealed the man within; and they also reflect the *via dolorosa* of environment that the individual has followed. Dialogue in Balzac's novels is given verbatim, with all its oddities; it is rarely reported. And Baron Nucingen's Jewish consonants, laboriously reproduced in successive novels, are only one of several crosses that the Balzac enthusiast has to bear.

While Balzac's professed aim was to create characters that were representative of certain categories and occupations, it must also be recognised that he could rarely overcome his penchant for the monstrous and extraordinary. He was continually drawn to the hardbitten obsessive, who had outfaced society or pursued his inclinations beyond the bounds of normality. As Baudelaire was to remark,

> All his characters are endowed with the blazing vitality that he himself possessed . . . every character in Balzac, even the hall-porter, is possessed of genius. Every soul is stuffed with willpower to the throat. They are all Balzac himself.

If this reflected a Romantic's delight in strength, it may also have been indirectly coloured by Balzac's earlier propensity to regard willpower as a quasi-independent force (see p. 32). The willpower of his more masterful creations, such as Vautrin, seems to possess a quasi-hypnotic quality that transcends their physical being. Underlying Balzac's faith in science, one is conscious of a strong emotional suspicion that life is also shaped by powerful forces that lie beyond the analysis of material reality—a suspicion that is not confined to his overtly 'spiritual' novels such as *Séraphita* (1835).

Stendhal too made a cult of willpower; but, unlike Balzac, he achieved an intellectually satisfying reconciliation between his respect for willpower and his recognition of the material basis of mind. As a disciple of Destutt de Tracy, he brought together willpower and material determinism on the same plane of physical reality, and was therefore never tempted to give willpower an autonomous 'spiritual' status. Nor did he have recourse to a dichotomous view of life on the split-levels of 'objective' and 'subjective' reality, in the manner of later Realists such as George Eliot (see pp. 94–6). Balzac, conversely, always retained something of a divided view of mind and matter, despite his periodic declarations of faith in the material unity of life. Whereas for Pascal, Man was '*ni ange, ni bête*', Balzac at times was inclined to regard him as something of both.

To concede this is not to deny the seriousness with which Balzac took the physiological content of his fictional writing, however hesitant the modern reader might be to share it. It was not mere pretentiousness that prompted him to group part of it under the general titles of 'Etudes philosophiques' and 'Etudes analytiques'. Nor was his fondness for medical metaphors mere affectation: *Physiologie du mariage, Pathologie de la vie sociale, L'Anatomie des corps enseignants, Monographie de la vertu*, etc. It reflected, if not always felicitously, the respect that an increasingly secular age felt towards the science of the human body (see pp. 23–30); and it also reflected its growing awareness of the close interrelation of medicine and social advancement (see pp. 59–60). Nor was it just whimsy that prompted Balzac to describe himself in *La Cousine Bette* as 'a simple doctor of social medicine, a horse-doctor of desperate social ills'. This, and much else, was to spur Hippolyte Taine (see pp. 128–30) into calling Balzac '*un beau champignon d'hôpital*'.

Even so, there remained within him a deep dichotomy, which can be sensed even among the semi-scientific claims of the foreword to the *Comédie Humaine*. In the same pages where he extols Geoffroy Saint-Hilaire and Gall, he denies belonging to the pantheist '*école sensualiste et matérialiste*', and is at pains to point out that belief in God need not be affected by the knowledge that the mind consists of 'cerebral and neural phenomena'. In Balzac, the metaphysician battled with the determinist, and the periodic admirer of Emmanuel Swedenborg lived uneasily with the committed disciple of Geoffroy Saint-Hilaire. The 1830s, moreover, found him increasingly interested in the Church (see pp. 50–1), an interest which was primarily, but not exclusively, linked with what he saw as the needs of society. 'Of all methods of government, is not religion the most powerful of all, for making the people accept the miseries and constant labour of their lives?' (*La Situation du Parti Royaliste*, May–June 1832). For, although contemporary philosophers might seek to restore some sort of meaning and quality to life, 'You cannot get a whole nation to study Kant.'

5 *Une Société Embourgeoisée?* Balzac's France

While Balzac believed that every niche in the jungle economy produced its own social type, he was critically aware that the jungle itself was undergoing rapid change. The later novels of *La Comédie Humaine* portray a society where men of all classes were being shaped by the forces of money-seeking and ambition—forces that found their most successful exponents in the bourgeoisie. It was here that Balzac's determinism and his sense of period came closest together; and it was also here, ironically, that his own, overemphatic perspectives can now be seen as partly the product of his time and milieu. If this, for Balzac, was a period when the objectives of a class became those of a whole society, it likewise reflected the fact that his imagination was creating a society that was in part a self-portrait: a hazard that every Realist was to encounter in some form.

Even so, Zola was later to acclaim Balzac's maturer work, notably *La Cousine Bette*, as a model of clinical observation, exemplifying the sovereign forces of *race et milieu* in a society where Man was being remorselessly moulded in new shapes. If this perhaps says more for Zola's enthusiasm than his judgement, it illustrates the lasting impression that Balzac was to make on later writers who similarly addressed themselves to depicting the determining forces of society.

With *La Cousine Bette* particularly in mind, this chapter discusses why Balzac and many of his generation regarded themselves as living in *une société embourgeoisée*, and whether they were justified in doing so.

The ethos of an age may leave its spoor in unexpected places. Explorers of the deeper gorges of the Massif Central will remember with wistful pleasure a hotel, built on a bridge, with views that defy description. The first proprietor in the 1830s wanted a name that might do justice to the splendour of the situation: *L'Hôtel du Torrent? L'Etoile des Montagnes?* With unerring assurance, he called it *L'Hôtel du Commerce.*

If writers in the 1830s and 40s lived in a shifting society that was moulding men in new shapes, they saw that money-making and ambition were dominant among these shaping influences. There was nothing new about the pursuit of wealth and influence; but the political and economic changes that followed from the French and Industrial Revolutions afforded unparalleled chances for its achievement. And the main beneficiaries were the middle classes.

The writer and middle-class perspectives

There were admittedly more obvious and immediate reasons for the Realists' interest in middle-class subjects. Both readers and writers themselves were largely of this milieu. Readers liked reading about themselves, or about the type of person they aspired to be, and writers found it easiest and most satisfying to write about the milieux they knew. The few early Realists who wrote about the working classes had either lived among them, like Mrs Gaskell (see pp. 80–5), or went out of their way to acquire information about them.

The market was always a major consideration. The novel-reading public was obviously much smaller in the 1840s than contemporary literacy estimates would suggest. The fact that some 60 per cent of the British population, and perhaps 50 per cent of the French, were said to be 'literate' meant very little, when it was enough to be able to read a few sentences and write one's name to qualify for this epithet. Only a minority could cope with a novel—even of the genre that made few demands on the intellect or the imagination. And when Balzac decided to emulate Eugène Sue and Alexandre Dumas, and hit the public in a big way through newspaper serialisation, the readership he envisaged was modest by modern standards. *Le Constitutionnel*, which serialised *La Cousine Bette*, had 25,000 subscribers—markedly more in fact than *Le Journal des Débats*, which had handled Dumas's highly successful *Le Comte de Monte Cristo* (1844–5). With newspapers of this quality selling at the equivalent of about 15 per cent of an average workman's daily wage, Balzac's readers were clearly of a well-heeled walk of life.

This is also reflected in Balzac's treatment of working-class conditions, where his appeal is to his readers' curiosity, rather than to their sympathy. Like Sue, his purpose was to make their flesh creep. The Paris proletariat had become sufficiently large by the 1840s to be a subject of growing apprehension—a fear which Balzac shared. His references to them became increasingly less sympathetic, as the decade progressed. It can paradoxically be argued that the early Realists were less interested than the Romantics in working-class life. It is true that the Romantics made little attempt to portray its material detail. They were content to depict what they saw as the spiritual desolation of urban life (as in William Blake's *London*), or the sensation of fatigue through long hours of labour in wretched conditions (as in Thomas Hood's *Song of the Shirt*). At the same time they tended conversely to idealise the rural worker, as supposedly embodying a primitive goodness, uncontaminated by urban society; Wordsworth's *Michael* being but one of many familiar examples. But whatever aspect of working-class life the Romantic chose to evoke, he could do so at a distance. Indeed too close a contact with the subject might complicate or blur the impression that he wanted to create.

When the early Realists wrote of the working classes, it was only occasionally to treat them in their own right. As often as not, their aim was to emphasise some point of criticism that they were making about the middle or upper classes. Their propertied readers, for the most part, accepted this quite cheerfully since the bulk of them assumed that the novelists' criticism was in no way applicable to them personally—though it was a remarkably perceptive description of the family next door. And, no doubt, scores of Crevels and Dambreuses shook their heads in disapproval at the egoism of their counterparts in Balzac and Flaubert. Conversely there were others who found the subject of themselves so absorbing that they preferred to see their fictional counterparts described as knaves or fools rather than not written about at all. Nor can one discount the modest but enthusiastic number of masochists who enjoyed the *frisson* of self-disgust as they recognised themselves and their associates in the vices and foibles pilloried in the book.

Yet, whatever type he was, the middle-class reader had the comfortable sensation that the author accepted the basic structure of society, and was inveighing against its sharp corners rather than calling in question society itself. However much the writer might castigate the bourgeoisie, he was not suggesting that the working class would manage matters any better. With the exception of Büchner (see pp. 59–65), the leading figures among the early Realists contained no committed socialists. There were admittedly a certain number among Realism's minor lights; but the motley collection of socialist novels that the early nineteenth century produced mainly belonged to other *genres*.

In the later half of the nineteenth century, however, the growing size of the urban working class was to thrust itself more forcibly on middle-class minds; and literature inevitably came to reflect the fact. At the same time the spread of 'Naturalism' among writers (see Chapter 12) was to focus their attention on the animal nature of Man and encourage them to look to working-class life as a potential source of illustration (see pp. 132–3).

L'Embourgeoisement

Writers observed with mingled feelings the spread of bourgeois attitudes and methods to other classes. To a large degree it was a matter of self-defence. Middle-class ascendancy was being won at the expense of other classes; and it seemed to some of the potential victims that only action of the same calibre could guarantee survival. The landed upper classes found their economic and political pre-eminence challenged by the money-makers of commerce and industry, who rallied electoral support to themselves on an ambiguous programme of cheap food, democratic progress and an end to outworn privilege. On the other hand, the traditional skilled artisan found himself unable to compete with the cheap production methods of new factories; and he was increasingly driven into joining the uniform ranks of factory labour where his superseded skills could no longer command a superior wage. A small but significant number of artisans—with business acumen, technical imagination and moneyed acquaintances who were prepared to make them loans—might seek to emulate the pioneers of industrial change. And some of the most noteworthy names in industry were to spring from unpretentious origins. But these men were by their very nature exceptional. More characteristic, in relation to their class, were the landowners and long-established merchant families who decided to invest their revenue in the new enterprises that were making the futures of the up-and-coming business-men and industrialists. In this way their interests became identified, to some extent, with those of the middle classes. They naturally resented middle-class competition, just as the bourgeois businessmen resented the competition of each other. It was also inevitable that they should resent the increase in middle-class political power. But when it came to the big issues in parliament 'that affected their economic interests, they tended to vote with the progressive bourgeoisie. This was particularly true of land-issues—of which the biggest was whether the laws that favoured the old traditional landed economy should be maintained or repealed. Those nobles whose wealth now lay primarily in commerce or industry generally voted for the abolition of the laws protecting the old order, and thereby came to be increasingly identified with middle-class interests.

It was therefore understandable that writers should be acutely conscious of a thrusting, money-making ethos in society, which affected many of the aristocracy as well as the middle classes. Wordsworth wrote in 1817:

I see clearly that the principal ties which kept the different classes of society in a vital and harmonious dependence upon each other have, within these thirty years, either been greatly impaired or wholly dissolved. Everything has been put to market and sold for the highest price it would buy.

Similarly in *La Cousine Bette* Balzac comments:

Under the Restoration the aristocracy has . . . become economical, careful, and provident: in fact bourgeois and inglorious. Now, 1830 has completed the work of 1793. In France, from now on, there will be great names but no more great houses, unless there are political changes, difficult to foresee. Everything bears the stamp of personal interest. The wisest buy annuities with their money. The family has been destroyed.

Le paysan petit-embourgeoisé

Balzac was but one of many writers who also saw the money-making ethos spreading to the peasantry. France differed from Britain and much of Germany, in that the first French Revolution had seen a large number of the noble and ecclesiastical estates split up among the bourgeoisie and peasantry. At the same time the feudal payments and restrictions which landlords had traditionally imposed on the peasantry were abolished, and many peasant landholders (notably those who were not rent-paying tenants) became in effect freeholders. The outcome was that much of France in the early nineteenth century was a patchwork of tiny peasant holdings, each owned or rented by a peasant proprietor who was proud of his independence, but who had to work extremely hard to make a living from it. He also had to provide for his children; and since the Revolutionary and Napoleonic laws stipulated the division of property among heirs, much of the peasant's spare time was devoted to scheming how to enlarge his holding or make it more productive. The calculating peasant is a familiar enough figure in French literature, from Balzac to Zola and beyond, and his problems found a certain counterpart in those other countries that retained the Napoleonic *Code Civil* after 1815: notably the Low Countries and parts of Germany and Italy (although the peasantry of many of these regions had more serious indigenous problems of their own).

In Britain and Prussia, however, there had been the reverse process in agriculture. Instead of large estates being split up, it had been a case of small tenants being evicted or moved around by landlords who wanted to turn the land over to new progressive types of farming. Moreover, in those continental countries where the peasantry had gained, or retained, little from the Revolutionary period, the rural masses could still be a disruptive force. Germany and Italy were to see periodic peasant riots, culminating in and contributing to the events of 1846–8. And in sizeable stretches of Central Europe, 1848 was to do for the land-holding peasantry what the 1790s had done for rural France; even if the landless farm labourer continued to be a more characteristic feature of Central Europe than of France.

Most of the French peasant holdings, however, were too small for modern farming methods to be effectively applied to them; and although the peasant now shared the tight-fisted, property-owning mentality of the middle classes, he had little material progress to show for it. Nevertheless, with the reinstatement of universal male suffrage in 1848, the French peasant was shortly to exercise a decisive political influence in France, which paradoxically was to strengthen still further the *embourgeoisement* of French society (see pp. 71–2).

Balzac and the July Monarchy

Balzac was never to know the Industrial Revolution in the way that English writers such as Mrs Gaskell knew it (see Chapter 8). His only experience of transformed landscapes came from Belgium and certain of the affected areas in France—which were as yet fairly limited. It was the commercial and financial consequences of the Industrial and French

Revolutions that he knew best, with what he saw as their insidious effect on social attitudes and loyalties. The narrow Paris streets of *La Comédie Humaine*, with their leprous façades, were little different from what they had been in previous centuries, despite Balzac's sharp eye for what was new or fast disappearing. It was essentially the life within and its motivation that he saw as changing.

His unhappy *début* in the business world of the 1820s left him in no doubt as to the harsh *realpolitik* that governed it. His initial legal studies found him articled to a lawyer for several years—an episode which brought him first-hand experience of the emotions and material interests that underlay human relations in a competitive society. Once his student days were over, however, he devoted himself to writing and to various ill-judged business enterprises. In his mind the two activities had much in common: 'We have no more works, we have products' (*Béatrix, 1839*). His first novels were aimed, unsuccessfully, at the quasi-popular market; and his various ventures as printer, publisher and paper-maker were based on the principle of cheap products and wide sales. By 1828 he was facing the threat of bankruptcy. Rescued by his family and friends, he abandoned these enterprises and consigned his energies more or less exclusively to writing—deeply in debt, but rich in experience of the unedifying world of business.

While he had few illusions about the selfishness that governs most men in any age, the regimes that had governed France before the July Monarchy (1830–48) had ostensibly subscribed to certain ideals that they publicly upheld, however much they might betray them in practice. The *ancien régime* and the Restoration outwardly honoured Christianity, and tried, after a fashion, to preserve an ordered society in which employer and employed had responsibilities towards each other, even if the arrangement proved in reality very one-sided. The Revolution, for all its mistakes and bourgeois self-interest, had embodied concepts such as equality before the law that could be respected by men of all classes, if not necessarily welcomed or approved. With Bonaparte, on the other hand, there was a sense in which order and vitality were brought together. France reached the peak of her power and influence. And although the Empire might uphold ambivalent ideals of respect for the Revolutionary achievement on the one hand, and respect for the Church and an ordered society on the other, it nevertheless inspired Frenchmen to extremes of energy and self-sacrifice that no subsequent regime would witness. The July monarchy (1830–48), by contrast, appeared to have no ideals, other than a general exhortation to self-aggrandisement. As Crevel tells Baroness Hulot in *La Cousine Bette*

You're deluding yourself, dear angel, if you imagine that it's King Louis-Philippe that we're ruled by, and he has no illusions himself on that score. He knows, as we all do, that above the Charter there stands the holy, venerable, solid, the adored, gracious, beautiful, noble, ever young, almighty franc!

—an echo in fact of Balzac's remark in *Splendeurs et Misères des Courtisanes*, 'The Charter has proclaimed the reign of money, success justifies all in an atheistical age'.

The restored Bourbon monarchy had been overthrown in 1830, largely because of Charles X's attempts to increase royal power by reducing the electorate to a quarter of its former size. Radicals hoped that the time had now come for a massive increase in the franchise and the initiation of a far-reaching programme of political reform, with perhaps long-term social implications; many hoped for a republic. These, however, were far from the intentions of the junta of *haut bourgeois* liberals who had taken the initiative in the events of 1830, and who had installed a more constitutional brand of monarch in the shape of the Duke of Orleans.

The men who brought the new King, Louis Philippe, to power included eminent businessmen and bankers; and it used to be fashionable to call the reign of Louis Philippe 'the bourgeois monarchy'. Up to a point this was justified. The *grands seigneurs* of Charles X's last cabinets had to retire jobless to their estates, while the new ministers were mainly Napoleonic officials, with a sprinkling of bankers and businessmen. Balzac was not exaggerating when he said in *La Cousine Bette* that 'Louis Philippe was levying a kind of conscription among the old Napoleonic adherents'. On a less exalted political level, Stendhal was one of the ex-Napoleonic officials who came back into favour. However, the biggest visible change of personnel came among the mayors of towns. Whereas the Restoration mayors had been mainly landowners, the new ones were predominantly businessmen—Balzac's Crevel in *La Cousine Bette* being a case in point. Nevertheless one must not misconceive the change that the 1830 revolution brought about. If the Orleanist regime dismissed many of the landowners from office, it was career officials rather than businessmen who were to provide Louis Philippe with most of his ministers and senior adminis-trators. Similarly the franchise and eligibility to sit in parliament were still subject to a tax qualification which politically favoured landowners at the expense of businessmen. Even so a businessman does not have to be a minister or to sit in parliament to be influential: it is sufficient for him to have contacts there; and the current fashion of 'de-bourgeoisifying' the Orleans monarchy needs to be treated with some caution. The important point is that, whatever their influence, the bourgeoisie found a lot to appreciate in the negative policies of the Orleanist monarchy. Its maintenance of the laws against trade unions and its refusal to reduce adult working-hours were approved by the employers, while its reluctance to spend public money on social reform kept taxes down and likewise pleased the bourgeoisie. If the historian is to accuse the Orleanist monarchy of failing to care for the masses, his accusation must rest on what the government neglected to do, rather than on what it did. For however important the political factors, the forces that shaped society in these years rested largely on the economic activities of private employers.

Balzac in fact was more interested in occupations than regimes as moulders of men (see Chapter 4). Yet, as *La Cousine Bette* exemplifies, Balzac saw each regime as reflecting and intensifying the ethos of the dominant class within it—an ethos which was itself a product of the occupations of the members of this class. *La Cousine Bette* makes the point in the continuing contrast the novel draws between the Hulot-Fischer family and Célestin Crevel. As *fournisseurs* to the French armies, Balzac's Hulot-Fischer family rose from modest beginnings under the Revolution to wealth and honours under Napoleon. Crevel, by contrast, is the quintessence of the sharp-eyed bourgeois investor, the vulgar self-seeker, who according to Balzac found favour and respect under the July Monarchy.

Crevel's initial commercial experience was gained in the old-style perfume business of César Birotteau, who for Balzac symbolised the honest, hard-working, traditional businessman, pushed to the wall by the ruthless get-rich-quick mentality engendered by the Industrial Revolution, the social consequences of the French Revolution, and the erosion of Christian values. The profits of Crevel's subsequent career as a perfume manufacturer are invested in railways—for as Cousine Bette herself remarks, 'this is a railway age'. Balzac admittedly exaggerated the attractiveness of railways as a rapid road to riches. Each mile of track required three hundred tons of iron; and the investor could expect no significant return on his money until the line was in service. Even in Britain where the network was bigger and brisker, the average investor was receiving only 3.7 per cent at mid-century. Indeed Balzac himself was to discover the extent of his overoptimism shortly after writing *La Cousine Bette*, when his own shares in the Chemin de Fer du Nord proved disappointing; it was only after his death that they started to justify the investors' expectations.

The difference in ethos engendered by the Napoleonic Empire and the July Monarchy is reflected on all levels in the novel, even in the sexual activities of the Hulots and Crevel. In contrast to Baron Hulot's womanising, which has a certain generosity in its self-destructiveness, Crevel's sensuality is always kept within the bounds of prudent calculation. When his long-felt ambition to seduce Baroness Hulot is finally offered him, but at the price of helping the Hulots with a substantial sum, his reaction is characteristic: 'a retired businessman . . . has to be, lordly with some method . . . He opens an account for his sprees . . . earmarks certain profits for that purpose—but to make a hole in his capital . . . that would be madness!'

Society and salvation

If *La Cousine Bette* condemns Baron Hulot as an obsessive lecher, it is quite clear where Balzac's sympathies lay between the two men. Believing that different societies produced different men, Balzac preferred the ornaments of the Empire to those of the July Monarchy. His nostalgia for the Empire partly reflected the fact that as a *fournisseur* to the French armed services, his father's prosperity had waxed and waned with the fortunes of the French army. And yet, although 'Bonapartist' was the label that perhaps fitted Balzac best, this was not the direction that his formal political allegiances were to take. His eclectic views on the nature of life (see pp. 32–3 and 35–41) had ill-disposed him towards the throne-and-altar ethos of the Restoration—as long as the regime lasted. But what he then saw as the dreary materialism of the July Monarchy gave him second thoughts. Not only did it appeal to the worst in human nature, but its weary succession of short-lived ministries consisted, in Balzac's view, of tired old men who lacked the enthusiasm and imagination that the nation needed. Quite what he wanted in its place is far from clear. There undoubtedly existed in his political outlook something of the Romantic bloody-mindedness, or divine discontent, that characterised the outlook of so many writers of his generation. Their commitment too often took the shape of a destructive allegiance to an unborn state of affairs, or a barren nostalgia for something dead.

Disillusioned with business, and similarly convinced that all governments were basically 'an insurance-contract drawn up between the rich against the poor' (*Traité de la vie élégante*, 1830), Balzac increasingly saw society's problems as lying in human nature rather than in the inadequacies of institutions. Appealing to the 'spiritual' side of his nature (see pp. 40–1), this conclusion encouraged him to look towards religion as a salvation; or at least as a preservative, since his pessimistic assessment of the times inclined him to believe that the best one could do was to prevent matters getting worse. And from 1831 his writing revealed a growing interest in Catholicism. This in turn caused him to look to the Legitimists with less disfavour. For all their stupidity under the Restoration, their government had at least been committed to the defence of the Church, albeit for self-interested motives, and in Balzac's current frame of mind, this was enough to commend them. It remained, however, a theoretical Legitimism—a conceptual belief in the ideals of the Bourbon monarchy, rather than a subscription to its tangible forms. This could be crudely summarised by saying that if people would only turn back to the traditional concepts of an ordered society, based on Catholicism and respect for authority, all might be well. It remained, however, a theoretical solution, which Balzac did not really believe was realisable. For one thing the bourgeois society of the 1840s could not be transformed by a mere change of political regime. The restored Bourbon monarchy of 1815–30 had scarcely embodied the ideals that Balzac now professed; and he thought that the new Bourbon Pretender to the throne was far from being the man to be able to achieve a miraculous transformation of French attitudes. Indeed Balzac's position was not dissimilar from those of members of Action Française who in the 1930s supported the ideal of monarchy, without believing that the current royalist claimant was the man to embody it. Similarly one could argue that Balzac's somewhat utilitarian attitude to Catholicism had a suggestion of Action Française in it—a belief in the social necessity of Catholicism without personally subscribing to its claims to authenticity. As he himself put it, in one of his colder moments, 'the Catholic Faith is a lie with which we deceive ourselves'; but for the bulk of people, it was a necessary deception, since Catholicism was 'a complete system for repressing the depraved tendencies of Man' (Avant-propos to *La Comédie Humaine*).

PART TWO

Facing Reality: Determinism and the Realist Response

Büchner, Flaubert, Mrs Gaskell, George Eliot, Turgenev, Tolstoy

6 Pessimism

The eighteenth-century determinists had been, for the most part, an optimistic bunch. The excitement of intellectual innovation and an increased understanding of the human mind shielded their midnight thoughts from the bleaker implications of their work. Similarly the Idéologues of the 1790s who blossomed and fructified in the rays of government esteem were too happily preoccupied with official commissions and their newfound freedom of expression, to spend melancholy days contemplating what had been lost with Christianity and the concept of free will. Nor, for the most part, were they of a temperament to regret lost innocence; they were men of intense curiosity, with a firm faith in the redemptive powers of science. The Empire, and especially the Restoration, put them once more in the position of being a distrusted sect, but gave them the inner sense of corporate militancy that characterises minorities who have to fight for intellectual survival. The task of preserving and asserting their beliefs gave them little inclination to initiate major debates on whether their beliefs were, in the last analysis, conducive to human happiness. And when they did, they strenuously argued that Man can thrive only on Truth, however unpalatable it may be.

The 1830 revolution, however, inaugurated a regime which was more sympathetic to their outlook; and, in relieving determinists of the necessity to be always justifying themselves, it gave them more time to survey dispassionately the stony prospects that they had opened up.

The secular drought

The July Monarchy has commonly been called 'Voltairian' in outlook—a term that is likewise often applied to the French middle classes in the same period. The term, however, suggests a degree of cerebral application which only a minority were prepared, or able, to indulge. It becomes more acceptable if it is thought of as an attitude adopted as much through fashion as personal conviction. Undoubtedly the middle and upper classes produced the bulk of the writers whose work challenged the premises of traditional beliefs and attitudes. But then, as now, it was only a minority of men who were seriously preoccupied with such questions as the nature of Man and his purpose, if any, in life. Under the *ancien régime*, the scepticism of the eighteenth-century rationalists had been kept from spreading as widely as it might have done by government restrictions and social convention. The Revolution, however, broke down many of these restrictions; and what the Restoration rebuilt after 1815 was swept away in 1830.

It can be said of all classes that under the *ancien régime* much of what had passed for religious observance was little more than social convention, enforced by fear of employers and local magnates, or of what people would think. Underpinning the whole structure was the traditional alliance between throne and altar. In so far as religious observance was more than this, love of God probably played less a part than did a vague apprehension of what might happen after death.

When the Church was persecuted under the Revolution, only the convinced Catholic was prepared to hear Mass said by a virtual outlaw. And it was only in those areas of France that resisted the Revolution that social convention kept the churches full. Elsewhere, however, the habit of churchgoing, once broken, was not easily mended—even under the Bourbon Restoration. Although the timid Catholic resumed church attendance under Napoleon, the indifferent one remained lost to the Church.

What the French Revolution had begun, the Industrial Revolution continued. The growth of industrial towns in western Europe took young men from their families and settled them in communities where social conventions had no traditional roots, and where there was little social incentive to go to church. At the same time the Industrial Revolution accelerated the whole process of communication. By the middle decades of the century, railways and newspapers put the rural provinces in increasing contact with the secular attitudes of the main centres of population. City newspapers were dumped on the platforms of country railway stations on the day of printing; and the Homais of the local press were able to model their editorials and political comment on the latest Paris opinion.

For the reading public, religious faith was also undermined by the moral implications of what scientists were saying about the nature of life. Steely-nerved evolutionists were now portraying life in all its forms, including Man, as a struggle for survival, a continual conflict in which the wastage and suffering were enormous. Moralists looked into this furnace, and were appalled at what they saw. Not only was the suffering enormous, but it seemed to serve no 'moral' purpose, other than to perpetuate a material existence which itself had no apparent *raison d'être*. Nature red in tooth and claw offered them little proof of a loving Creator; and they became increasingly scornful of traditional Christian claims that even the suffering of children and animals had its place in the economy of salvation. Poetry and fiction gave birth to a growing literature of protest against the moral outrageousness of a creation that belied the gospel virtues. Indeed, Jesus in conflict with the Creator became an overworked poetic cliché, especially in France; *'le silence de Dieu devant la misère du monde'* proved to them that God was either a monster or a void; and the void was the preferable explanation. The Christian churches gradually learnt, after a fashion, to assimilate the unpalatable evidence of science, and to ward off the attacks of moralists and men of sensibility. But it created doubts in the minds of many thinking Christians, and the casualties on the way were great.

Secular thought responded in varying ways to the harsh vision of life that science had produced. A pessimistic stoicism characterised the attitude of many of the more sensitive creative writers. Others, however, especially those who were conscious of the great advances made in science, saw hope in human progress. Though an animal, man's intelligence and self-consciousness would enable him to advance far beyond the imagination of traditional Christianity, provided that he followed the light of reason and knowledge and ignored the irrational prohibitions and beliefs taught by the Church. This was the view of many Positivists, and was a major reason for their prominence in nineteenth-century thought, especially the middle-brow world of the periodical-reading bourgeoisie.

There are often difficulties in distinguishing between Positivism as such and a more general attitude that was gaining currency in nineteenth-century educated circles; an attitude which amounted to a cheerful vote of confidence in empiricism and scientific observation. Positivism is usually associated with Auguste Comte (1798–1857), who was at one time the inventive, and retentive, secretary of Henri de Saint-Simon (1760–1825), many of whose ideas found their way into the hard core of Positivism. Saint-Simon had insisted that since progress depends on the advance of knowledge, proper scientific methods must be applied to the study of Man and society. He envisaged a new '*science de l'homme*', which would gradually acquire the exactitude of astronomy and physics. With the advance of this science from the conjectural to what Saint-Simon called 'the positive' stage, Man would be able to order his existence in a way which would completely transform society, thereby establishing material and moral standards that had hitherto been thought unattainable. 'In a positive state', Comte had added,

> the human mind, recognising the impossibility of obtaining absolute truth, renounces the search for the origin and determination of the universe and gives up the attempt to find the ultimate causes of phenomena. The human mind in the positive state will devote itself exclusively to discovering through a continuation of reasoning and observation, the effective laws that govern these phenomena.

La Mettrie and Cabanis had said as much in the previous century (see pp. 31–2 and 23–4), but less obtrusively and to a less receptive audience.

Comte's first *Système de politique positive* appeared in 1824; but it was his *Cours de philosophie positive* (1830–42) which made his major impact. George Eliot was to say in 1851 that Positivist science offered the only hope of extending Man's knowledge and happiness (*Westminster Review*, January 1851); and her sharp-eyed consort, George Lewes, described Comte's *Cours* as the greatest work of our century, . . . one of the mighty landmarks in the history of opinion.' (*Biographical History of Philosophy*, 1845–6). If it is perhaps a little hard for the modern reader to subscribe to each superlative of Lewes's verdict, these accolades nevertheless reflect the extent to which Comte successfully responded to what many of his generation were asking. Like Herbert Spencer (see pp. 164–5), Comte had a breadth of outlook and a gift for synthesis which excited the reader seeking a comprehensive view of life, in an age when so many former certainties were being eroded.

The expulsion of religious belief from many intellects, and the loss of faith in Man as an autonomous individual will, had left an emotional vacuum which both thinkers and poets found hard to fill. The problem was how to give back to life meaning and emotional content. Men wanted the sweet sensation of enthusiasm, but wanted a sound rational basis for that enthusiasm. To enthuse because one was happier enthusing seemed an unsatisfying reason. So poets and thinkers looked for a God-substitute in art, humanity or the universe: anything that would give a satisfying answer to the question, 'why bother?' Comte himself attempted to formulate a religion of humanity; but, in the experience of most of its short-lived adherents, its effect was to underline rather than assuage the predicament of Man without God.

Romanticism was one response, with its cult of sensibility and self-assertion; but as Flaubert was to demonstrate in the shape of Frédéric Moreau and Emma Bovary, its dangers outweighed its consolations for the ordinary person of no particular talent. *L'Education Sentimentale* and *Madame Bovary* were to delineate with merciless perception the solitary self-isolating character of the cult of sensibility; while the cult of self-assertion, in art or public life, was likewise shown by Flaubert to be a fundamentally introspective exercise, of limited value to others, and ultimately of limited value to oneself (see pp. 70–3).

Rejecting the cult of self as egotistical and masking the realities of life, Realists were more favourably disposed to those who tried to give content to life by improving the material lot of others. While philanthropic and charitable work was scarcely a matter for disagreement, arguments arose as soon as writers considered major transformations of society. Some, like Stendhal and Balzac, doubted the need for any significant redistribution of wealth, however much they might denounce individual cases of hardship or exploitation. Others, such as Büchner, were convinced of the fundamental injustice of society as they knew it, and the need for measures that transcended the capabilities of philanthropic individuals. For a generation that had not yet seen the sorry outcome of the 1848 revolutions, revolutionary politics still seemed to offer a practical solution. Whether they wanted a social revolution, like Büchner, or a more democratic society, like Ibsen in his salad days, several Realists had close connections with the clandestine political movements of the pre-1848 period. Others, such as Flaubert, viewed the reform movement benevolently, but with more detachment. In most cases, however, experience of revolutionary activity was followed by disillusion; as with Büchner in the mid-1830s (see pp. 62–3) and Ibsen in 1851 (see pp. 159–60). After the debacle of 1848, revolutionary activity came increasingly to be dismissed by Realists as unproductive: so much so that it came to be a cliché of Realist fiction that violence brought little but misery to its intended beneficiaries.

Parliamentary politics were viewed less pessimistically, but with a strong streak of scepticism, as exemplified in the cool ironic eye which George Eliot cast over the parliamentary Reform campaign in Britain (see pp. 87–8). In the last analysis they saw democracy as no answer to society's problems, unless the electorate was educated into a constructive awareness of what needed to be done. Indeed, in so far as the Realists had faith in anything, it was in education—and its corollary, science. Education and Science, in whose name so many men have since been salaried, were the Isis and Osiris of Realism. Even Büchner, prince of pessimists, came nearest to hope when contemplating the solace they might afford. Even so, it would, by its very nature, be a slow redemption. And, as the nineteenth century wore on, with only modest gains in the battle for a more enlightened humanity and a more humane society, it was not surprising that later generations of Realist writers should display less of the ebullient optimism of a Balzac or the urbane confidence of a Stendhal.

Georg Büchner

Although only two or three decades separated the childhood of Büchner (1813–37) and Flaubert (1821–80) from that of Stendhal and Balzac, they nevertheless represent a darker state of mind. Temperament had much to do with it. Neither had the zest for life of their elders; and although both had the advantage of a congenial childhood, neither enjoyed good health. Their view of Man was also more deeply rooted in a first-hand scientific knowledge, to which neither Stendhal nor Balzac could lay claim. Despite their poetic vision, neither of them let it colour their sceptical assessment of human capabilities.

There is, however, a sense in which both reflected something of their generation. Both embarked on their literary careers in periods of political disillusion—Büchner in the aftermath of the German risings of the early 1830s, and Flaubert after the short-lived Second French Republic. They likewise lived in a period which had been granted sufficient opportunity to assess the slim chances of finding anything half so consoling as religious belief.

Büchner and Flaubert both came of well-established medical families. Büchner's paternal and maternal grandfathers were doctors, as was his sturdy, and somewhat domineering father, Ernst, who was a living examplar of that favourite figure of nineteenth-century Realism, the military doctor who had served in the Napoleonic wars. Stendhal had provided the fictional prototype in Julien Sorel's boyhood mentor, the old army surgeon who leaves Julien his collection of books. Military doctors were to play a significant role in Realism, both in the novels it produced and in the lives of their authors. In common with their civilian counterparts in the plays of Ibsen, Hauptmann and Chekhov, they were professionally well aware of the physiological basis of human nature; and, as such, were often used by authors as spokesmen of rugged common sense on the fundamental issues of life. But the army doctors of the Napoleonic wars had the further qualification of having seen the human lot at its most brutal, and of having been participants in the enormous changes which these years brought about in Europe. Amputating limbs without anaesthetic, and dealing with a daunting variety of diseases in the wake of armies that had traversed and retraversed the Continent, such men knew more about the extremes of life than most of their contemporaries.

Like Julien Sorel's mentor, Büchner's father combined the outlook of a freethinking liberal with a great admiration for Bonaparte although later life was to find him increasingly cautious and conservative in his political outlook. By the time of Georg's birth in 1813, he had left the Grande Armée—to which his native Hesse-Darmstadt had contributed men—and returned to civilian practice. Intended by his father for a medical career, Georg was reared in a milieu similar to Flaubert's, surrounded by medical books and journals. And, as with Flaubert, his father's freethinking liberalism outweighed, without excluding, the quietly *bien pensant* influence of his mother, from whom he developed a strong interest in folk poetry and German cultural unity. As an adolescent, Büchner already shared his father's atheism, despite his continuing close ties with his mother's Lutheran friends and relatives.

The Büchner family was itself an impressive monument to the influence of *race et milieu*. Georg's younger brothers included the distinguished scientist and materialist philosopher, Ludwig Büchner, whose *Force and Matter* (1855) was to be a bible of nineteenth-century determinism (see pp. 107–8). Of the others, Wilhelm Büchner became a chemist and manufacturer, with strong political interests which were eventually to take him to the German Reichstag after the unification of Germany. The other children's inclinations were closer to their mother's. After a fairly bohemian youth, Alexander attained celebrity as Professor of Literature at Caen, while Luise was a well-known novelist and an early supporter of women's rights.

Georg himself was enrolled in the medical school of Strasbourg University in 1831, where he studied zoology and comparative anatomy. After a disturbed but fruitful undergraduate career (see pp. 62–3), his intentions moved away from medical practice towards university teaching. It was a measure of his breadth of interests that he was initially unable to make up his mind as to whether to present himself as a teacher of zoology or philosophy. His thesis in fact was on the nervous system of the barbel fish;

and when he was eventually appointed as a zoology lecturer in the University of Zürich (1836), his first course of lectures was on the comparative anatomy of fishes and amphibians.

Büchner's creative writing owed a great deal to his scientific training and discipline. Speaking of Büchner's medical background, a friend remarked 'I believe you owe to it your greatest strength, I mean your extraordinary freedom from prejudices and prepossessions, I might almost say: your autopsy, which is evident in everything you write'. As an atheist, convinced of the evolutionary materialist character of existence, Büchner had no time for the proponents of 'purpose' in nature: teleology was contrary to his experience and view of life. It was symptomatic of his preoccupations that his first lecture for the University of Zürich should be 'On the nerves of the brain'—albeit within the context of his study of fishes and amphibians. And it was particularly indicative of his evolutionary view of Man that he should energetically subscribe to Lorenz Oken's views on the nature of the brain. Oken, himself a Zürich biologist, believed that the skull was no more than a developed vertebra and that the nerves of the brain were fundamentally spinal nerves. With its emphasis on the unpretentious origins of mind, this hypothesis had a particular appeal to Büchner, who consistently opposed the attempts of contemporary Idealists to keep 'the human spirit' in exalted isolation from other living matter.

Admired by his students for the clarity and originality of his lectures, Büchner's life amid the acrid odours of the Zürich laboratories did not keep him from the spare-time literary activities that had helped to make his student days so full and fraught. Certain aspects of his writing were stormy premonitions of Naturalism (see pp. 123–33), particularly in their emphasis on the animal nature of Man. While it is arguable that this emphasis merely lifted the slab from what was already implicit in early Realism, his literary work was nevertheless much nearer the world of Zola than of Balzac. And, like Isben, Büchner's personal view of Man was heavy with a profound pessimism. As a biologist Büchner accepted determinism as a scientific fact, but as an artist he was revolted by it.

The uncompleted *Woyzeck* is a dark distillation of these feelings. Written in Zürich in 1836–7, these dramatic fragments are partly based on fact: like the earlier *Dantons Tod* (1835) and his novelle, *Lenz* (written in 1835). Büchner's main sources were three cases of *crime passionel*, two of which he found described at length in contemporary medical journals, while the third may well have come his way more directly, when the corpse of the murderer was sent to the dissecting laboratory at Giessen, where Büchner was studying. Of these cases, it was the earlier one of Woyzeck, executed in 1824 for killing his mistress, that had excited most interest and argument among doctors and psychiatrists.

The Woyzeck of Büchner's play appears throughout as the helpless victim of his inherited limitations and the circumstances that shape his life.

The ineluctable nature of his destiny is underlined on all levels of the play, in its grim humour as elsewhere. It is for instance the determinist in Büchner which ridicules the grotesque doctor who tries to convince Woyzeck that willpower can control the body. In Naturalist drama of the later nineteenth century, doctors are often made the mouthpiece of the author and the voice of objective commonsense (see pp. 134–8). The doctor in *Woyzeck*, however, is not intended as an authoritative representative of the medical profession or scientific thinking, for which Büchner had the highest respect, but as a caricature of the standpoint of the German Idealists. While the doctor claims that man can control nature, Woyzeck's life is a continual demonstration of the contrary, not least when nature obliges him to disappoint the doctor's hopes in him by urinating in the street.

> I saw it all, Woyzeck . . . You were pissing on the wall like a dog! . . . 'But, doctor, when Nature calls.' 'What has Nature to do with it? Didn't I prove to you that the *musculus constrictor vesicae* is controlled by your will? . . . Woyzeck, man is free! In Mankind alone we see glorified the individual's will to freedom!

In Büchner's analysis, morality too was at the mercy of hard material facts, especially in the case of the labouring poor. As Büchner remarked when a student: 'it is no great feat to be an honest man when one has soup, vegetables and meat to eat every day'. But, in Woyzeck's case,

> with us poor people it's money, money! If you don't have money . . . Well you just can't have morals when you're bringing someone like yourself into the world. People like us can't be holy in this world—or the next. If we ever did get into heaven, they'd set us to work on the thunder.

Like the Naturalists of a later generation, Büchner saw the working classes as epitomising Man's animal nature at its clearest and most vulnerable; utterly stripped of the protective veneer of culture and 'civilised' behaviour with which the comfortably-off concealed from each other the animal that lurked within each of them.

Büchner's working-class sympathies were already apparent in his student days, when his concept of revolution envisaged a full social revolution, not the mere liberalising of existing government; it was only by changing social conditions that there was any hope of changing Man. The revolutionary student groups with which he was connected in Strasbourg and Giessen (Hesse-Darmstadt) were both remarkable for the close contact they tried to maintain with local working-class militants, whereas most student groups made little impact outside the universities.

Yet, like Ibsen in 1851 (see pp. 159–60), the implications of Büchner's political enthusiasms were to undergo a savage *mise au point* in 1835. He had published with Pastor Friedrich Weidig an anonymous revolutionary pamphlet, *Der Hessische Landbote* (1834), attacking the autocratic nature and social injustices of the Hessian regime. Listed by the police, Büchner fled to the safety of Strasbourg, while the unfortunate Weidig was arrested. After many months of beatings and interrogation, Weidig eventually died in prison, having opened his veins with a piece of glass; while another colleague was systematically beaten and tortured. Büchner was overwhelmed by the appalling contrast between the price paid by his friends and the insignificant fruits of their activity—a price made more disproportionate by the fact that Weidig's politics had been more moderate and less socially-orientated than Büchner's. From the time of his return to Strasbourg in 1835, Büchner never again involved himself in politics.

Biographers are divided on the nature of this step. Some argue that it was not a repudiation of the principle of revolution, but rather a recognition that Germany was not yet ripe for it. Others, conversely, have taken their cue from the pessimism of *Dantons Tod*, written while Büchner was lying low during the early months of 1835. The mood of this play had already been foreshadowed in a letter of the previous winter to his fiancée (written between November 1833 and March 1834),

> I was studying the history of the Revolution. I felt myself as though utterly crushed under the frightful fatalism of history . . . The individual a mere froth on the wave, greatness a mere chance, the dominance of genius a puppet's game, a ridiculous struggling against an iron law, the recognition of which is the highest achievement, but which to control is impossible . . . The word *must* is one of the curses with which mankind is baptised. The saying: 'It must needs be that offences come; but woe to him by whom the offence cometh' is terrifying. What is it in us that lies, murders, steals? I no longer care to pursue this thought.

While the vision and energy of the historical Danton had made him the hero of Stendhal, and also of Büchner's own adolescence, *Dantons Tod* presents him at the end of his career, bleakly contemplating the pointlessness of life. Robespierre, by contrast, attempts to give meaning to life through activity. But fundamentally it is only his narrow-mindedness and lack of subtlety that enable him to act; and, unlike Danton, he thinks in abstractions. Danton, conversely, is paralysed by the human reality that lies behind the abstractions and the impossibility of knowing what people really are and what they need. 'We're thick-skinned creatures who reach out our hands towards one another, but it means nothing—leather rubbing against leather . . . Know one another? We'd have to crack open our skulls and drag each other's thoughts out by the tails'—a grim restatement of the point *Tristram Shandy* (1759–67) had made seventy years earlier under the benign guise of humour (see p. 178). And even

Robespierre in his darker moments of introspection comes near to Danton's despairing vision. 'Truly the Son of Man is crucified in us all; we all wrestle in bloody agony in our own Gardens of Gethsemane; but not one of us redeems the other with his wounds . . . the world is empty and void—I am alone.'

In common with many writers of his generation, Büchner's rejection of God was based on the cruelty of life, rather than on the implications of scientific enquiry: important though these were for Büchner. As Tom Payne exclaims in *Dantons Tod*, 'why do I suffer? That is the very bedrock of atheism. The least little flicker of pain . . . is enough to split the creation wide open from top to bottom.' And, as a measure of how far the onus of the atheist charge had shifted, Büchner has Payne conclude 'only reasoning can prove God, feeling rebels against it'—an epigram that might have appeared a perverse paradox to eighteenth-century atheists, but which was a fair reflection of what many men of sensibility felt in the 1830s. As Büchner himself bitterly remarked after his first major illness, 'This groaning on our torture-rack, could it be there only that it may pass through the gaps in the clouds and, echoing further and further on its way, to die like a breath of melody in celestial ears?'

The same issues dominate his novelle, *Lenz* (written in 1835): anger at God, did he exist, followed by black laughter at the fact that he doesn't. As Lenz makes his way through the mountains,

> He felt capable of clenching an enormous fist, thrusting it up into heaven, seizing God and dragging him through his clouds; capable of masticating the world with his teeth and spitting it into the face of the Creator; he swore, he blasphemed . . . Thus he arrived at the highest point of the mountains . . . and the heavens were a stupid blue eye, and the moon, quite ludicrous, idiotic, stood in the midst. Lenz had to laugh loudly, and as he laughed atheism took root in him and possessed him utterly, steadily, calmly, relentlessly.

Büchner had no illusions about the barren consequences of atheism. In Woyzeck's words, 'When God goes, everything goes', with the inescapable conclusion, uttered by Danton, 'Life isn't worth the effort it costs us to keep it going'. Nor is Büchner prepared to make do with the Flaubertian solution of stoicism. As Danton comments, 'Those Stoics gave themselves a good sort of feeling inside, you know. It's not bad fun to pull your toga on and have a quick look round to see what sort of a shadow you're throwing.'

With every panacea shrivelling under his scrutiny, the only crumb of comfort that Büchner would allow humanity was the distant promise of science and education, which might at least blunt some of the harsher edges of the indignity of life. And, as in so much else, he here foreshadowed Naturalist writers such as Ibsen, who as a young man likewise dropped political activity in favour of the slower but less erratic forces of science and education (see pp. 171–2).

Such moments of solace, however, could do no more than briefly assuage the bitterness of existence. What life itself amounted to, in Büchner's canon, is summed up in the old woman's story in *Woyzeck*, written in the year before Büchner died of typhus at the age of twenty-three.

Once upon a time there was a poor little girl who had no father and no mother. Everyone was dead . . . And because there was no-one left on the earth, she wanted to go to Heaven . . . And when she got to the stars, they were little golden flies, stuck up there as if they were caught in a spider's web. And when she wanted to go back to earth, the earth was an upside-down pot. And she was all alone. And she sat down there and she cried. And she sits there to this day, all, all alone.'

7 More Pessimism: Flaubert

Existence would seem to hold much for a man who unhesitatingly recognised that 'the sea, *Hamlet* and Mozart's *Don Giovanni* are the three finest things in creation'. (Had Flaubert added Vermeer's *View of Delft*, the list would have passed any committee of immortals.) At the same time, the rich meticulous texture of his novels, and their conscious aestheticism, suggest an artist who took more than a consolatory pleasure in living. Yet, at the end of the day, his conclusions on life were no less sombre than Büchner's or Ibsen's.

The family scalpel

Reviewing *Madame Bovary* in 1857, the avuncular Sainte-Beuve jovially commented 'Anatomists, physiologists, I find you everywhere'. Had Flaubert been allowed a free choice of career it would have been medicine, like his father. Since childhood he had wanted to be a writer; but family and friends had pointed out the necessity of an assured professional income to enable him to write in comfort. Although his personal inclination was to seek this material support in medicine, his elder brother had already embarked on a surgeon's life, with, as it turned out, the prospect of eventually succeeding his father as head of the Hôtel Dieu teaching hospital in Rouen. Flaubert was therefore sent to Paris to study law, which he found boring and uncongenial. A mysterious illness, variously described by biographers as epilepsy, or more vaguely and more fashionably as 'a nervous disorder', took hold of him in 1844, which resulted in his father prescribing a quiet life at home, far from the hated manuals of legal codes and cases. He was now able to devote himself exclusively to writing, and the rest of his life, apart from occasional excursions abroad and to Paris, was to be spent in the cloistered but congenial atmosphere of his mother's home at Croisset, overlooking the sinuous sweep of the lower Seine. But as he was to say fifteen years later, 'it is strange how I am drawn to medical studies—I want to dissect. If I was ten years younger, I would set about it.'

His childhood in Rouen had been spent in an apartment adjoining the hospital wards and overlooking the courtyard where the dissecting rooms were situated. In a famous letter of 1853, he described how

> Many times my sister and I climbed the trellis and, hanging in the vine, stared curiously at the stretched-out corpses—the same flies which settled on us and the flowers, also settled on them, and came back

buzzing . . . I can still see my father, raising his head from his dissecting, and telling us to go away.

Not only was Flaubert a constant witness of his father's professional devotion, which he subsequently immortalised in Dr Larivière in *Madame Bovary*, but he lived amid the sights, sounds and smells of illness and death. As an adolescent he would occasionally accompany his father when engaged in dissecting a particularly interesting case; 'the most beautiful woman is scarcely beautiful on a theatre table, with her entrails on her nose, her leg skinned and a cigar-butt resting on her foot' (letter of 1837).

This direct acquaintance with exposed nerves and ganglia—and his own later experience of the mental delusions that accompanied his bouts of illness—made him vulnerably conscious of the slender physical scaffolding that kept the mind in being, an awareness that was deepened when he made the acquaintance of a number of eminent medical figures in Paris. He also shared, from adolescence, his father's determinism. Flaubert *père* belonged to the new school of medical thought engendered by the Idéologues, more particularly Cabanis (see pp. 23–4), whose colleagues and disciples included seminal figures such as Pinel and Bichat. Philippe Pinel (1745–1826) had been a pioneer of psychological methods in curing the mentally ill; and it was from his writings that Stendhal had tried to teach himself the art of disciplining the emotions. Francois-Xavier Bichat (1771–1802), for his part, was best known for his exploration of body-tissue—work which George Eliot was to refer to, in *Middlemarch*, where Dr Lydgate is presented as an evangelist of Bichat's thinking.

Although Flaubert and his father had little in common in aesthetic matters, it was through his father that Flaubert developed his life-long interest in the Idéologues. In René Dumesnil's words

it was in reading the Idéologues of the end of the previous century that the young Gustave received his formation. He was won by the theories of Destutt de Tracy and always held them in the same admiration . . . Similarly attracted to Cabanis, Flaubert was imbued from adolescence with the idea of physiological determinism . . . What satisfied him in Cabanis, Bichat and Pinel was the application of analytical methods to the study of phenomena which had hitherto been the province of the risky speculations of metaphysicians.

Flaubert's determinism was a matter of sensation as well as knowledge. 'I deny individual free will, because I do not feel myself to be free' (letter of 18 September 1846). In this he differed from many determinists, who had to admit that subjectively they experienced life as though they had free will: illusory though the feeling might be. For Flaubert, however, there was no conflict on this score between what he knew and what he felt.

Of the twin forces of *race et milieu*, he believed that heredity was unduly neglected. 'I believe in heredity more than upbringing' (letter of 12 June 1846); and it is arguable that the hereditary element in Flaubert's characters was stronger than in Stendhal's or Balzac's. Even so, this was only a relative shift of balance, environment continuing to loom large in both his creative and non-fictional writing. Towards the end of his life, he told the Goncourts that he had plans for a book which would 'follow the fortunes of two or three Rouen families from pre-Revolutionary times to the present day . . . It would trace the ancestry of men like Pouyer-Quertier, who was descended from a weaver' and would have 'very detailed *mises en scène.*'

When it came to the origins of Man, his fellow Rouennais included, he had no doubt that 'apes are our ancestors' (*Voyage de Famille*, 1845). And he believed that the highest manifestations of humanity, such as art and religion, were as amenable to scientific analysis as the rest of living matter; 'perhaps, like mathematics, it is just a question of finding the method'.

> Aesthetics are still awaiting their Geoffroy Saint-Hilaire . . . A great step will have been taken when the human mind is consistently treated with the objectivity of the physical sciences in their study of matter. That is the only way humanity has of rising above itself . . . It will be applicable, above all, to art and religion . . . and in taking account of the relevant contingencies of climate, language etc., one can rise, step by step, to the art of the future and to a clear conception of what Beauty is.

Written in 1853, these somewhat sanguine aspirations may seem at odds with the *désabusé* Flaubert who castigated what he saw as the facile attempts of Positivist philistines to reduce life to the regimented simplicity of a school text-book. But Flaubert's quarrel was with oversimplification rather than with explorations of this sort. Although Flaubert's devotion to creative literature came near to being a surrogate religion, he regarded nothing as being beyond the realm of scientific enquiry—provided it was done with the humility and open-mindedness of the true scientist. Indeed his letters spoke of the need for literature to base itself on the principles of natural science and biology, especially in their insistence on complete accuracy in observation and description. This was a precept that was to help to make each of his novels the labour of many years. His efforts to establish a detail, such as how Frédéric and Rosanette would have travelled from Fontainebleau to Paris in *L'Education Sentimentale*, involved hours of research: so much so that in this instance he wearily admitted 'my bugger of a novel is wearing me to the marrow'.

Like Büchner, however, he saw limits to the redemptive powers of science. Whatever understanding and improvement it might bring to the human lot, he doubted whether the underlying *mauvaise plaisanterie* of life would be fundamentally altered. Zola was later to recall discussions with him:

> When I affirmed my faith in the twentieth century, when I said that our vast scientific and social movement must culminate in a flourishing of humanity, he would look at me fixedly with his large blue eyes, then shrug his shoulders.

This was the basis of Flaubert's quarrel with Positivism, especially with what he saw as the insensitive optimism of its high priests. He dismissed Comte's *Essai de philosophie positive* as '*assommant de bêtise*', containing '*des mines de comique immenses, des Californies de grotesque*' (letter of 4 September 1850). And in so far as he shared the Positivists' rejection of the search for first causes (see p. 57), his inspiration here was his father's friend, the nerve specialist François Magendie, not Comte.

Like Büchner, temperament and illness were factors in his pessimism. At the same time, the early loss of close members of his family was uncompensated by marriage or a satisfying sexual attachment, despite two prolonged love affairs.

> When I was quite young, I had a complete presentiment of what life was going to be like. It was like a sickening kitchen-smell escaping from a ventilator. You did not need to eat to know that it would make you vomit.

Moreover, the semi-sequestered nature of his life deepened this overcast conviction. As his friend, Maxime du Camp, remonstrated,

> It has given you the pernicious habit of living through others, and of being capable only of dealing with your *subjective self*, and never with your *objective self*. It has imprisoned you in the narrow circle of your own personality. You know how you live, but you don't know how others live. However much you look around you, you see only yourself, and in all your works, you've never done anything but yourself. These are the two greatest errors of your life, which, when all is said . . . bore you, and which have made people believe that you hate life, whereas it is only your own life that you hate (October 1851).

It was symptomatic of Flaubert's wariness towards life, and his fear of personal commitment to others, that he dreaded the possibility of his mistress, Louise Colet, becoming pregnant. 'The idea of giving birth to someone *fills me with horror*. I'd curse myself if I became a father. A son of my own! Oh! no, no, no! Let my flesh perish with me, and let me not transmit to anyone the boredom and the ignominiousness of life.' He awaited her menstruations, 'the redcoats', as he called them, with all the apprehension of a penniless newly-wed: 'God be praised, there is nothing further to fear, and blessed be the redcoats!'

L'Education Sentimentale

His pessimism, however, had roots in the period as well as in himself. 'I want to write the moral history—sentimental would be truer—of the men of my generation.' The result was *L'Education Sentimentale*, the novel which occupied him, on and off, from its first inception in the 1840s to its final publication in 1869.

Like Flaubert, Frédéric Moreau belongs to a milieu that has lost religious certainty but has found nothing to put in its place. Flaubert was profoundly aware of what mankind had lost when it rejected religious belief: 'I am mystical at heart, and I believe in nothing'. Although his mother was a practising Catholic and had had her children baptised, she had made no attempt to protect them from the abrasive scepticism of their father, once they had reached adolescence. Like Goethe's Faust, Flaubert's religious temperament was to be continually at odds with his own sharp intellect, reared in an ambience of scientific unbelief. Describing religious sentiment as 'the most natural and the most poetic of humanity', he despised Voltairians as 'people who laugh at great things', and was contemptuous of those nineteenth-century materialists who, he claimed, rejected sentiments, of which they had never felt the force.

Flaubert's comment on Alfred de Musset might have been made about his own creation, Frédéric Moreau: 'He's an unfortunate young man! One can't live without religion' (January 1852). With no creed or guiding principle in his life, Frédéric is obliged to create his own rules; but his personality is unequal to the task. The alternatives open to him are those of his generation, and one by one Flaubert shows them to be inadequate.

The demonstration is admittedly obscured by Frédéric's own indecisiveness, for it is arguable that the alternatives available to him rarely get a fair run. Yet the survey is nonetheless wide-ranging; and Frédéric's indecisiveness is itself part outcome of the times, despite close links with the difficulties of his own personality. His temperament inclines him towards the Romantic goals of love (*un grand amour*) and the cult of sensibility. And there are many points in the book where the reader is tempted to assume that the gentle, patient Madame Arnoux offers Frédéric his strongest chance of happiness and self-fulfilment. Yet Flaubert, as always, disdains to proffer an easy verdict; and his private letters indicate that he never saw love as a supreme fulfilment. 'For me, love is not, and cannot be, in the forefront of life . . . There are other things . . . which are, it seems to me, nearer to the light, nearer to the sun' (April 1847). 'I believe, moreover, that one of the causes of the moral degeneration of the whole of the nineteenth century has been the exaggerated "poeticisation" of woman' (December 1859).

Flaubert found his own salvation in creative art: 'art, the only true and good thing in life. How can you compare a human love with it?' But if this was a viable haven for someone with the creative talent of Flaubert, it was no solution for a man of the mediocre ability of Frédéric, or indeed the majority of men. Romanticism, for all its democratic utterances, had arguably done no more than replace an aristocracy of birth with an aristocracy of sensibility. A Lamartine or an Hugo could legitimately invite the reading public to share his perceptions of the beauties of nature or the rapture and despair of a self-styled *grand amour*. But for the ordinary untalented mortal to invest his meagre moral capital in plumbing his inner self was to condemn him to a life of barren introspection that would deflect him from helping others, and ultimately lead only to disillusionment with his own inadequacies.

Working for others was a more promising path. Yet for men of Frédéric's and Flaubert's generation, it was too often enmeshed with that other insidious Romantic cult: the cult of self-assertion. This, in the France of the late 1840s, might well take the form of a career in politics. The 1848 revolution, with its rapid turnover of personnel, not only created new opportunities for men of thrusting ambition, but it offered them on a scale that had been unparalleled since the upheavals of the 1790s.

The opportunism and charlatanry that seemed to be the stock in trade of many of the more successful politicians, were not of a nature to commend politics to a severely honest mind like Flaubert's. Nor could he condone the manipulation of many enthusiasms that too often accompanied revolutionary movements. 1848 was full of ironies: more than are explicitly stated in the novel. It may be that Flaubert felt it more prudent to leave these to the eye of the discerning reader. Having already endured one trial over the alleged obscenity of *Madame Bovary*, he knew himself temperamentally ill-suited to the upset and publicity that might arise from a seeming critique of the political past of the reigning Emperor—detested by many as the assassin of the short-lived Second Republic (1848–51/2). In any case, for Flaubert, the futility of the 1848 revolution sprang mainly from the fact that life itself was futile.

For the well-informed reader, however, who was still prepared to discern some virtue in life, the perverseness of the revolution lay largely in the fact that it produced contrary results to what its most militant instigators wanted. The institution of universal suffrage was a striking case in point: far from opening the door to social reform, it proved to be a major obstacle in its way. Louis Philippe had abdicated in February 1848 as a result of the coming together of two very different movements. On the one hand, there was the largely middle-class campaign for the extension of the franchise; and on the other, there was mounting desperation among the working classes, arising from the economic crisis of 1846–7. The republican government that succeeded Louis Philippe was mainly representative of the first of these movements, and aimed at political rather than far-reaching social reform. To pacify the working-class militants, whose participation in the demonstrations of February had given teeth to these events, it instituted several important social measures, and promised more. But it had no intention of implementing the extensive social programme that for many working-class elements was the main reason why they had supported the campaign for universal suffrage.

Paradoxically enough, it was precisely the establishment of universal suffrage during 1848 that destroyed the chances of social reform. For the main beneficiaries of the measure were not the urban working class, who totalled only one in seven of the population, but the peasantry and the lower middle classes. Numbering two-thirds of the nation, the peasantry were now wielding the vote for the first time since Napoleon. While they might have little love for the bourgeoisie, their interests were more akin to the cautious concerns of the middle classes, rather than the wild-eyed demands of the urban masses. Although they had little money, they had land, which was a heavily taxable item. And like the bourgeoisie, they feared that if the champions of the urban proletariat came to power, they would establish an expensive programme of public works and social reform which would result in heavier taxes being put on their land. They also feared that the mild-mannered liberals of the Republican government of 1848 were insufficiently strong to keep the urban proletariat under control. It was for this reason that they voted for Louis Napoleon as President in December 1848. And it was their massive vote, together with that of the propertied bourgeoisie, which led indirectly to the overthrow of the Second Republic in 1851–2, and the acceptance of Louis Napoleon as the Emperor Napoleon III (1852–70). In this way universal suffrage led to the indefinite postponement of social reform. It was only when the continued growth of industry made the urban working class a much greater percentage of the electorate in the twentieth century that socialist ideals had a chance of fruition in France. And for the historian, this gives Flaubert's portrayal of the 1848 revolution an added irony that goes beyond the sardonic vision of the master.

Even so, Flaubert's characters run reality pretty close, when it comes to perverse twists of fortune. It is symptomatic of his grey assessment of life that his most militant reformers find themselves on the wrong side of the barricades at the decisive moments in the republic's brief life-span, not because they are turncoats, but because they are misled by the complexity of events into miscalculating where the best interests of their cause happen to lie. This is true of Dussardier in June 1848, and arguably, of the much less sympathetic Sénécal in December 1851. It is a further indictment of life that the characters who come nearest to political success are the self-seekers, such as Frédéric's friend, Deslauriers, whose democratic ideals are little more than a vehicle for personal ambition.

The most striking example is Dambreuse, who embodies the social phenomenon that Balzac saw as particularly characteristic of the period: the aristocrat-turned-businessman (see p. 45). Like Balzac, Flaubert saw the *embourgeoisement* of France as a striking demonstration of social determinism at work. He himself was far from immune: as he knew very well. His style of life and aloofness from servants and tradesmen were that of a *'philippotard'* whose material values epitomised those of the July Monarchy of which he was very much a product. He married his niece to a seemingly prosperous lumber merchant, saying that he would sooner have her marry a rich Philistine than a poor artist; and then, ironically, he later had to sacrifice his own wealth to bail them out of financial difficulties.

Needless to say, Frédéric's attempts to find self-fulfilment in politics are no more rewarding than his love affairs or his undiscerning role as patron of the arts. Yet Flaubert recognised politics as a necessary evil—necessary, that is, as long as life was considered necessary—which was itself debatable. In so far as he had preferences in such a philistine game, his sympathies were with reform. He had attended a reform banquet in December 1847 at the time of the mounting campaign for a wider franchise. And in his own comments on *L'Education Sentimentale*, he admitted that he had been harder on the 'reactionaries . . . because they seem to me more criminal'.

Brothers in pessimism, Flaubert shared Büchner's deep-felt sense of the impossibility of communication between persons, and the ultimate loneliness of Man. When Frédéric comes closest to inspiration, as at Fontainebleau, it remains an interior experience that he cannot communicate. It is also true of his relationship with Madame Arnoux, the only woman he really loves and yet who only comes near to understanding him when it is too late. The most poignant demonstration of this isolation occurs when Madame Arnoux eventually offers herself to him, years later. Although this might seem the realisation of his aspirations, he nevertheless finds himself unable to accept her, for fear of shattering the inward ideal he has cherished of her.

As, one by one, Flaubert shows each of life's consolations to be meagre or false, the reader is left wondering what is left for the ordinary man who has no creative gifts to give meaning to his life. The nearest Flaubert came to giving an answer was in a letter of 1859.

One must be equal to one's destiny . . . By dint of saying 'That is so! That is so! That is so!' and of gazing down at the deep black hole at one's feet, one reaches calm.

8 The Industrial Revolution

If the work of the early French Realists was fairly free of factory smoke, this was not true of England. Even before Flaubert had witnessed the political events that provided the setting for *L'Education Sentimentale*, Mrs Gaskell was in the process of finishing *Mary Barton. A Tale of Manchester Life* (1848). Large parts of Britain were already undergoing major physical transformation, which, as yet, had no parallel in France. Much of the French industrial shift of population was directed towards existing major towns; and, although the coalfields of the north and east were fast becoming industrial belts, there was nothing comparable in size or character with the Lancashire and Yorkshire textile sprawl, the Black Country or the Clyde valley.

L'Education Sentimentale says little about industry as such; and, when it does, Flaubert's concern, like Balzac's, is for the state of mind it engenders, rather than for the sort of physical transformation that Mrs Gaskell described two decades earlier. What sticks in the mind is the materialistic opportunism of Dambreuse, or the philistinism of the industrialist-cum-art-patron, Jacques Arnoux, whose periodical, *L'Art industriel*, tacitly sums up in its title Flaubert's contempt for the mass production that enabled manufacturers to fill the homes of bourgeois and artisan alike with *objets d'art* at popular prices, that cost neither the maker nor the purchaser the effort and dedication that traditionally underlay creative art and its appreciation. In the same vein, there is Pellerin's painting of 'the Republic, or Progress, or Civilisation, in the form of Jesus Christ driving a locomotive across a virgin forest', epitomising for Flaubert what he regarded as the facile optimism of the Saint-Simonians and all those who saw in industry the regeneration of mankind.

Not that a Flaubert living amidst the grime of Mulhouse or St Etienne would necessarily have had more to say about industrial society. He could in any case see the chimneys of the Rouen textile belt from the windows of his home at Croisset, as well as the endless barges carrying manufactures and raw materials up and down the Seine. Yet it was nonetheless true that the few French writers who examined industrial life before Zola were very much of the second rank. Paradoxically it was a German, Georg Büchner, who provided the first striking example of a leading Realist confronting the predicament and mentality of the exploited classes. Yet its reflections in his literary works did not concern the Strasbourg textile workers, who were part of his political concern as a student in France. It was the Hessian peasant and the private soldier who feature there: victims of society whose problems had existed for millennia. Büchner's perceptions into the bewilderment and helplessness of the uneducated wage-earner were to be echoed by the later Realists who dealt with the industrial working classes; but it was not industry that provided Büchner with these insights in the first instance. It was largely his physician's mind, his socialist conscience and his poet's imagination that permitted him to see more deeply into the problems of the manual worker than most of his contemporaries.

Mrs Gaskell, by contrast, arrived at her concern for working-class subjects through finding herself in an industrial community where she encountered a kind of life that was entirely foreign to her previous experience. Encounters of this sort, between literary sensibility and industrial life, came earlier in Britain than in countries where industrialisation took wing less quickly. It was no accident that Marxism should find its factual inspiration in the same town as Mrs Gaskell's novels of working-class life. When Engels visited his father's factories in Manchester, he and Mrs Gaskell breathed the same unfamiliar air; they may have passed each other in the street.

Alberich's cave

The Industrial Revolution was arguably the greatest changer of Man since the Neolithic Revolution several thousand years earlier—when archaeology's little swarthy men, running over the downs, started to exchange the day-to-day uncertainties of hunting in packs for the planned existence of living in settled agricultural communities. Many of the inventions that made it possible originated in the later Middle Ages. It was then that belt-drives, cranks and treadles enabled the harnessing of one mechanical motion to another; and it was on these techniques that the first stage of the Industrial Revolution was largely based. The cotton-spinning inventions of Augustan England were largely rearrangements of parts of the mediaeval spinning-wheel—Blake's satanic mills having their mechanical roots in the Ages of Faith, rather than in the Age of Reason. It was only in the nineteenth century that the large-scale application of steam to textiles and transport gave industrialisation an impetus that technologically was radically new.

Yet several centuries divided the Industrial Revolution from its mechanical base. As always, technological advance was a response to demand; and it was not until the eighteenth century that circumstances provided a demand of sufficient magnitude—and the labour, finance and organisation to meet it. In a world where the mass of the population lived off the land, manufacturers' sales depended on a thriving agriculture. In past centuries farming families had traditionally made their own clothes and implements; and unless they grew more produce than they ate, they could not afford to do otherwise. It was therefore no accident that the

Industrial Revolution of the eighteenth century followed a period of growing agricultural productivity.

Historians are divided on the reasons for this increase. They are agreed that it sprang from the interaction of improved agricultural methods on the one hand, and a substantial increase in population on the other. More food permitted larger families, and larger families demanded more food. But which of the two factors initiated the spiral remains the subject of absorbing debate.

This self-stimulating combination was first clearly observed in the Netherlands; but it was in Britain that it later became most marked. Although France and Germany had their share of improving landlords, they were hampered by the surviving customs and traditions of a feudal past, which often prevented continental landlords and peasants responding with sufficient flexibility to the opportunities afforded by new farming methods. British agriculture, on the other hand, had undergone a process of competitive consolidation in the sixteenth and seventeenth centuries, when 'enclosures' and other developments had created larger units which were more amenable to eighteenth-century progressive methods.

The industry that initially responded to this situation in the post-1760 decades was still largely characterised by the self-employed artisan; or by the cottager working for a merchant who supplied the material and marketed the product. Both artisans and entrepreneurs put a great deal of thought and ingenuity into devising ways of improving the output of the apparatus at their disposal; and it was not until water-power, followed by steam-power, was harnessed on a large scale to this evolving machinery, that industry came to be largely housed in factories rather than in homes or workshops. It happened first in spinning, then in weaving; but the process was gradual. Indeed it was only in the 1840s that British factory weavers finally outnumbered the home-based handloom weaver.

The early textile factories were relatively modest in their financial requirements. The new looms and spinning contrivances were not particularly expensive to make. Even as late as 1846 a weaving factory of four hundred looms, including the land and buildings, could be established for as little as £11,000 (about £140,000 today). With labour cheap in a period of growing population—and with expanding markets at home, in Europe, and overseas—the owner could reasonably hope to offer his patron a relatively swift and handsome return. The oft-quoted case of Robert Owen offers the example of a man who borrowed £100 in 1789, and was able to buy out his partners for £84,000 twenty years later. Success of this kind spread confidence in industry as a form of investment, and permitted the development of the later, more costly, stages of industrialisation, notably in iron and the building of railways.

The financing and marketing of the British Industrial Revolution was indirectly aided by the overseas empire which Britain acquired during the course of the eighteenth century. This provided her with a rich variety of products that were much in demand on the Continent. Not only did this create fortunes for a number of merchants, fortunes that were later to provide some of the capital for industry, but it created an organisational network of trade that helped to grease the tracks for British industrial exports to Continental and other countries. This network, moreover, developed an attendant network of underwriters and finance houses, so that when Amsterdam fell to the French in 1795, London became the financial capital of the world. Moreover, in the nineteenth century, Britain's overseas empire, especially India, was increasingly to play the role of a market for her manufactures, as well as a supplier of cheap produce for British merchants to export elsewhere.

Another advantage that Britain enjoyed over her Continental competitors was her less encumbered system of communications. A heavily indented coastline and a fair number of navigable rivers were supplemented in the later eighteenth century by a rapid increase in turnpike roads and a remarkable spate of canal building. What was particularly advantageous to Britain, however, was her relative freedom from the internal customs barriers and obsolete toll charges that made transport so expensive on the Continent. This itself reflected the developed sense of commercial opportunity that characterised Britain in the eighteenth century. As already indicated (see pp. 9–10), there were not the marked class distinctions that had partly inhibited the Continental aristocracy from engaging wholeheartedly in the commercial and industrial activities that were to make the fortunes of the more enterprising members of the middle classes. It is true that Continental industry was to owe much to noble landlords who exploited the mineral deposits and manufacturing potential of their estates; but the traditional responsibilities that they held in a highly hierarchical rural social structure deprived them of the manoeuvrability that could do so much for the businessman with no traditional role to play in local society.

And yet it was to just such an established role that many of the Continental bourgeoisie aspired. Successful merchants in France and elsewhere invested their money in land, in the hope of social advancement as well as financial return. Under the *ancien régime*, however, such advancement could only be partial; and even partial assimilation often involved modifications of attitude and behaviour that might make the *parvenu* less of a thrusting businessman. In Britain, the middle classes had similar aspirations; but the social climber paid a much smaller price in self-metamorphosis, since the landed aristocracy were not a quasi-caste, as in so much of eighteenth-century Europe. Younger sons of English noble families became virtual fringe members of the middle classes, while their elders who inherited the land and title were often prepared to learn the business ways of the bourgeoisie. The frontiers of the upper and middle classes were therefore being continuously crossed in both directions, without there being much conscious need for adaptation.

Although textiles in the 1840s employed three-quarters of the British industrial population, it was iron that was to be the backbone of the Industrial Revolution: the *sine qua non* of technological advances elsewhere. Like much else in the Industrial Revolution, the changes that took place in the iron industry stemmed in the first instance from healthy agricultural progress. Horseshoes, new ploughs, and ironshod wheels all created a demand that encouraged the iron producers to try to by-pass the expense of wood fuel by experimenting with coke. Success in the 1780s led to a steady increase in production, until the railway boom of the 1830s sent it rocketing. Whereas in the 1780s Britain produced less iron than France, by 1848 her output outdistanced the rest of the world put together. Like textiles, it owed its progress to the trial-and-error methods of practitioners who used the experienced instincts of the culinary arts, rather than the speculative calculations of science.

Closely connected with these advances in the eighteenth century was the evolution of the steam engine. Although from the mid-1780s it was increasingly harnessed to cotton spinning, it nevertheless remained overshadowed by the water-wheel until well after the Napoleonic Wars, when the power and convenience of the steam engine increasingly persuaded industry to migrate from fast flowing rivers, with their dependence on the uncertainties of rainfall, to the proximity of coalfields and centres of population, where fuel, labour and markets were all close to hand. Britain's wealth of coal, compared to France, was an added inducement. In 1800 there were probably no more than a thousand engines in use in Britain, averaging perhaps ten horsepower each, and even this was far more than in the rest of Europe. By 1870, however, Britain's steam-power was equivalent to the strength of six million horses, or forty million men. And the great advantage of steam-power was its compactness: the country could have provided neither the food nor the uninterrupted space that yoked teams of horses or men in these numbers would have required to do the same amount of work.

The social repercussions of these changes are familiar enough. And the degree of their magnitude is indicated in Tables 1 and 2, which

TABLE 1   Occupations of the British population (approximate percentage of the total occupied population)

	1811 % (*tentative*)	*1851* %
Agriculture and fishing	30–35	22
Industry	c. 30	43
Services	c. 37	35

TABLE 2 The population of some major British cities (in thousands)

	1800	*1850*
Birmingham	71	233
Glasgow	77	345
Liverpool	82	376
Manchester	75	303
National population	10.5 million	20.8 million

demonstrate the expansion of the industrial population and the consequent growth of towns. It is nevertheless worth commenting that the mounting influx of countrymen into industry was primarily an outcome of the population increase that accompanied the agricultural revolution of the eighteenth century. It was this that created a large reservoir of rural labour, much of which was attracted by the relatively higher wages in spinning and weaving in a period of rapid industrial expansion. As is familiar to any reader of nineteenth-century English literature, the consequent pressure on urban accommodation and sanitation created conditions of squalor and misery that showed the impact of economic change on society in a new and disturbing way.

The Industrial Revolution in France

All this came more slowly to the Continent. Lacking many of Britain's current advantages, France remembered with some wistfulness that for two centuries she had been the world's leading manufacturer. The requirements of industrial change, however, put a premium on factors and commodities that had hitherto counted for less.

The French Revolution, and the wars that followed, had exercised an ambivalent effect on the French economy and that of her satellites. On the one hand it removed many of the social and legal limitations that had hampered economic enterprise; and for a while it permitted middle-class control of government, despite the complex, divided and limited nature of this control especially in a period of upheaval at home and abroad (see pp. 10–12). At the same time, the expansion of French frontiers had increased the material resources at France's disposal, and Napoleon's Continental System had given her, for several years, a protected market for her manufactures. Defeat brought these to an end, however, and left her facing the cost of the disruption and expense that even victorious wars entail. Moreover, she lost all but the last vestiges of her overseas empire, which, together with the destruction of a substantial part of her navy, took the lustre off her position as a great trading nation, even if only in the short run.

The collapse of the Continental System also brought a renewal of British industrial competition. New protective tariffs, under the Restoration, encouraged French manufactures to try to meet the demands of the domestic market by increased mechanisation; but protection also created a certain complacency which helped to prolong old methods. Complacency on a wider scale was also encouraged by the relative richness and profitability of French agriculture. Although the potential of peasant farming was severely limited by the small size of their holdings (see pp. 45–6), the high yield of the larger properties, especially now that they were emancipated from the restrictive traditions of the *ancien régime*, was a constant temptation to the upper and middle classes to regard land as a sound investment, as well as a key to social esteem. France therefore did not see, to the same degree, the rapid transfer of financial interest to industry that characterised Britain at this time. Indeed, when the July Monarchy usurped the reins of power in 1830, French industrial production was probably little more than a third of Britain's. Her cotton industry was only a quarter the size; her pig-iron production was little more than a third; and her total coal consumption, including the coal she imported, was less than a fifth.

This discrepancy in industrialisation made for a very different landscape. The proportion of the British population living in towns of over 10,000 inhabitants was 40 per cent in 1851, as compared with a mere 14 per cent in France. Indeed by 1851, the total British urban population (i.e. living in communities of over 2000) had already outstripped its rural counterpart; something which did not occur in France until eighty years later, in 1931.

Mrs Gaskell

The British industrial experience found perhaps its most powerful reflection in Romantic poetry, while among novelists, Dickens was the first major figure to give it sustained attention. Realism's opening performer in this field was arguably Mrs Gaskell—an unusual figure among Realists in being a committed Christian, whose determinist views were qualified by her religious faith.

Her Christianity preceded her determinism. But her prolonged and intimate contact with working-class life in the industrial North convinced her of the awesome role of environment in shaping the individual. After a childhood divided between rural Cheshire, Stratford-upon-Avon and Park Lane, she married a Unitarian minister in 1832, which brought her to Manchester, where she was to live intermittently for the rest of her life. Unlike the French Realists of the 1830s, her faith in the Christian promise was never in doubt; and the otherworldly dimension that exists in her books lent a certain optimism to even her most depressing accounts of Manchester slum-life. Her confidence in a supreme judge who knows, and allows for, the difficulties of the labouring poor was implicit in her view of the human condition; and like many women novelists, not least George Eliot, she tended to be merciful in exercising her own omnipotence over her fictional characters. She shrank from consigning them to destruction, either in the hereafter or the here-and-now. Writers like Büchner and Flaubert, however, had stared into the void of a world without God (and a world without ultimate meaning) and were less hesitant about treating their characters as the world treated them. Her determinist leanings were therefore all the more interesting, in that they were the reluctant result of experience and observation, rather than a reflection of long-held intellectual convictions or inclinations.

As a voluntary visitor of the Manchester and Salford District Provident Society, she knew the poor in a way that lay beyond the experience of Disraeli, or even Dickens (despite his early poverty in London). They, like Zola several decades later, relied on published reports and the occasional personal expedition. *Mary Barton* (1848) was the outcome of fourteen years of direct experience, in which she had seen the region grow from 280,000 inhabitants to 380,000. She had been a witness of the trade recession of 1839–41 and its impact on a population that was outstripping domestic food supplies; at a time, moreover, when foreign grain imports were discouraged by the Corn Laws. She herself claimed that the book came to her one evening when she was trying to console a labourer, and he had replied, 'Ay, ma'am, but have ye ever seen a child clemmed to death?'. As she says in the preface,

I had always felt a deep sympathy with the care-worn men, who looked as if doomed to struggle through their lives in strange alternatives between work and want; tossed to and fro by circumstances, apparently in even a greater degree than other men.

Man, the victim of economic circumstance, is a *leitmotiv* of the book.

The most deplorable and enduring evil that arose out of the period of commercial depression [1839–41] . . . was this feeling of alienation between the different classes of society . . . the sufferers wept first, and then they cursed.

Mary Barton and *North and South* (1854–5) were monuments to milieu. She sees the different demands of urban and rural living imprinted on the faces of the population. The cotton millworker, John Barton, has 'an acuteness and intelligence of countenance, which has often been noticed in a manufacturing population'. His wife, however, 'had the fresh beauty of the agricultural districts; and somewhat of the deficiency of sense in her countenance, which is likewise characteristic of the rural inhabitants in comparison with the natives of the manufacturing towns.'

Both novels treat Manchester as the quintessence of the industrial

North. Mrs Gaskell herself continually complained about 'foggy Manchester, which gives me a perpetual headache very hard to bear', and her excursions south were frequent and eagerly taken. *North and South* is nevertheless a tribute to what was good in Manchester: its constructive energy, its directness, and the material benefits that it gave to the rest of the country, including those areas where Manchester was despised for being dirty, money-minded and uncultured. Hampshire-bred Margaret Hale begins by despising the Manchester manufacturers and businessmen for 'testing everything by the standard of wealth'. Her father is 'no longer looked upon as Vicar of Helstone, but as a man who only spent at a certain rate' (a phrase worthy of George Eliot).

It is, however, the manufacturers' view of their workers as mere instruments of financial gain that becomes Margaret's prime objection to them. Anticipating Zola (see pp. 139–40), Mrs Gaskell does not condemn the manufacturers as immoral, but sees them, like the workers, as the product of the regions and the economic circumstances that have made them what they are. The Manchester of *North and South*, set in 1854, is clearly more prosperous than that of *Mary Barton*, largely set in 1839–41. The women 'prefer the better wages and greater independence of working in a mill' to domestic service—while a weaver earning sixteen shillings a week in Manchester was still doing better than the ten shillings-a-week farm labourer in the South. Yet Margaret tells the millowner, Thornton, 'in the South we have our poor, but there is not that terrible expression in their countenances of a sullen sense of injustice which I see here'. Thornton, however, believes that the workers' genuine grievances are a thing of the past. In the light of his own personal history of financial misfortune and recovery, he maintains that any hardworking man with a modicum of commonsense can better himself in Manchester: 'it may not be always as a master, but as an overlooker, a cashier, a book-keeper, a clerk, one on the side of authority and order'. Margaret dismisses these counsels of self-help as beyond the capacity of many working-class families. It should be the employer's duty to help them, not to despise them for failing to help themselves.

> God has made us so that we must be mutually dependent . . . Neither you nor any other master can help yourselves. The most proudly independent man depends on those around him for their insensible influence on his character . . . And the most isolated of all your [Lancashire] Egos has dependants clinging to him on all sides; he cannot shake them off

Thornton, however, is not impressed. He points out that when faced with competition,

> there must always be a waxing and waning of commercial prosperity; and that in the waning a certain number of masters, as well as of men,

must go down into ruin, and be no more seen among the ranks of the happy and prosperous.

And, as the author comments, 'He spoke as if this consequence were so entirely logical, that neither employers nor employed had any right to complain if it became their fate'. Mrs Gaskell's own rejoinder is to ask

has everything been done to make the suffering of these exceptions as small as possible? Or, in the triumph of the crowded procession, have the helpless been trampled on, instead of being gently lifted aside out of the roadway of the conqueror, whom they have no power to accompany on his march?

If many employers were blinded by their own problems, Mrs Gaskell saw their families as often living in ignorance of the workers' conditions; and in this also she anticipated Zola (see pp. 139–40). Preferring country houses or salubrious suburbs to the locality of the factory and its workers, they were more remote from the sources of their wealth than the average landlord or earlier generations of English manufacturers.

Underlying these various social questions, Mrs Gaskell saw a more fundamental issue, which haunts the pages of *Mary Barton* like a persistent ghost. Reappearing in various shapes and sizes, it repeatedly asks whether human nature is neutral clay, to be moulded for good or evil by circumstance, or is Man's nature basically good and owes its perversion to the pressures of society? There are times when the determinist in Mrs Gaskell seems driven to accept the first alternative: the *tabula rasa* view.

The actions of the uneducated seem to me typified in those of Frankenstein, that monster of many human qualities, ungifted with a soul, a knowledge of the difference between good and evil . . . Why have we made them what they are; a powerful monster, yet without the inner means for peace and happiness? (*Mary Barton*)

And then, in discordant antiphonal reply, the Christian in her asserts her belief that

the most depraved have also their Seed of the Holiness that shall one day overcome their evil. Their one good quality, lurking hidden, but safe, among all the corrupt and bad. (*Mary Barton*)

Moreover, she also suggested that God was merciful in the circumstances that he put in Man's way to guide him back to the path of salvation. When in *Mary Barton*, the desperate union committee delegate John Barton to murder their employer's son, both Barton and the bereaved employer are subsequently saved from lifelong bitter self-absorption by their chance encounter and gradual appreciation of each other's problems. And if, in the final analysis, life was full of cases where God chose not to shape circumstance in this benevolent way, there sill remained his sovereign role as a merciful judge in the hereafter.

Consolation in the hereafter was clearly no solution for the agnostic reader. Yet he could at least give Mrs Gaskell credit for recognising and conceding the problem of evil. She saw that among much else the ruthless nature of contemporary economic progress was a challenge to the existence and benevolence of God. John Barton attempts to discern a meaning in life by reading the Bible, but is progressively disillusioned by seeing the misery of those who try to follow its precepts, and the prosperity of those who ignore them. He turns from the Bible to trade union activity; and when the failure of Chartism seems to indicate that peaceful parliamentary reform can offer no solution, he finally turns to violence and murder. Similarly in *North and South*, the genial Bessy Higgins finds her faith under pressure when she loses her mother and takes stock of her condition and that of her fellow millgirls.

> Sometimes I'm so tired out I think I cannot enjoy heaven without a piece of rest first. I'm rather afeard o' going straight there without getting a good sleep in the grave to set me up

—a distant and less despairing echo of Woyzeck's remarks on heaven being no place for the poor (see p. 62).

There is also an unexpected, and equally unconscious, echo of Büchner (see p. 64) in Margaret Hale's thoughts as she looks out of the window at the sky

> seeing at every moment some farther distance, and yet no sign of God! It seemed to her at the moment, as if the earth was more utterly desolate than if girt in by an iron dome, behind where there might be the ineffaceable peace and glory of the Almighty: those never-ending depths of space, in their still serenity, were more mocking to her than any material bounds could be—shutting in the cries of earth's sufferers, which now might ascend into that infinite splendour of vastness and be lost—lost for ever, before they reached His throne.

If, for Mrs Gaskell, the ultimate answers lay with God, she was not without temporal solutions, oversanguine though some of them may seem. Her novels periodically suggested that the 'alienation between the different classes' was more the product of misunderstanding than antagonism of interest. She claimed for instance that few contemporaries understood the factors underlying the depression of 1839–41; and her main criticism of the employers was their failure to explain to the workers the manufacturers' problems. Even so, she recognised the obstacles to mutual understanding, especially when either side resorted to collective militant action against the other. Individuals she trusted; but men in indignant groups were no longer themselves. The riot that provides the dramatic high-point of *North and South* turns the workers into a Zolaresque pack of animals. They surge forward with 'the demoniac desire of some terrible wild beast'; they were 'gaunt as wolves, and mad for prey'—phrases that were to be staple fare with Zola (see pp. 132–3).

And when the millowner, Thornton, eventually mellows to his workers, it is not as a result of their collective action, or indeed through mature reflection on his part. It is rather through the influence of Margaret Hale, with whom he has fallen in love. For redemption, in a temporal sense, is seen by Mrs Gaskell very much with the same eyes as George Eliot. Love, or suffering, are frequently the means by which self-centred or unfulfilled people are made aware of others, and thereby find their own better selves. Like Fred Vincy in *Middlemarch* (see pp. 179–80), the amiable but callow Jem Wilson confesses that his love for Mary Barton 'is the groundwork of all that people call good in me'; and through it, he achieves a moral stature unsuspected at the beginning of the novel. On the other hand, it is suffering that brings salvation to both John Barton and Carson: the spectacle of Carson's grief moving Barton to compassion and understanding, and Barton's response moving Carson to forgiveness. Each comes to appreciate the other's difficulties, and Carson develops into a more benevolent employer. The change, however, is gradual and unstartling; unlike Scrooge, there is no overnight transformation.

George Eliot—and England before the railway

George Eliot described Dickens as Britain's

> one great novelist who is gifted with the utmost power of rendering the external traits of our town population; and if he could give us their psychological character—their conceptions . . . their emotions—with the same truth as their idiom and manners, his books would be the greatest contribution Art has ever made to the awakening of social sympathies. But . . . he scarcely ever passes from the humorous and external to the emotional and tragic, without becoming as transcendent in his unreality as he was a moment before in his artistic truthfulness . . ., encouraging the miserable fallacy that high morality and refined sentiment can grow out of harsh social relations, ignorance, and want; or that the working-classes are in a condition to enter at once into a millennial state of *altruism*, wherein everyone is caring for everyone else, and no-one for himself. (1856)

These comments pinpoint the essential difference between Realists like herself, and novelists like Dickens, who are sometimes thought of as Realists because of their social concern. In the same way she deplored as counter-productive Harriet Beecher Stowe's idealisation of the negro slaves in *Uncle Tom's Cabin*. 'If the negroes are really so very good, slavery has answered as moral discipline'; and in presenting this one-sided view of them, Stowe thereby missed 'the most terribly tragic element in the relation of the two races—the Nemesis lurking in the vices of the oppressed'. It was Mrs Gaskell's avoidance of this pitfall, despite the occasional near-lapse, that was one of her several claims to George Eliot's admiration. As Eliot wrote, 'my feeling towards Life and Art had some affinity with the feeling which had inspired . . . the earlier chapters of *Mary Barton*.'

Like Flaubert she had precise ideas of what was entailed in social observation. She once expressed the wish that someone

> would devote himself to studying the natural history of our social classes, especially of the small shopkeepers, artisans, and peasantry, the degree in which they are influenced by local conditions, their maxims and habits, the points of view from which they regard their religious teachers, and the degree in which they are influenced by religious doctrines, the interactions of the various classes on each other, and what are the tendencies in their position towards disintegration and towards development . . .

She herself came near to such an enterprise, albeit in fictional form, in *Felix Holt, the radical* (1866) and *Middlemarch* (1871–2).

Both novels are set in the early 1830s, during the preparation and aftermath of the Great Reform Bill. Yet she wrote with the perspective of someone who knew the industrial Midlands of the 1860s and could see how short-lived were the features that the novels describe. Middlemarch (Coventry) and the Treby Magna of *Felix Holt* (Nuneaton) were both communities whose social autonomy would not survive the coming of the railway. Their closely knit character and resistance to outside influences belonged to a pre-railway age whose end is already foreshadowed in *Middlemarch* by the arrival of the surveyors to prepare the ground for the railway. Only in the Indian summer of the turnpike and stagecoach could the arrival of outsiders like Lydgate and Ladislaw create such a stir in what was after all a manufacturing community, no mere village where events were few and far between. Similarly it was only in such a period that local gossip could loom so much larger than the great national issues that were transforming the country around them. Within six years of the end of the novel, Coventry (Middlemarch) would be on the main line from London to Birmingham. The London newspapers would arrive on the morning of publication, and innumerable Lydgates and Ladislaws would pass through the town, some staying, others moving on, without exciting attention. Moreover the town would find itself drawn into the orbit of Birmingham with its mushrooming industry, its attractive shops and its cultural amenities (which, in proportion to its size, were better then than now).

As a girl, George Eliot (Marian Evans) knew both towns in the 1830s; her time being divided between a boarding school in Nuneaton and her parents' home near Coventry. Their pre-steam autonomy, however, did not represent for her a lost idyll to be remembered with nostalgic regret, despite her affection for rural England. As she was well aware 'selfish instincts are not subdued by the sight of buttercups . . . To make men moral something more is requisite than to turn them out to grass.' They represented an insular world, self-interested and resentful of outsiders. Their recent history was remarkable neither for generosity nor goodwill.Treby Magna (Nuneaton) 'had lived quietly through the great earthquakes of the French Revolution and the Napoleonic Wars'. Indeed during the wars the farmers 'played at whist, ate and drank generously, praised Mr. Pitt and the war as keeping up prices and religion'. The 1820s, however, brought falling prices; it also brought miners and tape-weavers to neighbouring districts. The end of wartime prosperity and the influx of alien elements were quickly if illogically linked in the popular mind. The attitudes, behaviour and religion of the new arrivals became a target for resentment, as the high prices and fat pickings of Napoleonic times receded beyond recall.

> Mr Tiliot, the Church spirit-merchant, knew now that Mr. Nuttwood, the obliging grocer, was one of those Dissenters, Deists, Socinians, Papists and Radicals who were in league to destroy the Constitution . . . and even the farmers became less materialistic in their view of causes, and referred much to the agency of the devil and the Irish Romans.

The sum impression given by both novels, *Middlemarch* in particular, is that the changes wrought by the Great Reform Bill of 1832 were insignificant compared to those about to be ignited by the coming of the railway and the growing industry of the central Midlands. Characteristically, she does not labour the point: her readers in the 1870s were well aware of the situation. But of the enormity of the economic changes to come, she leaves no doubt, brief though the references are. When Mr. Solomon contemplates extorting money from the railway company by seeming to obstruct it, she describes 'his cunning' as 'bearing about the same relation to the course of railways as the cunning of a diplomatist bears to the general chill . . . of the solar system'. And indeed the cumulative pressure of industrial changes on the enclosed traditional life of towns like Middlemarch was to be no less devastating in its effect than the coming of a new ice-age, even if it was to engender new life on an unparalleled scale.

Eliot had a healthy sense of the uselessness of politics unless they improved the quality of life. She significantly portrays the local Reform Bill candidate in *Middlemarch* as a well-intentioned but negligent landlord who fails to keep his tenants' cottages in repair. The farm labourers of the neighbourhood share Eliot's scepticism:

> the rumour of Reform had not yet excited any millennial expectations in [the village of] Frick, there being no definite promise in it, as of gratuitous grains to fatten Hiram Ford's pig, or of a publican at the 'Weights and Scales' who would brew beer for nothing, or of an offer on the part of the three neighbouring farmers to raise wages during winter. And without distinct good of this kind in its promises, Reform seemed on a footing with the bragging of pedlars, which was a hint for distrust to every knowing person. The men of Frick were not ill-fed, and were less given to fanaticism than to a strong muscular suspicion; less inclined to believe that they were peculiarly cared for by heaven, than to regard heaven itself as rather disposed to take them in—a disposition observable in the weather.

9 A *Modus Vivendi?*
George Eliot

George Eliot knew better than most the arguments for expecting little of life and human nature. She had an acute mind, and few contemporary novelists could match her conversance with the intellectual issues of the time. As a translator, critic and editor, she initially made her living through reading other people's work, much of it quasi-philosophical or quasi-scientific; and her subsequent liaison with the insatiably curious George Lewes made her the partner of his extraordinarily wide interests.

Like most Realists, she had rejected Christianity as intellectually unacceptable and emotionally suspect. She had subsequently examined most of the secular alternatives and found them wanting. Yet, despite the sharp scepticism that comes of successive disappointments, she came nearest, of all the major Realists, to formulating a *modus vivendi* that was both subjectively satisfying and useful to others.

Like Tolstoy, Eliot was primarily concerned with finding a foundation for morality in a determinist world. But whereas Tolstoy ultimately turned his back on the intellect and put his trust in collective traditional experience (see pp. 114–20), Eliot continued to look the intellect straight in the eye and built her moral system in the inhospitable alien realm of what her intellect told her were the realities of life. Her achievement was to some extent the outcome of temperament and upbringing; but it was also the consequence of her subsequent intellectual odyssey, the various stages of which had each left its imprint on her thought and attitudes. Her development was something of a dialectic, in which religion was the first term and science the second, the synthesis that came in later life owing much to both.

Religion

Eliot regarded her childhood and upbringing with a discerning gratitude, in which her critical faculties were nonetheless active. Stendhal, Büchner and Flaubert had all rejected Christianity in their boyhood, in accordance with (or, in Stendhal's case, as a reaction against) paternal influence. They had never had the opportunity of experiencing its emotional depths in adolescence and early manhood; although Flaubert had a strong awareness of what he had lost, despite the fact that his intellect denied him the necessary conviction to ignite his religious inclinations. Eliot, however, had experienced a deeply felt religious faith during the early part of her life. Church of England by baptism, she subsequently encountered a strong evangelical influence at her boarding school in Nuneaton; and it is not without interest, in the light of her later deterministic views, that her religious convictions began to lean towards Calvinism. Indeed, by the time she was twenty, she was strongly arguing the case of predestination against her Methodist aunt's more voluntarist opinions.

Her loss of Christian faith three years later arose partly from her critical reading, but also from the influence of what could almost be a figment of Realist fiction, a freethinking ribbon-manufacturer from Coventry, Charles Bray, who made her aware of current developments in secular thought. He was himself an admirer of Holbach's *Système de la nature* (1770) and of the Idéologue, Constantin Volney, and it was he who also developed her existing interests in phrenology. Much was to come of their acquaintance. His brother-in-law, the Unitarian Charles Hennell, was the author of *An Inquiry concerning the Origin of Christianity* (1838), a book which was to have wide repercussions on Eliot's beliefs when she read it in 1841—far more than Strauss's *Das Leben Jesu* which she subsequently translated. While claiming that Christianity was 'the purest form yet existing of natural religion', it questioned the factual authenticity of much of the gospel story, but without impugning the evangelists' good faith. It nevertheless destroyed her Christian belief.

She continued to admire Christianity's insights into the subjective world of inner needs, but felt that it failed as soon as it tried to project these insights into the external world of hard reality. She likewise disliked its inbuilt system of rewards and punishments, 'disturbing that spontaneity, that choice of the good for its own sake, that answers my ideal' (August 1842). Characteristically she turned to pantheism which enabled her to retain something of the spiritual baggage of her former Christianity; but this too she soon found suspect, and from 1849, she was increasingly turning to humanism. As she was to say, twenty years later,

> Pantheism . . . could not yield a practical religion, since it is an attempt to look at the universe from the outside of our relations to it . . . As healthy, sane human beings we must love . . . what is good for mankind, hate what is evil for mankind.

She found a congenial expression of many of her inclinations in Ludwig von Feuerbach's *Das Wesen des Christenthums* which she translated in 1854. Asserting that 'God is for man the commonplace book where he registers his highest feelings and thoughts', Feuerbach's concern was that Man should not sacrifice his highest feelings to the fictitious God which he had created out of these feelings: particularly love and charity. She also experienced a short-lived interest in Comte's religion of humanity (see p. 58), an interest that partly arose from her difficulty in coming to terms with the death of friends. But like many others who admired Comte's general assessment of the human condition (see pp. 57–8), she rapidly found that his religion of humanity did less than justice to the main body of his work. She thereafter described her position as *meliorism*, the belief that the world can be improved by judicious human endeavour. As she said in 1853, 'I enjoy life more than I ever did before . . . because I have better learned that as Comte and other wise men have said, "Notre vraie destinée se compose de *résignation* et *d'activité*".'

Science

While Eliot was sloughing off these successive skins of religious enthusiasm, she became assistant editor of the *Westminster Review*, with the function of finding contributors on issues of current intellectual interest. This brought her into direct contact with contemporary writing on the physiological basis of mind, and was to lay the intellectual foundations of her determinism. It also led to her lifelong liaison with George Henry Lewes (1817–78), who was then one of her contributors, regularly reviewing recent French publications in physiology and philosophy. Their relationship was subsequently to draw her into his main literary activity of producing readable syntheses of current developments in science, psychology and sociology. Their life of jointly reading and discussing the works he was describing resulted in her rapidly becoming heir to his knowledge on these matters; indeed when he died, she undertook to edit the unpublished sections of his *Problems of Life and Mind*.

Lewes had studied medicine before becoming a writer; and he was subsequently to return to the university dissecting laboratories when he embarked on his psychological study, *Problems of Life and Mind*, in the late sixties. 1870 was to find him visiting a number of mental hospitals, as well as taking Eliot to watch an eminent Oxford anatomist perform a brain dissection for them. He was conversant with most of the major French determinists. His *Biographical History of Philosophy* (1845–6) had criticised Condillac for excluding innate impulses from his theory of knowledge, while his *Problems of Life and Mind* was to involve him in a particular study of Cabanis. He shared Eliot's interest in phrenology, Gall's *Anatomie et Physiologie du Cerveau* being one of the many books they read together. Eliot in fact had carried this interest further than most: as a young woman she had cut off her hair to enable the phrenologist, George Combe, to examine her skull. And although she later expressed reservations about Combe's views, she continued to regard phrenology as a respectable area for investigation—as did a number of other eminent Realists, including Balzac and Turgenev.

Both Eliot and Lewes were familiar with the French evolutionists from their *Westminster Review* days, notably Lamarck and Geoffroy Saint-Hilaire. They were likewise early enthusiasts of Darwin and Herbert Spencer (see pp. 164–5), Spencer being a close personal friend who, before

Lewes's ascendancy, came near to occupying a special place in Eliot's affections. Eliot regarded Darwin's *On the Origin of Species* (1859) as making 'an epoch . . . So the world gets on step by step towards brave clearness and honesty'. Both she and Lewes believed that moral impulses and judgements were the product of the interplay of innate and acquired characteristics. Like Lamarck and Darwin, they held that physical change could bring moral change: in Eliot's words, 'character is based on physiological organisation'. But their belief in the physical transmission of acquired attitudes and behaviour from the generation which first acquired them to its successors was arguably closer to Lamarck than to Darwinism. Like Herbert Spencer, who was also a Lamarckian, they held that society itself was in a process of institutional and moral evolution, which was itself both a cause and a product of the changing attitudes and behaviour of its individual members. This they understood not only in Lamarckian terms of biological transmission, but also in terms of environment, the traditions of society creating a distinctive milieu that is experienced by successive generations. In this way people of a certain race have certain *a priori* forms of thought and moral predispositions—as Eliot was later to suggest in *Daniel Deronda* (1876).

Eliot's evolutionary view of society had its counterpart in the gradualism that increasingly characterised her political opinions. 'There is a perpetual action and reaction between individuals and institutions; we must try and mend by little and little—the only way in which human things can be mended.' 'You remember me as much less of a conservative than I have now become. I care as much or more for the interests of the people, but I believe less in the help they will get from democrats.' (1878) Like Ibsen, Eliot was often canvassed to give support for female suffrage; but, like Ibsen she always refused, on the grounds that the need for emancipation lay at a deeper level than mere vote casting. The answer was 'a sublimer resignation in woman and a more regenerating tenderness in man'.

Eliot never became Lewes's wife: a legal technicality prevented him divorcing the *de jure* Mrs Lewes, despite the fact that she had two children by another man. Although his relationship with Eliot was overwhelmingly salutary, he was not to everyone's fancy. A visitor said of him,

> he looks and moves like an old-fashioned French barber or dancing-master, very ugly, very vivacious, very entertaining. You expect to see him take up his fiddle and begin to play . . . I have heard both Darwin and Sir Charles Lyell speak very highly of the thoroughness of his knowledge in their departments . . . He has the vanity of a Frenchman; his moral perceptions are not acute and he consequently often fails in social tact and taste . . . there is something in his air which reminds you of vulgarity.

While he may not have been the quintessence of English gentility, his influence on Eliot was remarkably productive; among much else it was he who first encouraged her to try her hand at novel writing in 1856. Their joint reading in psychology and what would now be called the social sciences gave precision to many of the ideas and perceptions that underlay her later novels. And, as she said in 1879, 'the Social Factor in Psychology . . . [is] the supremely interesting element in the thinking of our time'—a conviction that has its reflection in her mature fiction. As she mordantly observed in *Felix Holt*,

> there is no private life which has not been determined by a wider public life . . . Even in that conservatory existence where the fair Camellia is sighed for by the noble young Pineapple, neither of them needing to care about the frost or rain outside, there is a nether apparatus of hot-water pipes liable to cool down on a strike of the gardeners or a scarcity of coal.

Synthesis

If the 1850s emancipated Eliot from the intellectual grasp of religion, the end of the decade found her emotions feeling the cold. Writing in July 1859 she remarked

> I have had heart-cutting experience that *opinions* are a poor cement between human souls: and the only effect I ardently wish to produce by my writings is, that those who read them should be better able to *imagine* and to *feel* the pains and the joys of those who differ from themselves in everything but the broad fact of being struggling, erring, human creatures.

Again, in *Middlemarch* (1871–2): 'There is no general doctrine which is not capable of eating out our morality if unchecked by the deep-seated habit of direct fellow-feeling with individual fellow-men.' This was to be a recurring theme in Tolstoy's novels, as indeed in those of many other Realist writers who found that the promised land, revealed by the liberated intellect, was not so sunny as they at first expected. While her mind continued to reject Christianity, she had to admit that 'on many points where I used to delight in expressing intellectual difference, I now delight in feeling an emotional agreement'.

Her novels of the sixties and seventies were to be remarkable, among much else, for the reconciliation she attempted between determinism and morality, a morality that had emotional affinities with the religious beliefs of her youth. Traditional morality was inextricably linked with choices between 'good' and 'evil', a relationship that posed problems for the determinist who saw freedom of choice as a subjective illusion. Like most determinists, Eliot defined as 'good' whatever was conducive to the wellbeing of mankind, including the individuals whose actions and thoughts were being scrutinised. And, by extension, she classified attitudes and states of mind as 'good' or 'bad' according to the effect they had on the general disposition of the individual towards others.

As a determinist, she accepted that the individual is impelled to what is 'good ' or 'bad' by factors originating outside him, hereditary and environmental: he is not an autonomous moral agent. As *Middlemarch* continually demonstrates, his ability to change his life for the better is largely dependent on extraneous elements, such as the influence and encouragement of others, or events and developments that act as a salutary example or warning. And the emergence or not of these benign influences is itself dependent on pre-existing factors. She recognised that there was no point at which the iron ring of determined existence could be broken and entered. All of which might lead the reader to suppose that moral judgements of the traditional sort could have no place in a world where the decisive factors lie outside the individual's control.

Yet on the level of subjective experience, which is where the individual consciousness lives out its life, most men have the sensation of free will, however illusory this sensation may be. And it is on this subjective plane that Eliot believed that the individual can, and must, cultivate his sense of moral awareness, while still recognising, on the level of objective reality, that he and the rest of mankind are directed by forces over which he has no control. To act as though he has free will enables him to conduct his life 'responsibly', without falling into discouragement or apathy. But his fundamental awareness of the determined nature of the human condition enables him to be more tolerant of the shortcomings of others, and also less impatient with his own limitations. It increases both his capacity for sympathy and his practical sense of what is possible, while avoiding the numbing sense of futility that may come from a too exclusive view of the objective facts of determinism. When a lady of Eliot's acquaintance confessed that her acceptance of determinism had drained life of its meaning, Eliot replied,

> As to the necessary combinations through which life is manifested, and which seem to present themselves to you as a hideous fatalism, which ought logically to petrify your volition—have they, *in fact*, any such influence on your ordinary course of action in the primary affairs of your existence as a human, social, domestic creature? (*Letters*, VI, 98.)

> I shall not be satisfied with your philosophy till you have conciliated necessitarianism—I hate the ugly word—with the practice of willing strongly, willing to will strongly (*Letters*, VI, 166)

And, as Eliot confided to her note-book,

> It is rational to accept two apparent irreconcileables, rather than to

reject tested processes in favour of a reasoning which tends to nullify all processes. ('More leaves', p. 365.)

Although Eliot was arguably doing no more than state explicitly what determinists had traditionally assumed (and in some cases enunciated), her double vision of subjective experience and objective reality enabled her to give moral significance to life, without turning her back on the material realities of existence.

At the same time Eliot believed that it was moral awareness on both these levels, and a readiness to evaluate the actions of others in moral terms, which provided mankind with its most potent factor for self-improvement. The fact that a man's conduct is ultimately not of his own making, should not deter others, or himself, from passing moral judgements on it, since it is precisely judgements of this sort that may well influence his subsequent behaviour. This belief had its parallel in Darwin's assertion that the sympathy underlying 'the approbation and disapprobation of our fellows . . . forms an essential part of the social instinct and is indeed its foundation stone' (*The Descent of Man*). In the same way, while recognising herself as fundamentally no more than a link in a chain of cause and effect, Eliot hoped that her novels would themselves incline people towards attitudes and courses of action that would bring happiness to others and to themselves. A few months before embarking on *Middlemarch*, she confessed that

> the inspiring principle which alone gives me courage to write is, that of so presenting our human life as to help my readers in getting a clearer conception and a more active admiration of those vital elements which bind men together and give a higher worthiness to their existence . . .

Eliot's split-level concept of human existence, corresponding to subjective experience and objective reality, was not easy to convey in a novel. Her characters, of necessity, live out their lives on the level of subjective experience, and so do her readers. If her readers are to feel empathy for her characters, her commentary, as well as her dialogue, must be of a kind to appeal to the reader's experience and emotions; which in practice obliges much of the commentary to be given in the language and metaphor of subjective experience, even if the content may aspire to something more 'objectively' analytical. The intellectual focus of the commentary may shift from one level to the other, but its style and presentation cannot shift so quickly: it has to preserve a certain continuity of mood and texture.

Nor does Eliot regard the omniscient narrator as holding a monopoly of objective truth. Her characters too may succeed in groping their way towards a truer understanding of life, even if they cannot aspire to the breadth of view of the narrator. As Bernard Paris has suggested in *Experiments in Life*, her characters can be understood and grouped in terms of the progress they achieve towards an objective view of their relationship with others. In Paris's analysis, those who come nearest to this are those who acknowledge their smallness as a part of human society, and who endeavour to apportion their sympathies and efforts accordingly. Yet Eliot is very insistent that the individual, in being generous to others, must not exclude himself from the sphere of his own beneficent activities, nor from those who wish to help him. Selflessness does not mean self-abnegation. Although the man who aspires to objectivity sees the smallness of his part in society, he nevertheless remains a part of it; and he has a duty to receive as well as bestow the benefits that human beings in society confer on each other, even if his just share is a modest one. How this concept is applicable to *Middlemarch* and *Felix Holt* is demonstrated in Appendix C (see pp. 179–81).

The status Eliot gave to the realm of subjective experience enabled her to restore to life many of the consolations that seemed lost with free will. Even the Christian promise of individual immortality had its counterpart in Eliot's view of existence; for not only did she seek to give meaning and quality to life, but she sought to console those who were reluctant to leave it. As death increasingly depleted her friends, and the oblivion of the tomb became a growing preoccupation, she came to believe that the Christian concept of the eternal fellowship of heaven had a secular counterpart. It had been a traditional commonplace of popular sentiment that great men enjoy a certain immortality in their achievements: artists lived on in their works; and most institutions commemorated their benefactors, many of them long dead. Yet these were men whose achievements were publicly known or tangibly survived their deaths.

Eliot, however, saw the principle as equally applicable to the ordinary acts of undistinguished people. She argued that a word or act of kindness, or malevolence, affected not only the recipient; but, in colouring his current frame of mind, it also affected those whom he subsequently encountered, however indirectly and however imperceptibly. Like the widening ripples of water, displaced by a falling stone, the impact of the act in question would diminish as its effects were passed from individual to individual—indeed the act and its agents might be forgotten in a matter of minutes. But its indirect effects were nevertheless passed on, however much they might be modified by other lateral factors. A man's life was composed of many such actions, each sending out a widening if weakening succession of ripples.

It is in this sense that Eliot saw the individual as enjoying a certain immortality, since even the least significant of men leaves the world a slightly different place from what it was before, however imperceptible and anonymous the difference. Whether this immortality is a matter of consolation depends on whether his influence has been on balance beneficial or not. As Eliot said in one of her poems

> O may I join the choir invisible . . .
> Of those immortal dead who live again
> In minds made better by their presence.

The same thought provides the conclusion to *Middlemarch*, where she says of Dorothea:

> Her full nature . . . spent itself in channels which had no great name on the earth. But the effect of her being on those around her was incalculably diffusive: for the growing good of the world is partly dependent on unhistoric acts; and that things are not so ill with you and me as they might have been, is half owing to the number who lived faithfully a hidden life, and rest in unvisited tombs.

Eliot recognised that these 'unhistoric acts' and their faithful performers are themselves merely links in a causal chain anchored in the past. But, for anyone who wished to feel part of life and to experience a fellow feeling with the rest of humanity, it was consoling rather than disappointing to sense one's role as that of a link rather than a prime cause. It enhanced the individual's sense of solidarity with humanity and the living world. It was here in particular that the past stages of Eliot's intellectual and moral development, Christian, pantheist and humanist, came together to form a coherent *modus vivendi*. She contrived to salvage many of the more attractive furnishings of the abandoned ship of traditional religion, and loaded them, not unskilfully, into the faster, safer, but arguably less comfortable vessel of nineteenth-century secular thought.

The effect she had on contemporary readers is reflected in a letter she received from a Cambridge don, shortly after the publication of *Middlemarch*:

> now that there is no longer any God or any hereafter or anything in particular to aim at . . . you seem now to be the only person who can make life appear potentially noble and interesting without starting from any assumptions. De Stendhal [sic], perhaps, while himself detached from all illusions, has painted life in the same grand style. But he remains too much outside his characters, and though in his books nobleness seems possible it seems possible only as an aberration.

10 Russia and the Realist Response: Turgenev

The Russian Realists, no less than their western counterparts, acknowledged society as a regnant shaping influence in a determinist world. Those who travelled in the West not only saw social change in full spate, but had daily proof, exhilarating, saddening or amusing, that the ethos of western society was very different from that of Russia. Few could doubt the familiar commonplace that different societies fashioned different men. The 'Westerners' among them, however, such as Turgenev, believed that Russia's destiny lay precisely in this shifting foreign terrain that was being laid bare of belief by the secular West wind of rationalist thought and material progress. And although part of Turgenev's sensibilities felt a nostalgic regret that this was so, he and his colleagues regarded the change as not only inevitable but desirable. The Slavophils, on the other hand, both feared and despised the growing materialism of western culture, and hoped that Russia could fashion her own future along the lines that her traditions had already established. Like Balzac in the 1840s, they looked to the old cohesive forces of an established religion and a deep-rooted paternalistic monarchy.

An ordered society

Money-making and ambition, which loom large in western Realism, are not a major presence in the Russian novels of the pre-1890 period, although warning signs are there (see pp. 116–17). With the Russian Industrial Revolution yet to come, the Russian economy was still predominantly based on land, which, for the most part, was in the hands of a relatively static class of hereditary landowners. Although financial mismanagement obliged quite a few to sell their land to parvenus, this did not alter the basic pattern of landownership. Compared with the West, the opportunities for social mobility through money-making were fairly limited. Agriculture did not offer the spectacular changes of fortune which were possible in industry and commerce. And it was difficult for the man of modest means to buy land in any quantity on borrowed wealth, since financiers were hesitant about making substantial loans to would-be-farmers, when the percentage returns were so relatively unexciting.

The other ladder of western social mobility, *la carrière ouverte aux talents*, likewise afforded limited prospects in Russia. The achievement of certain grades in the army and civil service automatically conferred membership of the Russian nobility—a class that differed markedly in concept and composition from the aristocracies of Western Europe. But the higher offices of state were largely the preserve of established families. Ability accelerated promotion; but the influence of friends and relatives was a dominant factor, as Tolstoy observed in *Anna Karenina*. It goes without saying that political conformity was also an essential requisite for office—a number of nobles being *personae non gratae* in the public service because of their liberal opinions.

In these circumstances, ambition mainly took the form of achieving esteem and advancement in the aspirant's own particular profession and acquiring a similar esteem in the social circle where birth had placed him. While Anna Karenina's husband and her lover, Vronsky, are both of an ambitious temperament, theirs is the ambition of the civil servant and the army officer, each determined to go far in his particular profession, and each determined to be well thought of in his own social milieu. Both are nobles and their ambition was of the type that consolidates rather than challenges the existing social structure and its conventions. Although Vronsky briefly considers joining a friend's political faction, that too was a perquisite of his class.

Such a society had little room for Balzac's ambitious young climbers, or his upstart businessmen. *Anna Karenina* discerned the growth of a parasitic fringe of middle-class speculators, who sought to exploit the financial carelessness of the more feckless noble landlords. But Tolstoy portrayed them as a jackal class who primarily lived off others' mistakes, rather than developing and exploiting economic situations of their own making. Russia had its share of merchants, bankers and railway financiers—likewise indicated in *Anna Karenina*. But it was the industrial revolution of the 1890s that started to initiate the world of rapid fortunes that western Realism had thrived on since the 1830s. Even then the initiation was to be only partial and very brief, for the momentous events of 1917–27 were shortly to transfer industrial power from businessmen to the state.

The leisured landed society that predominates in nineteenth-century Russian fiction—with its relatively static composition and unspectacular economic expectations—had time for the contemplation of ideals and principles, and could afford to put some of them occasionally to the test: within the bounds of financial prudence and social propriety. The western reader, surfeited on Balzac and Zola, with their accounts of endless manoeuvres for financial advantage, experiences a certain relief on encountering *Fathers and Sons*, where thoughts on the purpose of life simmer slowly with the samovar. When not reading Pushkin or playing his cello, Nicolai Kirsanov spends his leisure hours perusing mildly liberal periodicals. He has put his serfs on a tenant footing; not primarily for profit, but largely as a gesture of personal commitment to humanitarian principles and progressive economic theory. Indeed like Turgenev himself, who commuted his serfs' labour services for a quit rent (see pp. 104–5), Nicolai loses money by it in the short run; and it is far from clear whether he will make it in the long. Not that Turgenev is suggesting that the benevolent if somewhat ineffective liberalism of Nicolai is characteristic of the Russian gentry as a whole. His own mother was the tyrannical owner of five thousand serfs, and had a child put to death because its crying got on her nerves; she likewise exiled two serfs to Siberia for neglecting to bow to her. Yet, as he said of *Fathers and Sons*, 'My entire novel is directed against the nobility as a leading class'. For him the Kirsanov family represented 'weakness, flabbiness, inadequacy'. They were better than most; but 'If the cream is bad, what can the milk be like?'

If western Realists such as Balzac disliked the thrusting ambition of the bourgeoisie, 'weakness, flabbiness, inadequacy' were the price that Russia paid for the absence of this productive if disagreeable force. Russians returning from abroad were aware of a prevailing ambience of inertia and resignation, thrown into relief by the ferment and startling changes they had witnessed abroad. Would-be reformers were appalled by the massive obstacles that seemed to lie in the way of any significant change in Russia, with the result that pessimism and a listless depression were frequent ingredients of Russian Realism, especially in its portrayal of the liberal intelligentsia. In *The Diary of a Superfluous Man* (1850) Turgenev epitomised the predicament of the intellectual reformer in an autocratic society—the man who had no effective means of criticism that did not involve serious personal risk. At odds with what surrounded him, he felt frustration at being unable to change it and contempt for his own fear of speaking too openly. At the same time his education cut him off from the masses, thereby confining him to a sort of limbo, disowned by both the establishment and the greater part of the population.

These obstacles were deep-rooted in the centuries. In the view of liberal observers, not only were the Tsarist monarchy and the bulk of the nobility determined to resist anything that might erode their entrenched authority, but, after centuries of autocracy, even the upper classes seemed incapable of taking any significant initiative. In the past autocracy had arguably been essential in a country of scattered communities that had few natural frontiers and was a prey to successive invasions from east and west. Alexander Nevsky, Ivan the Terrible and Peter the Great were probably the price Russia had to pay for national survival. But a people that had been crushed into submission by one ruler after another came to accept that all important decisions depended on the Tsar. And in the nineteenth century, such landmarks as the Emancipation of the Serfs in 1861, and the launching of the Industrial Revolution in the 1890s, were largely initiated by the Tsarist government. Any writer, committed to reform, could only view this passive attitude with pessimism, if not despair.

Ivan Turgenev (1818–83)

Turgenev's determinism was both an emotional and an intellectual response to what experience and his wide reading had taught him about the human condition. Like many nineteenth-century writers, his religious scepticism sprang from an awareness of suffering. As a child he had watched a snake trying to devour a toad alive: 'that for the first time made me doubt the existence of a merciful Providence'. And, as he later wrote, 'the nightingale can give us moments of indescribable rapture while some unhappy half-crushed insect is dying in agony in its crop'. The severity of his mother, Varvara Turgeneva, both to her serfs and to her family, had likewise accustomed him from an early age to a low expectation of happiness, even if, as one hopes, he may have been exaggerating when he said of his childhood 'I do not have a single happy memory of it'. Varvara herself was the victim of a savage, violent upbringing; and her passionate nature responded bitterly to the neglect and infidelities of her husband.

Like Flaubert, however, he knew what man had lost with religion. 'He who has religion has everything and cannot lose anything; but he who has not got it, has nothing, and I feel it all the stronger as I myself belong to those who have not got it' (1860). As Litvinov comments in *Smoke* (1867), watching the train smoke wreathing across the fields, 'Everything is smoke and vapour . . . everything hurrying, hastening somewhere—and vanishes without leaving a trace, without reaching anywhere'.

But if life is pointless, it is predetermined, however meaningless and unpredictable the pattern. Turgenev was familiar, if often at second hand, with much of the gamut of determinist thought. He read philosophy at Berlin University, and seriously considered becoming a philosophy lecturer before deciding on an administrative career. As it happened, this début in the Ministry of the Interior turned out to be short-lived, the uncongenial nature of an office life deciding him to live 'independently' on his mother's wealth, combining the occupations of landowner and man of letters. Being something of a philosopher by training, he took a wry amusement in the way determinist thought was bandied about as a subject of fashionable conversation in salon society. *Fathers and Sons* speaks of 'those statesmen of the time of Alexander who used to read a page of Condillac in the morning in preparation for a reception that evening in Madame Swetchine's in St. Petersburg'. Yevdoksia Kukshina, the self-conscious emancipated woman of the same novel, likewise bursts out 'George Sand . . . She's nothing more than an outdated woman ! . . . She has no idea of any kind about education, or physiology, or anything. I'm sure she hasn't even heard of embryology, and in our time—how can you do without it?' Kukshina's lunch-time conversation is typically about the Helvétian problem of 'what people are at birth—are they identical or not?—and what constitutes individuality?'

Turgenev himself was deeply interested in these issues. Like Balzac and Eliot, he was also fascinated by phrenology. Among much else, he made a meticulous study of Lavater's massive work on physiognomy (see p. 38), believing, like Lavater, that mental and physical attributes were closely connected, even if the precise nature of the connections was imperfectly understood. Most of the characters in Turgenev's novels were in fact observed from life; and when talking to people who interested him he kept a sharp eye open for physical and behavioural characteristics, hoping to discern identifiable connections with their personalities that would add verisimilitude to his creations.

The importance he accorded to the physical basis of mind was matched by a parallel respect for the formative influence of environment. In his view, all were subject to it, even the man of exceptional gifts: 'A man of genius is not a cosmopolitan: he belongs to his people and to his age' (1844); 'the chief fault of our writers is their insufficient contact with reality' (1856).

If life for Turgenev was no more than drifting smoke, he believed that the smoke while it lasted could at least be made less noxious. A curious feature of Russian Realism was its ambivalent response to the backwardness of Russian society. On the one hand this backwardness helped to create a characteristic mood of despondency, which often resulted in apathy or inertia. On the other hand it presented a clearly identifiable area where improvements in the human lot could positively be attempted, without soul-searching as to whether these improvements were ultimately in the best interest of mankind. Part of the pessimism of a Stendhal in the 1830s (see pp. 15–16) or a Flaubert in the 1870s (see pp. 71–3) was that they imagined that most of the necessary reforms in government and society had already been achieved, in France and Britain, at least, and yet people seemed no happier or better than before. In Russia on the other hand, although Turgenev and his fellow determinists held no optimistic brief for humanity. [Life in the long run being worth very little], they nevertheless saw that Life as it was currently endured in their own country could at least be made more tolerable.

Temperamentally Turgenev felt no pull towards politics. But as Vissarion Belinsky (1811–48) pointed out to him, any writer who chose to describe society under the Tsarist autocracy was *ipso facto* performing an act of political significance. Belinsky in fact was the lodestar of Turgenev's social conscience. *Fathers and Sons* was dedicated to his memory; and Turgenev was to say of Belinsky's open letter to Gogol (see p. 103) that it was his 'whole religion'. Like so many figures involved or portrayed in nineteenth-century Realism, Belinsky was the son of a doctor in the armed services: in this case a naval doctor. An admirer of classical antiquity and the French Revolution, Belinsky's credo, in Turgenev's words, was 'science, progress, love of humanity, civilisation; in short, the West'.

Turgenev subscribed to all but the violent, revolutionary element in Belinsky's thought. He could not share his admiration for Marat, nor his enthusiasm for a Russian republic. As he was to write in 1880, three years before his death, 'I am, and always have been, a gradualist, an old-fashioned liberal in the English dynastic sense, a man expecting reform only from above. I oppose revolution in principle . . .' Like Belinsky, however, he believed that reform in Russia depended on the nobility throwing in their lot with the bourgeoisie.

Belinsky made a clear distinction between the reforming roles of the capitalist bourgeoisie and the middle-class intelligentsia. In his view the capitalist bourgeoisie was a self-interested but historically necessary instrument of reform; but the guiding spirit must be the intelligentsia. He saw their contribution as particularly important in Russia where there was no constitutional means by which criticism could make itself officially heard. As he said in his open letter (15 July 1847) to Gogol, who had become increasingly conservative in his later years, 'I see you do' . . .

> not quite understand the Russian public. Its character is determined by the condition of Russian society, which contains, imprisoned within it, fresh forces seething and bursting to break out; but crushed by heavy repression and unable to escape, they produce gloom, bitter depression, apathy. Only in literature, in spite of our Tartar censorship, there is still some life and forward movement . . . The public . . . sees in Russian writers its only leaders, defenders and saviours from autocracy, Orthodoxy and the national way of life.

The dramatic events of February 1848 drew both Turgenev and Belinsky to Paris. Turgenev was characteristically much more circumspect in his sightseeing than his French counterparts, Balzac and Flaubert. Flaubert had roamed the streets during the fighting; and, at some risk to himself, with a certain stoical detachment, he had helped to carry a wounded man out of the line of fire. Balzac, on the other hand, like Flaubert, had witnessed the mob pillaging the Tuileries, but equally characteristically had discreetly joined in the looting, taking off several choice *objets d'art* for his collection. Turgenev, by contrast, preferred to observe events from a safer distance.

The visit, however, brought him into contact with Alexander Herzen. Herzen had followed an intellectual odyssey which in its initial stages had much in common with Belinsky's. After an early enthusiasm for Hegelianism which he tried to develop in a left-wing direction, seeing in the dialectic the 'algebra of revolution', he became increasingly interested in the *philosophes* of eighteenth-century France, and subsequently in French socialism. Yet, although he regarded the Russian Slavophils as muddle-headed and unconstructive on most issues, he also came to see that they had pinpointed a major problem in reforming Russia: the need to establish links between the intelligentsia and the mass of the population. While conceding that the bourgeoisie had served a useful instrumental role in the development of western democracy, albeit self-interestedly, he did not share Belinsky's view that they had a similarly important role to play in Russia's future. The defeat of French socialism under the Second Republic (see pp. 71–2), convinced him that the great obstacle to reform was the identity of interest between the possessing classes and the forces of a centralised state machine. This conviction increasingly channelled his thoughts into a populist, decentralising direction. Like the Slavophils, he saw the Russian agrarian commune as containing an enormous re-generative potential—but, for Herzen, this would take a revolutionary form. Moreover, since Russia had not yet reached western Europe's condition of bourgeois capitalism, Russia might well be able to dispense with bourgeois rule and move straight from feudal autocracy to a federal democracy of peasant communes.

In fact the peasant commune as it then existed offered a very slender basis for such hopes. Its prime function was to apportion the poll tax and arrange periodic redistributions of land among the peasants: duties which had effectively been delegated to it by the landlord. The periodic redistribution of land was designed to compensate for the varying fertility of the soil; a peasant with a poor plot might hope to receive a better one at the next rotation. But although this function and the allocation of tax gave the commune substantial control over the lives of the peasantry, it hardly equipped it for the role of democratic self-government that Herzen envisaged. Turgenev, as a landowner, knew the peasant communes at first hand; he knew them as ignorant conservative bodies, dominated by a handful of the richer peasants, who tyrannised over the rest. Herzen, in his view, had rejected 'the golden calf' of western capitalism, only to worship 'the sheepskin coat' of the Russian peasant. For the same reasons, Turgenev could not accept the enthusiasms of the Slavophils, who, from an opposing conservative standpoint, similarly idealised peasant institutions.

Herzen, for his part, became increasingly exasperated by the Anglo-Saxon moderation of Turgenev's liberalism. When Turgenev publicly assured the government that he was a lifelong monarchist, Herzen savagely dismissed him as 'a white-haired Magdalen of the male sex', unable to sleep at night for thinking that the Emperor might not have heard of his repentance. He would make no concession to the fact that Turgenev had earlier been confined to his estate for a year, as an indirect result of the implicit critique of serfdom contained in his *A Sportsman's Sketches* (1847–52). Indeed, his confinement might have lasted for much longer, had it not been for the intercession of a literary friend at court.

Unlike many of his critics, Turgenev was a practical reformer who sought to practise what he preached. During his brief career in the Ministry of the Interior, he had sent his supervisors a memorandum on the inefficiency of serfdom, with its absentee landlords and lack of incentive for the peasants. And although this venture was promptly consigned to oblivion, he instituted reforms on his own estate, notably by commuting the labour dues of his serfs for an annual quit rent in 1858, thereby effectively making them tenants of nearly half his land. The remaining half he farmed with hired labour. Although he was a firm believer in the long-term economic advantages of this measure, he anticipated losing a quarter of his annual income during his own lifetime as a result of his changes; a loss which did not deter him from providing his peasants with a school, a hospital and a home for the aged.

Land reform, however, and socio-political measures in general could do no more than bring Russian life a little nearer to the level that was normal in the west. There was nothing startling or regenerative about it. One would at best be merely arriving at the start of the weary western road, which might turn out to be no more than a circular path, which Flaubert and his fellow pessimists had been treading for decades. The victims of the Russian way of life would be less miserable, but there was no reason to suppose that there would be more happiness of the positive kind that characterises men whose lives have a new and hopeful meaning. Only those who still held a living vibrant belief could experience that; and religion was no solution for men who needed factual foundations for personal commitment. Indeed, with the withering of the credos that had given meaning to life, Turgenev saw only one force that might give humanity something approaching a new expectation:

> . . . life has crumbled into bits and pieces; there is no longer a general great movement, except perhaps industry which if one considers it from the point of view of the progressive submission of the elements of nature to man's genius, will perhaps become the liberator and the regenerator of humanity. Therefore the greatest poets of our time are, in my opinion, the Americans, who are about to cut through the Panama isthmus and are discussing the question of laying a telegraph cable across the ocean.

Like other Realists, Turgenev saw science, and its corollary, education, as humanity's best prospect, limited though it might turn out to be. 1860 found him drawing up schemes for a national system of universal elementary education; and when in 1858 it became clear that the government intended to embark on the emancipation of the serfs, he characteristically urged it to launch an agricultural journal, which would educate the landowning classes into seeing the potential advantages of the measure. (The government, however, equally true to form, turned down the suggestion as conducive to dangerous debate.)

Fathers and Sons
The great issue, however, was how were these regenerative possibilities to

be realised, and what price would Russia, and humanity, have to pay to obtain them? This was the crux of *Fathers and Sons* (1862).

The novel reveals Turgenev as both critic and defender of the society that had produced him. He was convinced that the existing social order in Russia was condemned to disappear, and his intellect rejoiced at the fact. Yet, as if in anticipation of this, he already felt a certain nostalgia for a society that did not have long to live; and much of the wistful atmosphere of the novel stems from his ambivalent feelings. Since, however, reason insisted on change, the question was whether it should come through piecemeal reform as envisaged by his own generation of liberal reformers: 'the Fathers' as they appear in the novel. Or were more fundamental alterations needed, involving a new society and new patterns of thought, as envisaged by the younger radicals: 'the Sons' in the novel?

Turgenev said of this choice of approaches, 'We, the people of the forties, based our philosophy of life on moral principles, but we lacked willpower—these others have the willpower but lack the moral principles'. The morality of the Fathers was based on their common acceptance of the values of propertied society. They were mostly of the middle nobility and university-educated. Reared on the classics and western culture in general, they stood for the familiar watchwords of western liberal democracy—equality before the law, freedom of the press, respect for property, etc—and, as far as methods went, they mostly preferred the education of public opinion to the short cut of a seizure of power.

The genteel dilletantism of many of 'the Fathers' stood in marked contrast to the dour root-and-branch-ism of 'the Sons'. This new generation of intellectuals, who achieved a certain notoriety in the later 1850s, were in many cases men of fairly humble social origins. They were often the sons of Orthodox priests (who were able to obtain financial concessions for the education of their children). Others were engineers, whom the government was prepared to train at public expense. Unlike 'the Fathers', few of them had family estates to keep them in pocket; and so the bulk took fairly menial white-collar jobs as clerks or teachers, their political views excluding most of them from more lucrative appointments. The better qualified became doctors or engineers. This was a generation that had grown up in the knowledge that the western revolutions of 1848 had failed. Unlike the well-heeled 'Fathers', they held no brief for middle and upper-class liberalism. Revolution, to mean anything, must be a social revolution. Affecting to admire the manners and attitudes of the common people, their ascetic philistinism had a certain *rapport* with England's 'Angry Young Men' of the 1950s.

Turgenev's closest experience of this generation came through his association with the *Contemporary* review, which in the late 1850s was dominated by two young radicals, Nicolai Chernyshevsky (1828–89) and Nicolai Dobrolubov (1836–61), who saw art primarily as a vehicle for reform: 'a text-book of life' as Chernyshevsky called it. Both sons of priests, their puritanical intransigence and integrity both attracted and repelled Turgenev; above all they had an energy and decisiveness which he found lacking in himself. Turgenev may have used Dobrolubov's rudeness and Chernyshevsky's 'hateful' views on art to provide some of the ingredients that he gave to Yevgeny Bazarov, the central figure of *Fathers and Sons*. But Bazarov's intellectual standpoint is considerably more radical than that of the two 'seminarists' of *The Contemporary*, and in many ways foreshadows the credo of Dmitri Pisarev (1840–68), one of the Grandsons of the 1860s.

Turgenev said of Bazarov in 1870, 'My personal feelings towards Bazarov were confused. (God only knows whether I loved him or hated him)'. And in 1862, 'I conceived him as a sombre figure, wild, huge, half-grown out of the soil, powerful, nasty, honest, but doomed to destruction because he stands in the gateway to the future.' With Bazarov, Turgenev came to grips with what was arguably the most basic question facing humanity in the nineteenth century. In a world divested of traditional certainties, how did one set about finding secure intellectual foundations on which to build a new society? The term 'nihilist', which Bazarov applies to himself, had a wider meaning in the early 1860s to what it was later to have in the 1880s. For Bazarov, it implies scepticism towards all things that cannot be proved by scientific enquiry; the rest is 'romantic rubbish'. As he says to Pavel, 'At present the most useful thing is to deny. So we deny.' 'Everything? . . . Not only art, poetry.' 'Everything.' 'So you destroy everything . . . but surely one must build too?' 'That's not our business . . . First one must clear the ground.' This is fundamentally an intellectual rather than a political argument, although it has political ramifications. The destruction envisaged is not that of the anarchist's bomb, but rather the clearing away of unsafe intellectual premises (political ones included) until bed-rock is reached—bed-rock in this case being scientifically demonstrable fact. Nor must the scouring process cease with the elimination of unsound ideas and institutions. One's own sense data and thought processes must be put to the acid test. One's very being must be scrutinised. 'You find this hard to swallow?—No, friend, if you have decided to knock everything down, you must knock yourself down, too.'

Like the Idéologues, Bazarov claims that all cerebrally-held principles are reducible to mere sensations; and symptomatically, it is Ludwig Büchner's materialist *opus*, *Force and Matter* (1855) that Bazarov recommends as salutary reading to the Kirsanovs. Ludwig Büchner was Georg Büchner's younger brother; and although there is no evidence to suggest that Turgenev knew anything of George Büchner (whose literary works remained largely unnoticed until the 1870s), Ludwig Büchner was a scientist and thinker of international reputation, his *Force and Matter* being regarded as a leading statement of biological materialism.

It is of a piece with Bazarov's determinism that he should have strong medical interests. Son of an army physician, like Georg Büchner, his intention is to be a country doctor. Like Buchner, he is an avid dissector of frogs which, like beetles, he believes to reveal more about the nature of life than art or poetry.

> As for the mystic relationship between a man and a woman? We physiologists know what constitutes that relationship. Study the anatomy of the eye; where does that—what you call—enigmatic look come from? That's all romanticism, humbug, rot, art. We'd do better to look at the beetle!
> A decent chemist is twenty times more useful than any poet.

Bazarov's scepticism has far-reaching political implications. Institutions and practices that cannot be justified according to the same strict basic logic must be cleared away. But how and when this is to be done, he does not specify. He pours scorn on the Slavophils' faith in the peasant commune, just as he scorns the hopes of the westward-looking liberals, with their belief in political constitutionalism. 'You know the proverb: "The Russian peasant would gobble up God himself".' As for the peasant's much-vaunted family life, the frequency of arranged marriages in Russia made it, in Bazarov's view, a source of misery rather than happiness. He is equally scathing about the liberal gentry, his sarcasm suggesting some of the anger felt by modern black-rights leaders, faced with the well-meaning sympathy of white liberals.

> Your type, the gentry, cannot get beyond noble humility, noble indignation, and that is nonsense. You won't for instance, fight, and yet you think yourself terrific . . . you still can't help admiring yourselves, you like castigating yourselves, and that bores us.

Bazarov's attitude to politics, however, is far from negative. His abrasive dismissal of contemporary solutions arises from what was to be the archetypal view of the later Realists that political reform is useless unless it is preceded by an interior revolution in men themselves. Change would come in the first instance through education and scientific advance. Only then could political activity achieve the massive transformation of society that Bazarov envisaged. This was a view that was implicit in the later Büchner, and, in a gentler form, underlies much of George Eliot's thinking on politics. In Bazarov's words, 'moral sicknesses are produced by bad education, . . . by the outrageous state of society . . . Reform society and there will be no sickness.'

The issue, however, presents a major procedural problem of the chicken-and-the-egg variety. Bazarov, in common with Ibsen and a number of the other later Realists, believes that there must be an inner reform of the individual before society can be changed. And yet if education is the means by which this inner reform can be effected, how can education be changed until society itself is transformed? On the face of it, the issue seems a closed circle, with no point of entry. Turgenev provides Bazarov with no answer to this problem; indeed the problem itself is not explicitly stated in the novel, despite its implicit presence. Had Turgenev chosen to pose it, Bazarov might have replied as Chekhov was later to reply: namely that the education of the individual and society can only be initiated by the diffusive influence of the enlightened few (see pp. 167–9). Those men, who see the world for what it is, will influence others through their conversation and examples; and, like oil on water, their views will gradually spread. Once public opinion is educated in this way, the political changes will follow of themselves, and massive reforms of institutions and society become possible. In Chekhov's view, this process might require many generations to reach fulfilment; and it is a matter for conjecture whether Bazarov would have been prepared to wait so long. But, had he been able to pursue his intended career of country doctor, one can imagine him doggedly fulfilling his duties to the community, grimly lecturing his patients on the stupidity and short-sightedness of the world around them, while they stand speechless or trouserless, as he examines their tonsils or boils, in the hope that not all his seeds of wisdom will fall on stony ground. Indeed the fanciful reader might well be tempted to regard Chekhov's Dr Astrov in *Uncle Vanya* (see pp. 168–9) as a mild-mannered embodiment of what Bazarov might have become.

If these conjectures come anywhere near the implications of Bazarov's views on the achievement of reform, they invalidate the common assertion that Bazarov was 'the first Bolshevik'. The Bolshevik believes that he can revolutionise Man by changing society: therefore, on his analysis, the political revolution can, and should, precede the educational revolution. For Bazarov, by contrast, the inner revolution must come first, in the liver-salts tradition.

On the more fundamental issues of determinism and the nature of man, there seems at first sight to be some contradiction in Bazarov's expressed opinions. On the one hand he is a staunch believer in scientific determinism, while, on the other, he makes a cult of the exercise of the will. For most of the novel Bazarov extols education as the only solution to Russia's ills. At other times he bursts out: 'Education? Every person should educate himself . . . and, as for the times, why should I be influenced by them? Rather let them be influenced by me. No, brother, that's all spinelessness'. In fact the two attitudes are not contradictory, as both Stendhal (see pp. 25–6) and George Eliot (see pp. 94–5) clearly demonstrated. In Eliot's schema, a person who believes in determinism is accepting a scientific fact on the level of objective reality. The cult of the will, however, as practised by Stendhal, and understood by Eliot, is a form of self-discipline, exercised on the level of subjective experience, which does not seek to deny that *why* we will, and *what* we will, are the product of factors outside our control.

The juxtaposition of these two attitudes in Bazarov partly emanated from the fact that he was an amalgam of several characters in Turgenev's mind. Two of these were a couple of doctors he encountered: one on a train journey in Russia, the other when on holiday at Ventnor in the Isle of Wight. The first had impressed Turgenev with his claim that he could sleep anywhere, through the exercise of sheer willpower. The other had been a proponent of some of the materialist views that made up a substantial part of Bazarov's intellectual baggage.

As Turgenev confessed, 'I could never invent my characters . . . I had to choose a living person and combine in this person many characteristics in conformity with the type of my hero.' 'All through my career as a writer, I have never taken *ideas* but always *characters* for my starting point.' And, characteristically, he said of Balzac, whose method was the complete converse of this,

> All his characters are so marvellously typical . . . and finished to the last detail—and yet not one of them has ever lived or indeed could have lived, and not one of them possesses even one particle of the truth which makes the characters of Tolstoy's *Cossacks*, for instance, so vitally alive.

This comment underlined, if it exaggerated, the essential difference between the observed presentation of character, as practised by the Anglo-Russian Realists, and the conceptual approach of their French compeers.

Even so, Turgenev was too much of a determinist and a systematic worker to neglect conceptual planning. He would compose for his own benefit a *curriculum vitae* of each character up to the point where the novel opens. 'The writer must be a psychologist, but a secret one: he must sense and know the roots of phenomena, but offer only the phenomena themselves—as they blossom or wither.' Whereas Zola would more or less push into the reader's hand a genealogy and *curriculum vitae* (see pp. 128–32), with Turgenev they were there, but remained in his own mind.

11 Experience versus the Intellect: Tolstoy

Tolstoy and the human condition

Tolstoy sits uneasily in any assemblage of Realists. He despised much of the mainstream of western intellectual thought, and his recipe for living was directly at odds with it. But for all that, he lived in a milieu that was influenced by western determinism; and the problems it raised are a recurring feature of his books.

His interior life was one of conflict: a continuous struggle between what his reason told him was the truth about life, and what his experience and emotions told him life could be like if properly lived. This struggle partly corresponded to the two main streams in his cultural formation: the traditional attitudes of rural Russia and the western legacy of the French Enlightenment. It was in fact an individual reflection of the great debate between Westerners and Slavophils that was dividing educated Russian society as a whole. But whereas most writers were, like Turgenev, drawn to one side or the other, the battle in Tolstoy's case continued within him.

Conflict characterised the whole spectrum of his attitudes. In Henri Troyat's words

> [he was] not one man but ten or twenty, all sworn enemies of one another: an aristocrat jealous of his prerogatives and a friend of the people who dressed as a peasant, an ardent Slavophil and a Westernising pacifist, a denouncer of private property and a landowner enlarging his domains, a keen shot and a protector of animals, a hearty trencherman and a vegetarian, an Orthodox believer of the moujik type and an enraged assailant upon the Church, an artist and a despiser of art, a sensualist and an ascetic.

Other Realists, like Eliot, went through conflicting phases of belief and scepticism; but the end result was usually some form of synthesis or *modus vivendi*, which was intellectually coherent, if not necessarily satisfying to the emotions. With Tolstoy, however, there was no ultimate arrival at a *modus vivendi*, however much a novel like *Anna Karenina* might suggest that there was. The solutions that sustained Tolstoy when he wrote *Anna Karenina* were to undergo further metamorphoses in the years to come, even though they may strike many readers as remarkably coherent and self-sustaining as they stand. And although *Anna Karenina*, like his other works, provided him with a static canvas on which he would partially resolve his problems, in a way that he found difficult in the moving context of his own life, the resolution is only partial.

The forces of heredity and environment are as strong in *Anna Karenina* as in any other Realist novel. Tolstoy knew and respected the scientific arguments in their favour; but it was his own experience, rather than scientific conviction, which shaped his portrayal of them in his novels. His characters are nonetheless determined for that; and are arguably the more convincing for being the fruit of observation rather than the conscious embodiment of an intellectual concept in a Stendhalian or Balzacian sense. His concern for environment is particularly apparent in his treatment of family life, while almost every page displays his remarkable awareness of how mood and attitudes depend on circumstance and physical wellbeing. A bright, crisp morning, luck at shooting, a filling sandwich, any of these can temporarily dispel the blackest cares, just as toothache or an irritating visitor can induce unmitigated pessimism. Similarly, he has a Sterne-like awareness of how people variously respond to the same information or circumstances, according to personal mood or situation. An oft-quoted example is the discussion between Pestsov, Karenin, Oblonsky and Dolly about women's rights. Only Pestsov comes near to having a disinterested view of the matter. Karenin, with Anna in mind, is hostile to women's rights. Oblonsky, thinking of a ballerina he has picked up, is in favour; his wife thinking of the same ballerina, is against. *Tristram Shandy* abounds in complex ensembles of this kind, but Tolstoy brings to his a remarkable spontaneity and freshness.

But if experience, rather than the intellect, has the upper hand in Tolstoy's portrayal of determinism, *Anna Karenina* also affirms Tolstoy's belief that experience is often wiser than the intellect. Moreover, the intellect, if allowed supremacy, is capable of destroying the happiness that is rooted in experience. 'Experience' for Tolstoy went far deeper than the lifetime of the individual. For him its surest and most rewarding expression was in the accumulated wisdom of past generations. *Anna Karenina* in effect is a celebration of the fruits of this collective experience: family life, traditional values, and the religious and social institutions that protect them.

Most Realists would share Tolstoy's respect for experience. Büchner, Flaubert and Eliot had all castigated would-be reformers who created cerebral solutions that took too little account of the nature and emotional needs of the people for whom they were intended. But Tolstoy's stance was to appear too anti-intellectual, and left too many issues unresolved, for it to offer the sort of inspiration that a large section of the educated public found in a writer like George Eliot. It was Tolstoy's perception rather than his prescriptions that made him appear to contemporaries as perhaps the greatest of the nineteenth-century Realists.

Tolstoy was nevertheless aware of the limitations of his solutions. They are specifically voiced by various of his fictional characters. He knew that collective experience was itself made up of the modifications and changes that earlier generations had made to the traditions of their predecessors. Each human situation had to be approached as a separate issue—not with traditional answers. And his own disputes with the Government, his fellow landowners and later with the Orthodox Church show him as pragmatic in his attitude to authority.

The contradictions in his nature owed much to his early life. As a member of the serf-owning landed aristocracy, he was steeped in the indigenous traditions of a despotic way of life. Yet it was a milieu strongly influenced by a cosmopolitan western culture. He himself was educated by a succession of French tutors; and, as a law student at Kazan University, he spent a great deal of his spare time reading Rousseau and Montesquieu. On an earthier level, his grandfather used to send the family washing across northern Europe to Holland, the sparkling reputation of Dutch laundries being but part of the family's respect for western civilisation.

Tolstoy claimed that it was his adolescent reading of the French *philosophes* that killed the remnants of his religious faith. In a schoolboy aphorism, worthy of Destutt de Tracy, he remarked that 'I *want*, therefore I am' was how human existence should be understood. Like Flaubert, he found his university legal studies boring, and made illness a pretext for leaving them. Again, like Flaubert, he felt drawn to medicine and medical theory and resolved to draw up a programme of spare-time reading in the subject. The inheritance of a large estate, however, brought him new responsibilities, and thenceforward his enthusiasm for progressive thought was diverted into the initiation of modern farming methods. A spell of military service gave him an opportunity for writing—work which quickly attracted the attention of Turgenev and other literary figures in St. Petersburg.

He was invited by Turgenev to share his apartment where despite a basic esteem and concern for each other, there soon developed the violent quarrels that were always to punctuate their relationship. Tolstoy still led the life expected of a young nobleman: whoring and gambling, paying his debts with serfs and suffering occasional doses of clap. Tolstoy would spend the morning sleeping off the excesses of the night before, and then proceed to castigate his host and his Westerner friends for what he called their political spinelessness. Their attempts to remain on good-humoured terms with him annoyed him further; and in fury he deserted the company of the Westerners early in 1856 to see if the Slavophils could offer anything better. They too proved disappointing. He disliked their religious Orthodoxy and their willingness to be patronised by an authoritarian government which was harassing intellectuals of other persuasions.

Despite his multifarious activities and the success that greeted his novels in the 1860s, he became increasingly tormented by the need to find a meaning to life. His temperament, if not his intellect, yearned for religious certainty. As he wrote in 1859,

> I have searched the gospels and found there neither God, nor Redeemer, nor the sacraments . . . There is no doubt that I love and esteem religion; I believe that without it, man can be neither good nor happy . . . But I have no religion and I have no faith. With me, it's life that makes religion and not religion that makes life . . . You make fun of nature and nightingales. But for me nature is the mediatrix of religion.

1869 brought a crisis. While on an excursion to buy some land, he spent a night in a hotel in Arzamas, where he suddenly awoke, overcome by a box-like horror: 'as though I was about to vomit', giddy with the thought that 'there is nothing in life, nothing exists but death, and death should not be'. As with Levin in *Anna Karenina*, times came when Tolstoy contemplated suicide. A happy marriage and literary success only served to underline for him the inevitability of death and the meaninglessness of life.

Science offered no answer to his search. After extensive reading in physiology, he found that 'Above all, my personal question "What am I with my desires?" remained quite unanswered' (*A Confession*). Philosophy, on the other hand, merely confirmed the meaninglessness of life. Socrates, Solomon, Buddha, Schopenhauer, all concluded that life was 'vanity and emptiness'. Levin in *Anna Karenina* is obsessed with the thought that 'if my senses are annihilated, if my body dies, no further existence is possible'. 'This whole world of ours is nothing but a speck of mildew, which has grown up on a tiny planet. And for us to suppose we can have something great—ideas, work—it's all dust and ashes'.

Tolstoy subsequently claimed that salvation came to him not from the intellectual few, the Solomons and the Schopenhauers, but from 'the real labouring people'. He saw that they endured conditions of life which he would have found insupportable. And yet they did not contemplate suicide. They had a simple faith which they accepted without question: and they were happy.

> Rational knowledge, presented by the learned and the wise, denies the meaning of life, but the enormous masses of men, the whole of mankind, receive that meaning in irrational knowledge, find that irrational knowledge is faith, that very thing which I could not [at that time] but reject (*A Confession*).

Walking through the spring woods, he reflected that he felt an ineffable joy whenever he unthinkingly assumed that God existed; but that as soon as he applied the corrosive force of his intellect to the matter, his happiness disappeared. As he noted in his diary in March 1870, 'As soon as man applies his intelligence—and only his intelligence—to any object at all he unfailingly destroys the object'.

Levin makes the same discovery in *Anna Karenina*. Talking to one of his farm-workers, he is impressed by the peasant's unquestioning assumption that the way to live is 'plain enough': 'living rightly, in God's way'. Levin contrasts the peasant's calm conviction with his own tortured thoughts, and realises that this is the way to accept life. It is this, rather than the religious content of the peasant's words, which came as a revelation. Levin has known the Christian message all his life. What is new is his realisation of the folly of subjecting this or any other source of happiness to the withering heat of intellectual scrutiny.

If this Tolstoyan 'truth' struck many contemporary readers as anti-intellectual, it was anti-intellectual in an indirect way. Tolstoy was not specifically turning his back on the intellect; he was claiming instead that there was a whole category of fundamental issues that lay beyond the range of scientific enquiry and were therefore not a subject where the intellect had pre-emptive rights.

Tolstoy felt it within the logic of his discovery that he should accept and follow the peasants' way of worship. He therefore embarked on his strange relationship with Russian Orthodoxy, meticulously observing its ritual, but periodically jibbing at various of its dogmas. The early 1880s were to find him questioning the Trinity and the divinity of Christ, until eventually, after a further decade of stormy exchanges, the Church officially excommunicated him in 1901.

Doctrinal difficulties apart, Tolstoy had never pretended that his new-found faith would resolve the many problems, general and personal, that beset him. On the universal level, Tolstoy like Levin was troubled by the question of whether other religions could be a road to salvation. If Orthodoxy was his own haven, 'the Jews, the Mohammedans, the Confucians, the Buddhists—what of them? Can those hundreds of millions of human beings be deprived of that greatest of blessings without which life has no meaning?' Levin's answer to this problem may strike the reader as no answer at all; yet it follows logically from his realisation of the limits of the intellect: 'I have no right to try to decide the question of other religions and their relations to the Deity; that must remain unfathomable to me'.

At the same time Levin understands that although his life now has a meaning, and in a sense is now transformed, he will still fall into the same petty transgressions as before.

> I shall still lose my temper with Ivan the coachman . . . I shall probably go on scolding [my wife] in my anxiety . . . but my life now . . . independently of anything that can happen to me . . . has a positive meaning of goodness with which I have the power to invest it.

Tolstoy and Russia

Tolstoy's respect for collective experience strongly influenced his view of Russian society and deepened certain of his prejudices. For him this experience was most faithfully reflected in the nobility and the peasantry, with their roots firmly embedded in the soil and Russia's past. For all their arrogance and selfishness, the nobility had the nation's history in their veins; their names were resonant with the achievements of past generations. The peasantry, for their part, despite their stupidity and reluctance to consider anything new, supposedly embodied the solidity and simple wisdom of tradition. Tolstoy believed it a matter of national urgency that the peasants' ignorance and apathy in technical matters should be dispelled by a programme of universal education. The 1860s and early 1870s found him busy experimenting in educational methods, both as the author of a children's reader, and as a teacher to the peasant children on his own estate.

> When I see these tattered, underfed, unwashed youngsters with their candid eyes, from which the soul of an angel often shines out, a feeling of apprehension and horror comes over me, as though I were watching someone drown.

The corollary of Tolstoy's belief in experience was his distrust of untried 'rational' solutions. It was symptomatic of his outlook that his extensive acquaintance with the French Enlightenment should leave him admiring most of all two of its least characteristic figures, Rousseau and Montesquieu, the writers who accorded most importance to the irrational in human nature. If, in his view, the untried figments of the inexperienced intellect were the prime threat to the hallowed institutions born of traditional wisdom, he saw the liberal intelligentsia as the hawkers, hucksters and fabricators of these insidious commodities. He called them '*la cuisine littéraire*', rootless men, many of them middle-class, knowing little, and understanding less, of the fundamental wisdom of the peasantry or the traditional responsibilities and loyalties of the landed nobility. Brash and arrogant in their ignorance, they presumed to criticise matters they did not begin to comprehend.

Symptomatically the middle class get short shrift in *Anna Karenina*. Levin refuses to speak to the land speculator who buys Oblonsky's forest: admittedly at an over-advantageous price. And the professional middle classes fare no better at Tolstoy's hands. He paints a particularly unsympathetic vignette of the doctor, 'the celebrated specialist' who insists on Kitty undressing; and he likewise mixes venom with his ink in his brief sketch of 'the famous Petersburg lawyer' who handles Karenin's marital problems.

Contemptuous of the middle class, Tolstoy reserved his bitterest feelings for the liberal nobility who betrayed their destiny by joining forces with them. Turgenev he saw as one of these. The mixture of admiration and exasperation that characterised their relationship was nowhere more apparent than in their differences over the emancipation of the serfs. Both were convinced of its necessity, yet they disagreed violently on the spirit in which it should be done. The Westerner, Turgenev, saw it as part of a self-evident programme of democratic reforms, that commended itself automatically to any right-minded liberal. Tolstoy, by contrast, had lived with serfdom for nearly thirty years, before seriously deciding that it must go; only on his return from Western Europe in 1857 did he see it with new eyes. Like Turgenev, he commuted his serfs' labour dues for a quit rent. But he was not prepared to regard Turgenev's concession as commensurate with his own. Was it not precisely the sort of legalistic gesture that one could expect from a man who saw little of his peasants and spent most of his time pursuing an unresponsive prima donna around Western Europe? Tolstoy, by contrast, laboured in the fields with his peasants; he scythed the hay with them and ate with them beneath the waggons at midday. Like most of his major decisions, this singular practice stemmed from his belief that experience was everything; only by sharing their lives in this fashion could he feel for himself what were their genuine needs. (It perhaps also reflected, if only unconsciously, an inward sense of guilt towards the men whose labours made his comfortable existence possible.) Whatever the underlying motivation, the net effect was to make him feel that he had already established a humane relationship with his peasants, which, if it still left their emancipation as a worthy objective, rendered it less urgent.

Turgenev's reform, by contrast, struck him as a barren cerebral gesture which brought him no nearer to his peasants and merely dispensed Turgenev from his previous guilty feelings, guilt perhaps being the only emotional link Turgenev had ever had with them (apart from amorous entanglements with serving girls). In Tolstoy's view, Turgenev's reform cost him no more than the rich man's subscription to charity, which enables him to enjoy his wealth without giving the poor another thought.

Turgenev, for his part, doubtless saw Tolstoy's labour in the fields as an absurd act of self-delusion, exorcising Tolstoy's own uneasy conscience but offering no tangible benefit to the peasantry. As a liberal Westerner, he did not share Tolstoy's contempt for cerebral gestures; the whole history of western democratic progress was built on them: constitutions, equality before the law, the rights of labour, all depended on laws which were the very framework of freedom, however remote and abstract the principles and the institutions that had brought them into being.

It was characteristic of Tolstoy that when the Emancipation Edict became law in 1861, he was in no great hurry to implement it on his own estate, despite his previous campaigning against serfdom. Now that it was an obligatory matter, incumbent on every landowner, it had somehow lost its savour: law deprived it of the spontaneous, heartfelt quality, without which it was hard to enlist Tolstoy's enthusiasm. Even so, when he belatedly got round to emancipation, he equally characteristically gave his serfs the maximum of land allowed under the system. Moreover, he was appointed as an official government arbitrator of the scheme in his locality and quickly made enemies among the gentry by consistently taking the side of the peasantry in disputed cases: so much so that he was driven to resign in April 1862.

There were other points of friction between Tolstoy and Turgenev. Tolstoy despised Turgenev's western manners, his manicured fingernails and dandified appearance—the features that the self-perceptive Turgenev partially parodies in the shape of Pavel Kirsanov in *Fathers and Sons*: Turgenev even goes to the point of saddling Pavel with *un grand amour*, painfully suggestive of his own debilitating passion for Pauline Viardot. Morever, Turgenev sent his natural daughter, the child of a young seamstress, to be educated with Pauline Viardot's family in western Europe. Tolstoy strongly disapproved of this uprooting of the child, which deprived her of the native background that Tolstoy considered essential to the happiness and self-fulfilment of any Russian. His provocative remarks on the matter so incensed Turgenev that the older man threatened to hit him. Despite Turgenev's apologies for his reaction, Tolstoy insisted on fighting a duel, a grotesque situation that was only narrowly averted after prolonged and difficult negotiation, fraught with the usual misunderstandings on both sides.

Tolstoy and responsibility

Tolstoy described *Anna Karenina* as 'a declaration of love for the idea of the family'. Not only was family life the oldest embodiment of collective experience, but it shapes all who participate in it, parents as well as children. It was for Tolstoy the foremost environmental force. Those who lack it, like Vronsky and Karenin, who knew little parental love in childhood, remain morally impoverished throughout their lives. And even Levin only narrowly escapes a similar deprivation through the good fortune of having the Shcherbatskys as a surrogate family.

Family life is a theme as old as literature; yet it acquired a certain acuity in the nineteenth century, since it was then that it was subjected to serious questioning for the first time in Russia. Russia was still a confessional state; but the popularity of Romantic literature in educated circles gave increasing, if limited, currency to the notion that love transcends everything, including the family. Marital infidelity, in the name of love, was no new phenomenon, any more than infidelity *tout court*. Indeed certain infidelities had traditionally been regarded as normal and even desirable. Tolstoy's own aunt,

> herself the purest of beings, always told me that there was nothing she so desired for me as that I should have relations with a married woman:

'Rien ne forme un jeune homme comme un liason avec une femme comme il faut'.

But this was the discreet sort of liaison that was tolerated in aristocratic society because it left the marriage outwardly intact. Its essence was its discretion: everyone knew about it, including the 'wronged' parties, but no one talked about it in public.

Romanticism, however, sought to justify *le grand amour* in the name of a higher good. Tolstoy not only rejected this claim, but firmly believed that no love could survive without the sustaining responsibilities of rearing children and running a household. The experience of Anna and Vronsky demonstrates that love and passion cannot by themselves create a permanent relationship; it needs to be buttressed by a joint task, the shared commitment and cares of creating a happy and productive household. Anna has staked all on her love for Vronsky, and having found that, for Vronsky at least, love on its own is not enough, she inflicts on him the terrible, indelible memory of her departure and suicide. Her bitter cry 'Are we not all flung into the world only to hate each other, and therefore to torment ourselves and others?' is the converse of Dorothea's declaration in *Middlemarch* at a similarly desperate moment of her life. What do we live for, if it is not to make life less difficult for each other?' But whereas Dorothea has wider commitments than her feelings for Ladislaw, Anna has risked all on her love for Vronsky.

The converse of this tragedy is the home life of Levin and Kitty, largely based on Tolstoy's own experience. For all its contretemps, their love is firmly based on the mutual, wider tasks of family and household, causing them to fuse into something greater than their individual selves: as Tolstoy says of Levin 'he could not now tell where she ended and he began'.

Yet this enlargement of Levin's being has a paradoxical counterpart in his refusal to involve himself in the much wider issues that lie beyond the boundaries of his estate, notably provincial politics and Russia's foreign responsibilities. The paradox largely resolves itself when it is seen in the light of Tolstoy's basic contention: that unless the emotions as well as the intellect are involved in philanthropic activity, the activity will remain sterile; one's whole being must be committed, not just the intellect. This, in fact, was the basic issue that underlay his earlier differences with Turgenev over the peasantry (pp. 117–18). Levin's family and estate are sufficiently limited to be within the capacity of his love and solicitude; he can feel for them and see the results of his care, in a way that is not possible with the huge impersonal issues of provincial politics and international relations. These matters can only be tackled with the mind and not the heart; and without the heart, philanthropic activity is ultimately barren. Moreover, it is only in the restricted sphere of personal relationships that the individual can hope to perceive what is good and what is not. There are too many unknown factors in large public issues for the individual to be able to commit himself to one side or the other, and feel confidence in his decision.

Looked at with these criteria, certain contradictions in Tolstoy's attitudes seem less puzzling. Levin's refusal to concern himself with Russia's war against Turkey is in keeping with Tolstoy's arguments. What superficially might seem less consistent is Tolstoy's own involvement in educational reform and his later activity in the nationwide famine relief of the 1890s. Yet ignorance and hunger were evils which Tolstoy could see and experience for himself on his own estate. It required no particular stretch of empathy to *feel*, as well as recognise cerebrally, that they must also be fought on a larger national scale. In the same way, earlier in his life, (see pp. 117–18), his participation in the nationwide campaign for Emancipation resulted from his own personal observation of peasant life.

Unlike Levin, Levin's half brother, the intellectual Koznyshev, is deeply committed to issues that lie beyond his immediate personal experience: in particular Russia's campaign against Turkey. But Tolstoy portrays this concern for national questions as the corollary to his unwillingness to risk his ego in the mutual self-giving required by marriage and family life; it is a function of his inadequacy.

> . . . the thought struck [Levin] that this faculty for working for the public good, of which he felt himself completely devoid, was perhaps not so much a quality as a lack of something—not a lack of kindly honesty and noble desires and tastes but a lack of the vital force, of what is called heart, of the impulse which drives a man to choose someone out of all the innumerable paths of life and to care for that one only . . . Koznyshev, and many people who worked for the welfare of the public, were not led by an impulse of the heart to care for the public good, but had reasoned out in their minds that it was a right thing to take interest in public affairs, and consequently took interest in them.

Turgenev's sympathies in this debate would have been largely with Koznyshev. Indeed, he said on reading *Anna Karenina*,

> [Tolstoy] has lost his way . . . It's the influence of Moscow, the Slavophil nobility, Orthodox spinsters, his isolation and lack of artistic work.

For Tolstoy, however,

> The question is not what kind of community life is best, but what are *you* going to do as a reasonable being appearing for a brief moment in the world, who may depart at any moment? I know nothing of the result. I only know what I must do.

PART THREE

Later Responses:
Zola, Ibsen, Fontane,
Chekhov

12 *La Bête Humaine*

Like many of its middle-aged readers, Realism had a capacity for growing more like itself with every year: which to many observers was synonymous with getting uglier and more morose.

If the impression was not without truth, it had several sources. With the later Realists the emphasis lay increasingly on social identity rather than on individual cast of character (see chapter 14, especially pp. 148–9), with the result that economic factors featured even more prominently than before. There was also a greater readiness to drag the middle-class reader into the unfamiliar, insalubrious haunts and homes of people living on the edge of subsistence—thereby subjecting his delicately tuned senses to the unappetising, and disturbing, facts of life as they were experienced by a substantial percentage of mankind. And, as if these unedifying excursions were not enough, the later Realists, particularly the so-called 'Naturalists', took a more uncompromisingly biological view of Man, showing him as an amalgam of bodily functions: Consumer Man, rather than spirit. In short they regarded him as a legitimate object of scientific study, no different, except in complexity, from other forms of life.

Early Realism had implicitly posed the general problem that concerned the Naturalists: the understanding of Man as the product of environment and inherited characteristics. But most early Realists had made a sharp distinction between Man and the rest of the animal kingdom. The difference they made might be one of degree rather than kind; but the distance was such as to put Man more or less into a separate category. When evolutionists, however, with increasing plausibility, linked Man's ancestry with that of the apes, the parallel paths of psychologists and animal behaviourists were seen to have much in common. And what had been regarded as puzzling similarities became compelling arguments for applying to Man the secular methods of science; eschewing all assumptions about Man's 'destiny' or 'purpose'. Indeed it was no longer necessary or relevant to ask whether Man had a purpose at all.

'*Darwinism*'

The intriguing question of whether Man's origins lay in more primitive forms of life had been a subject of speculation since the sixth century B.C., if not earlier. La Mettrie had savoured its implications in the mid-eighteenth century (see pp. 31–2), while the evolutionary theories of Lamarck and Geoffroy Saint-Hilaire had rekindled educated interest at the beginning of the nineteenth. Perhaps for this reason, Darwin's work created far less furore in France than in Britain. Even so, Darwin brought to the question a conceptual coherence and a wealth of evidence that made it no longer a matter of mere speculation. 'Darwinism' became the title popularly conferred on the whole corpus of evolutionary thought, in France as elsewhere.

The Lamarckian tradition of evolution had assumed that the acquired characteristics of one generation of animals could be passed on physiologically to the next. Lamarck assumed that giraffes had long necks because successive generations had stretched upwards in search of foliage, the lengthening achieved by the early generations being cumulatively passed on to the later. The difficulty of envisaging in physiological terms how in fact this could be done was one of several major factors that confined evolutionary thought to the realm of speculation. Although Darwin did not challenge this supposition – it was August Weismann who refuted it in 1889 – his achievement was to build alongside this hypothesis a more general concept that was to stand the test of subsequent scrutiny and scientific progress, even if its genetic aspects had to await the investigations of a later generation. The effect of this concept was to give evolution a less positive character. He stressed that change in a species came about through the more successful individuals gradually outnumbering the less. Giraffes that happened to have slightly longer necks than their neighbours would be more successful in acquiring food. They would breed earlier and live longer, thereby propagating more young than the shorter-necked individuals. With the passage of time, and the numerical growth of the long-necked population, breeding would increasingly take place between the long-necked variety, thereby making long necks the dominant feature of the species. It was basically an elimination process, and an extremely slow one at that. For such a gradual process to lengthen giraffes' necks to their present proportions would clearly take many more aeons of time than anything envisaged by Lamarck.

Not only was Darwin's concept plausible in contemporary terms, but parts of it were demonstrable: for one of the greatest strengths of his theories was that they were the product of observation rather than speculation. Darwin was intended initially for a medical career, then the Church; but his passionate interest in geology and natural history resulted in an unexpected invitation to accompany an Admiralty survey ship as an unpaid naturalist for five years (1831–6). What he saw during his extensive voyaging, and the thoughts it engendered, eroded his belief in a divine creator and convinced him of the mutability of species. As a student he had been familiar with Lamarck's evolutionary theories; indeed his own grandfather, Erasmus Darwin (1731–1802) had foreshadowed certain of Lamarck's hypotheses, notably on the inheritance of acquired characteristics. But Charles Darwin had begun his voyage with an open mind on the matter.

He found, however, that the various finches of the Galapagos Islands seemed to embody different developments of a basic type of bird. These differences, moreover, struck Darwin as the product, in some cases, of particular feeding habits, or the result of geographical separation in others. He was also intrigued by the differences between the extinct armadillos he found in his South American fossil hunts, and the living varieties that were still to be seen in the same continent. Within a few months of returning to England, he wrote: 'Animals . . . may partake of our origin in one common ancestor—we may be all netted together'.

He had likewise concluded that the development of some forms, and the disappearance of others, must reflect their respective abilities to adapt to their particular environment—the most efficient living longer and having more offspring. But what gave this conclusion a compulsive force in Darwin's view was the indirect support he found in the stern-eyed economics of Thomas Malthus (1766–1834). Darwin read Malthus's *Essay on the Principle of Population* (1798) in September 1838 on his return to England, and was immediately struck by its central thesis—that the reproduction potential of most animals is far greater than the food supplies on which they live—which, if true, would oblige animals to compete to survive. On this basis, the process of elimination and adaptation would take on a much sharper character, and would make the divergent development of so many different species a much more plausible concept.

Darwin was nevertheless chary of committing his conclusions to print, and it was only the parallel probings of Alfred Wallace (1823–1913) that eventually spurred him to do so. Wallace had travelled widely as a specimen collector in the Amazon forests and southeast Asia, where his findings impelled him towards similar opinions. Significantly enough, it was Malthus's *Essay on the Principles of Population* that confirmed his commitment to these ideas, and decided him to write to Darwin in 1858, outlining his beliefs. Papers by both men were read to the Linnaean Society in London in July 1858; but it was the publication of Darwin's *On the Origin of Species* in the following year which created the first major stir in educated opinion.

British churchmen expressed the same outrage that Cuvier's disciples had displayed against Saint-Hilaire thirty years earlier in France (see pp. 33–4). Among much else, Darwin's theories seemed to strike directly at the theologian's traditional claim that God's existence could be inferred from the presence of design in nature; Darwin had apparently replaced the divine plan with a world of warring egotistical forces, where the exercise of the gospel virtues would be a certain recipe for elimination, or so it seemed.

On the Origin of Species also made a major, if less spectacular impact in France. Not only was it more compelling than earlier evolutionary theories, but the link between Man's ancestry and that of the apes was much more explicit. *The Descent of Man* (1871) was to explore the matter in detail, stipulating, among much else, that Man's moral sense was a developed form of the social instincts of the higher animals. These he saw as containing the embryo of the principle, 'As ye would that men should do to you, do ye to them likewise'.

A more ominous respect in which Darwin struck the literary imagination was his adaptation of Herbert Spencer's slightly misleading phrase, 'the survival of the fittest' (see pp. 164–5). Lamarck's hypothesis had had a positive, quasi-optimistic ring to it, in that it had envisaged each generation inheriting the accumulated acquirements of its predecessors; a notion that had particularly appealed to George Eliot, who saw it as also embracing the moral development of Man (see pp. 91–2). Darwin's concept, by contrast, had a more negative, eliminatory equality, giving it a darker countenance in the estimation of the educated public. As Tennyson had asked in 1850

> Are God and Nature then at strife,
> That Nature lends such evil dreams?
> So careful of the type she seems,
> So careless of the single life;
>
> That I, considering everywhere
> Her secret meaning in her deeds,
> And finding that of fifty seeds
> She often brings but one to bear,
> $\qquad$ (*In Memoriam*)

Despite the plausibility and far-reaching implications of Darwin's theory, there still remained the question of how the first generation of successful individuals initially came by their advantageous characteristics. It was still widely assumed that they had acquired them through concentrated effort and exercise in coping with their particular environment. However, an Austrian monk, Gregor Mendel (1822–84), conducted a series of experiments which showed that distinctive features of this sort, appearing unexpectedly, were the outcome of patterns of heredity, which were themselves dependent on what are now called genes. Although Mendel published his findings on heredity as early as 1866, he did so in the transactions of a comparatively obscure natural history society; and it was not until 1900 that other scientists chanced on Mendel's work and realised its enormous significance. Darwin, however, died eighteen years too soon to share in this.

The Realist response

'The personalities of our *dramatis personae* are determined by the genital organs. It's Darwin! That's what literature is!' This declaration, allegedly made by Zola in 1868, not long after reading *On the Origin of Species*, vibrates with the exuberant exaggeration that often characterised him. If it was frequently a feature of the French 'Naturalists' to speak, or at least to be reported, in the language of manifestos, the more measured tones of a Chekhov or an Isben likewise testified to the profound impression that 'Darwinism' and adjacent concepts of Man made on the later Realists.

In the case of Zola and certain of his French colleagues, it was partly reflected in a less deferential attitude to the complexities of human nature. Balzac had always retained an awed respect for human capabilities, despite his fondness for deterministic explanation. This betrayed itself not only in his larger-than-life creations like Vautrin, but also in his refusal to penetrate what he regarded as the mysterious aspects of human nature; it was a function of his latent Romanticism. This respect is far less evident in Zola and in many of his contemporaries. There is a cutting-down-to-size of Man that leaves little room for the unexpected. When the unexpected occurs, it is largely the prerogative of circumstance; some twist of fortune, that has its roots in past factors but which is largely unperceived by the characters themselves, until too late. And although Zola in his way could be as Romantic as Balzac, his Romanticism was largely expended on man in the mass, notably in his crowd scenes in *Germinal* (1885), or paradoxically on man-made machinery, such as the pit-head apparatus in *Germinal* or the alcohol still in *L'Assommoir* (1877).

Like Zola, Chekhov knew Darwin's work at first hand, but with the perception and discrimination of a qualified medical man. In 1883 he had considered writing 'A History of Sex Dominance', based on the application of Darwinian principles to the role of women in society. Although nothing came of this project, Darwin continued to fascinate him: as he told a friend in 1886, 'I am reading Darwin. Magnificent! I simply love him'. Five years later he spent a long summer holiday with Vladimir Wagner, a future professor of zoology, whose strong views on natural selection were the subject of prolonged discussion, and were later to be incorporated in Chekhov's short story, *The Duel* (1891), where von Koren's forthright, at times extremist, opinions represent an intransigent distillation of Wagner's thoughts, taken to their ultimate conclusion. The two men also collaborated in writing an article condemning the mismanagement of Moscow Zoo, 'the graveyard of animals', which failed both to look after the inmates properly or to provide proper facilities for their scientific study.

As *The Duel* illustrates, Darwin's main effect on Chekhov was to throw into relief the conflict between the gospel virtues and what was ultimately in society's interest (see pp. 164–5). Mercy to the weak, and the survival of the fittest, were not easily reconciled; despite the attempts of Darwin and others to show that they were not necessarily incompatible. Ibsen too was conscious of this conflict and, as with Chekhov, it was an important ingredient in his pessimism (see p. 165). It also strengthened the conviction of both men in the ineluctability of life: the heavy hand of destiny on everything, and the vanity of supposing that it could be otherwise. Ibsen spent much of the winter of 1878–9 in the company of the novelist and botanist, Jens Peter Jacobsen, whose Danish translations of *On the Origin of Species* (1872) and *The Descent of Man* (1875) had introduced Darwin to Scandinavia. They drank and talked a lot: Jacobsen carrying Ibsen home in the small hours of the morning from the Scandinavian Club in Rome, Ibsen abrasively debating and dismissing the destiny of the human race.

Zola

If the influence of Darwinism on Chekhov and Ibsen was nonetheless real for being indirect, the vociferous nature of Zola's allegiance might tempt readers into suspecting that there was something false and rhetorical about it. He was certainly the most *insouciant* in his manipulation of facts: as he admitted in 1896, 'I resort to voluntary error without scruple, when the needs of construction necessitate it'. In his readiness to be careless or cavalier in scientific matters, he was somewhat reminiscent of Balzac—although Balzac had the excuse of an irrepressible (and at times naive) enthusiasm, and an earlier place in time which denied him much of the knowledge that was open to Zola.

Thérèse Raquin (1867) was Zola's first serious attempt to play the dispassionate clinical observer in a major piece of fiction. He described his characters as

> absolutely dominated by their nervous systems and heredity (*souveraine-ment dominés par leurs nerfs et leur sang*), without free will, led into every act of their lives by the fatalities of the flesh . . . *L'âme* is completely absent . . . each chapter is a study of a curious physiological case.

Inspired by Balzac and Flaubert, the preface claimed 'I have simply performed on two living bodies the analytical work which surgeons perform on corpses'. 'My aim has been above all scientific.' In fact the novel's continual moralising undermines the claim; but the intent is clearly present and pointed the way to the Rougon-Macquart series.

Thérèse Raquin was written in the full flush of Zola's enthusiasm for Hippolyte Taine (1828–93). Like George Lewes in England and Georg Brandes in Scandinavia, Taine was something of a bridge between the worlds of science and literature. Although Zola's active interest in the implications of science for literature predated his acquaintance with Taine's *Histoire de la Littérature anglaise* (1863), Taine's attempt to establish the scientific laws that determine the artistic production of a particular country had a profound effect on him, notably the famous passage

> whether phenomena are physical or moral does not matter; they always have causes. There are causes for ambition, courage, truthfulness, just as there are for muscular movement and animal warmth. *Vice and virtue are products just as are vitriol and sugar* [author's italics], and every complex fact

arises from the encounter of other similar facts on which it depends. Let us therefore seek out the simple facts underlying moral qualities, as one looks for the simple facts underlying physical qualities.

It was Taine, moreover, who encouraged Zola to transfer his attentions from individuals to society, advice which bore fruit in the Rougon-Macquart series, *Histoire naturelle et sociale d'une famille sous le Second Empire*. The project revealed the influence of Darwin as well as Taine, Zola having read *On the Origin of Species* just three years before the appearance of the first volume of the series, *La Fortune des Rougon* (1871). The divers destinies of the various members of the Rougon-Macquart family were an attempt to demonstrate how the inherited characteristiscs of the Rougons and Macquarts were to influence the type of niche that each was to find in the jungle of Second Empire society. The predatory self-interested Rougons were on the whole to do well for themselves in this opportunistic society, while the gentler, less selfish Macquarts were more often to find themselves its victims, as well as victims of the degenerate aspects of the family's inherited characteristics.

The problem remained, however, of demonstrating these beliefs in a way that was both plausible to the reading public and reasonably in accord with the main drift of scientific opinion: no easy task, since scientific opinion itself spoke with an uncertain and discordant voice. Not until Mendel's findings were published at the beginning of the next century (see p. 126) did there exist a working basis for systematic investigation. In any case Zola was neither qualified nor sufficiently endowed with free time to study the matter in depth and make a considered choice on scientific grounds. Nor could such a choice be guaranteed to survive the test of subsequent scientific advances. And even if it did, there remained the perennial problem that heredity did not lend itself to easy description. Having said that a character derived certain specific tendencies from his mother's family, and others from his father's, that was as far as novelists like Zola were usually prepared to go. Not only was little known about the biological facts of heredity, but it was not a subject on which an author's literary skill could easily be deployed. While environmental factors called into play his descriptive powers and psychological perception, genetics did not make compulsive reading for the general public, even had they been known or understood in the nineteenth century. It is only when parents and children appeared in the same novel or play, that the author had much chance of using his descriptive skills to demonstrate resemblances and differences. Otherwise he could only impart the information in a take-it-or-leave-it-fashion, as Zola did in his genealogies and occasional asides.

Zola in fact went to no great trouble to study the matter. He was content to acquaint himself in a general way with Prosper Lucas's *Traité philosophique et physiologique de l'hérédité naturelle dans les états de santé et de maladie du système nerveux*, a two-volume work published in 1847–50, which he found mentioned by Michelet and Taine. Zola's notes reveal him as interested in little more than the basic outline of Lucas's theories, while quick to seize on anything bizarre or anecdotal. He also drew on Charles Letourneau's *Physiologie des Passions* (1868). His aim was to inform himself well enough to avoid making the sort of mistake that would give a handle to critics; and at the same time he wished to acquire a stock of case-histories which could be drawn on, and embellished, for inclusion in his novels. As he wrote in a memorandum for his own guidance

> There must be logic and deduction. It does not matter whether the factual premiss is accepted as absolutely true; the premiss will be first and foremost a scientific hypothesis, taken from medical treatises. But once it is posed . . . as axiomatic, all the rest must be deduced mathematically, and be absolutely sure.

Lucas's principles intruded very little into the main text of the series—which perhaps was as well, since they were of a much contested and short-lived respectability. They nevertheless provided the basis of the two genealogical trees that Zola drew up in 1878 and 1893, illustrating the characteristics of the Rougon-Macquart family; and they likewise provided the substance of Dr Pascal's disquisition on his family, in the novel of that name (1893). Even so, Zola was prepared to manipulate them in a fairly cavalier fashion when the dramatic demands of the novels required it. As he confessed in the *Chronique médicale* in 1895, concerning the neurosis of one of his characters, 'No doubt, I've exaggerated a little, but as I was concerned only with verisimilitude and dramatic effect, that was good enough for me'.

It would nevertheless be wrong to see Zola as cynically indifferent to the scientific truth of his assertions. More than most writers, he was anxious to conceal his ignorance, and he was prepared, experienced publicist that he was, to make use of epithets and concepts that were then in vogue. As he replied to Flaubert in 1877, 'like you, I don't give a damn for this word *naturalism*, and yet . . . things need a name for the public to think them new'. He could at the same time, however, be guilty of the most extraordinary lapses in scientific matters, or in matters of simple commonsense. The saddest example was his essay, *Le roman expérimental* (1880), a misguided literary counterpart to Claude Bernard's celebrated *Introduction à l'étude de la médecine expérimentale* (1865). He claimed notably that the writer can explore human nature by confronting his fictional characters with given situations and then observing how they react: it was 'la méthode scientifique appliquée dans les lettres'.

Lucas's main attraction for Zola was that his theories provided him with a simple descriptive schema, rather than a scientific explanation understandable only to the professional. Lucas claimed that heredity expressed itself in three different ways. In the first of these, which Lucas described as '*élection*', the child inherited his distinctive features mainly from his father or his mother, but not from both. In the second, '*mélange*', the child inherited characteristics from both parents, but the legacy of each remained recognisably distinct within the child's overall make-up. In the last category, however, '*combinaison*', the elements inherited from each parent combined to produce an entirely different type, bearing little resemblance to either father or mother.

These were clearly classifications, rather than explanations. Lucas did not attempt to explain why a child's inheritance pattern should conform to one category rather than another, a deficiency that arguably suited Zola's purpose. Had Lucas ventured to suggest explanations, Zola would have found his freedom of manoeuvre much more restricted: his characters would have required specific types of antecedent that might not have suited Zola's creative inclination.

If Lucas's theories are compared with those of Mendel, his vision is seen to be very much centred on the characteristics of the child and his parents. He rarely looked beyond the parents to previous generations, except where a particular characteristic had been visibly passed on unbroken from generation to generation. If a child's personality was completely different from those of his parents, his answer was to say that elements of the father and mother had 'combined' to produce this strange new product. In a world as yet ignorant of Mendel, it did not occur to him that these unfamiliar characteristics might have been passed down in a 'recessive' way from earlier generations, without being visibly apparent in the parents or grandparents.

It must be confessed that Zola's creative energies fell short of even the modest possibilities that Lucas's scheme implied. In cases of *mélange*, Zola tended simply to give his characters the physical attributes of one parent and the mental attributes of the other, instead of permutating mental and physical together. The Rougon-Macquart family consequently presents a curious dichotomy between mental and physical characteristics, corresponding neither to Lucas's intentions on the one hand, nor to the normal experience of most perceptive people on the other. And for all the prominence that Zola gave to hereditary matters in his prefaces and genealogical trees, they make a somewhat lame appearance in the novels themselves.

As exemplified in Appendix D (see pp. 182–3), it is environment that consistently plays the dominant role. Jacques Lantier, the homicidal engine-driver of *La Bête Humaine*, is perhaps the only major character whose destiny unequivocally justifies the claims that Zola made for heredity (see p. 182). Even his mother, Gervaise, arguably Zola's most successful creation, is more the victim of environment than of heredity (see p. 182). Nor does Zola remain true to the types of inheritance with which he initially endowed his characters. To ease some of the inheritance problems of the later novels, his genealogy of 1893 puts both Gervaise and her son, Etienne, into markedly different categories from how they appear in the 1878 genealogy, despite the fact that he had already completed Gervaise's life in *L'Assommoir* (1877) before either genealogy was published (see pp. 182–3). It is a measure of how relatively little Lucas's theories matter to the substance of the novels, that this kind of alteration could take place without the reader being conscious of any significant violence being done to the concept of the character in question.

Animals, children and servants have always had a certain mutual affinity in the eyes of the propertied classes: if nothing else they were addressed as '*tu*'. Self-consciously aware of the animal origins and the animal nature of Man, it was not surprising that a number of the later Realists should look to the manual classes as fruitful ground for their investigations. Living nearer to subsistence, the worker and the peasant shared the danger, toil and insecurity of animal life; their hard existence, and lack of education and possessions, largely limited their activities and pleasures to the simple maintenance and gratification of the senses. Here, if anywhere, it was argued, Man's animal nature would be seen most clearly, uncomplicated and unadorned.

The middle and upper classes, by contrast, were seen as too thickly coated with the veneer of civilised behaviour for the animality within them to be so easily portrayed, except in certain basic situations such as the appearance of sudden danger or an unexpected chance of rapid riches, when the unedifying spectacle of well-fed figures scrambling and fighting for safety or advantage was always good copy for a few sardonic pages. But to keep a whole novel exclusively focused on the animality of the propertied classes posed serious problems, as is apparent if one compares Zola's *Nana* (1880) with his much more successful *Germinal* and *La Terre* (1887). To strip a cultured society down to its basic elements by removing and discarding its outer layers of convention, behaviour and civilised conversation runs the risk of leaving out a whole dimension of its life; the result is incomplete and unconvincing, as is only too clearly exemplified by the featureless automata whom Zola passes off as Nana's distinguished admirers. With miners in *Germinal*, however, the middle- and upper-class reader comes away with the sensation, however illusory, of having seen a totality of existence.

Germinal emphasises both the levelling effect of occupation and the animal-like state of being that it imposes: 'the never-ending round of poverty and bestial toil, the destiny of the animal slaughtered for its wool'. The individuality of the miners is lost in the uniform drudgery of their lives. Their reactions become stereotypes; men of very different temperaments behave in the same way. The novel describes

the snorting of the haulage girls as they reached the incline [of the both 2 and Lorteus view of women!

tunnel], all steaming like overloaded mares. It was at times like this one of those waves of bestiality ran through the mine, the sudden lust of the male that came over a miner when he met one of those girls on all fours, with her rear in the air and her buttocks bursting out of her breeches.

Indeed the lives and aspirations of the miners and the pit ponies became almost indistinguishable. The pathetic attempts of the pit pony, Bataille, to remember the outside world where he was born are paradoxically just as poignant as old Alice's evocation of her rural childhood in *Mary Barton*. And the highest compliment that is made to Bonnemort, the old miner, driven mad by hardship and privation, is that he had hitherto lived the respectable life of a beast of burden—perhaps the bitterest comment in the whole book.

13 The Ubiquitous Doctor

'Zola's aplomb . . . comes from his inconceivable ignorance' (Flaubert). 'Your Zola knows nothing; he invents it all in his study' (Chekhov). The exasperation which many of Zola's friends and admirers felt for his scientific pretensions was the greater for coming from men who in a number of cases had genuine professional knowledge. A striking feature of the later Realists is the first-hand acquaintance which several of the leading figures had with the world of medicine. Ibsen started to earn his living at the age of fifteen in an apothecary's shop, where he made up the prescriptions and spent his spare hours preparing himself to read medicine at Christiania University. Had he not failed his entrance examination, he might conceivably have embarked on a medical career, despite the fact that literary composition was already occupying much of his time and eroding his medical interests. Theodor Fontane (1819–98), for his part, was not only a pharmacist's son, but made it his profession for ten years, practising in Berlin, then Leipzig.

The most celebrated embodiment of medicine and literature, however, was Chekhov, who not only started life as a practising doctor but made a brief unsuccessful attempt to qualify himself for an academic career in medicine. As he claimed towards the end of his life

> the study of medicine has had a great influence on my literary work; it has considerably widened the field of my observations and enriched my knowledge, the real value of which for me as a writer can only be understood by one who is a medical man himself; it has also exerted a guiding influence upon me, and, I suppose, it is because of my knowledge of medicine that I have succeeded in avoiding many mistakes. An acquaintance with the natural sciences and the scientific method always kept me on the look-out for such mistakes, and wherever possible I tried to take the scientific data into account; and where it was not possible I preferred not to write at all.

Chekhov knew medicine from both sides: as patient as well as practitioner. Although he was twenty-four before he suspected that he might be consumptive, he underwent a major illness, peritonitis, when he was fifteen, thereby acquiring an early awareness of the dependence of attitudes and states of mind on physical factors. It was during this illness that long conversations with his doctor developed his interest in medical matters and resolved him to make it his profession. After graduating from Moscow University in 1884, he briefly became locum for a *zemstvo* doctor in Zvenigorod, which involved him in attending *zemstvo* meetings, as well as treating some thirty to forty patients each morning. This brought him direct experience of provincial politics as well as immediate involvement in the tragi-comic world of Russian public health, with its dirt and inadequate resources, so compellingly described in his later short stories. Although he established an impecunious practice in Moscow, writing provided the main source of his income, as it had during his student days; and with the success of *Ivanov* (1887) and the acclaim that met his steady output of short stories, he decided to make writing a whole-time activity. Thereafter he only intermittently exercised his professional skills; chiefly in his new-found role as country squire in Melikhovo (1892), where peasants came from fifteen miles around to his unofficial surgeries to receive free treatment and advice, while he, for his part, visited the sick in difficult travelling conditions. He was also entrusted with organising local preventive measures against the cholera epidemic of 1892, when he found himself in charge of twenty-five villages, four factories and a monastery—preparations which happily escaped the necessity of being put into operation.

One of the most interesting features of Chekhov's medical activities was their reflection of the growing interdependence of medicine and social studies during the nineteenth century. Doctors had long been aware that the roots of ill-health lay in malnutrition and inadequate housing and sanitation: so much so that the nineteenth century found a number of them making social studies of the areas in which they worked. Governments, for their part, both at national and local level, were increasingly resorting to medical opinion on matters of public health and on living and working conditions. Chekhov's medical interests had always had a strong social content. In 1884 he and two colleagues had questioned the inmates of a Moscow brothel as to their backgrounds and circumstances; and in the same year he had, more systematically, embarked on collecting material for 'A Medical History of Russia', a project that occupied his spare time for two years, but never reached the writing stage. His most remarkable venture into the sphere of social medicine, however, was the survey he made of the convict settlement of Sakhalin, an inhospitable island in Russo–Japanese waters, which he crossed Siberia by cart and carriage to visit in 1890. To compile it, Chekhov rose every morning at five, and made a house-to-house, cell-by-cell census of the whole convict population, entering his findings in a card-index (containing more than ten thousand entries) where he recorded among much else their occupations, education, illnesses and whether their children were legitimate or not, for prostitution and concubinage were endemic in a population where men outnumbered women two to one.

The result was a four-hundred page report, *Sakhalin Island* (1891–4) which Chekhov considered submitting to Moscow University as an academic dissertation, with the ultimate intention of applying for a lectureship. The Dean of the Medical Faculty, however, was not prepared to consider the matter seriously, and Chekhov's career was to remain primarily a literary one.

Among the lesser and more transient figures of later Realism, Gerhart Hauptmann (1862–1946) likewise professed an interrelated interest in social and medical matters. Although not himself a doctor, he had from 1888 close personal connections with a circle of Zurich medical men, and made frequent fact-finding visits to mental hospitals and other institutions in and around the city. Religious and metaphysical by inclination, he nevertheless came wistfully to feel that medical practice was the ideal vocation, since it applied scientific knowledge to the problems of humanity in a fashion that was direct and unambiguous, without being open to hostile accusations of political or religious motivation. Although it was not appropriate for him to strike out belatedly on such a career, he nevertheless determined to make his literary talents a vehicle for sound well-informed judgements on human problems. In many ways he spoke for a whole generation of Realist writers when he made the rather theatrical gesture of standing by Georg Büchner's grave and dedicating his literary future to the ideals that Büchner had stood for. If a corpse could register ironic amusement, no doubt the long-dead Büchner would have done so—even more had he known the tortuous and ambiguous path which Hauptmann's ideals were later to take. But in invoking the name of the writer who had most strikingly combined science, literature and social concern, Hauptmann was very much a man of his time, even if his Realism was to prove only one of several states through which his chameleon-like career was to pass.

Doctors and drink

These interests and concerns left a deep impression on later Realism, where doctors were increasingly used as the voice of truth and sanity. Doctors had admittedly played an important role in the plays and fiction of earlier centuries. Their education and the local gossip they picked up in their social and professional calls made them especially useful to playwrights as a vehicle of information to the audience. Denied the narrative voice of the novelist, the playwright needed an on-stage spokesman whose professional duties made plausible both his knowledge and the frequency of his exits and entrances. In the nineteenth century, however, an increasingly secular and scientifically conscious society was coming to prefer the doctor to the priest as a qualified commentator on human behaviour, especially at a time when medicine and medical training were making such advances. The doctor was now not only a channel of information between author and audience, a role he had often shared with the notary, but he was also the spokesman of the author's ultimate views on life and how it might be lived.

To underline the point that the doctor spoke in the name of a higher authority, and was not merely uttering personal opinions, dramatists often made him something of a personal failure: a disillusioned idealist with a fondness for drink and dismissive ironies, a man whose intelligence, knowledge and perception enabled him to speak with the voice of truth, but whose willpower and resilience to misfortune were not enough to carry him through life successfully. Science and commonsense spoke through him like grace through the whisky priests of Graham Greene.

The disillusionment and drinking that characterised the archetypal doctors of Ibsen and Chekhov also stemmed from their sharp awareness of the limitations of life. Seeing more clearly than most the abyss that lay beneath Man, they consoled themselves with alcohol, and then, with loosened tongues, gave vent to sardonic truths about the human lot. Their prescriptions for alleviating its misery were fairly modest. Ibsen's Dr Relling in *The Wild Duck* (1884) prescribes illusion (see pp. 172–3), while Gerhart Hauptmann's more sober Dr Schimmelpfennig in *Before Dawn* (1889) can claim no more than 'to make the situation as bearable as possible with medicine'.

If Dr Relling is the most striking example of this Realist device, there are others of a less obvious kind; and in Ibsen's plays, they always make a better showing than pastors and other spokesmen of traditional morality. Chekhov's Dr Dorn in *The Seagull*(1896) is an interesting variant, in that his character has been softened by social success, rather than failure; yet his training and perception enable his wisdom to survive. Even so, Chekhov frequently uses doctors for other, less didactic, roles that have little to do with his own concept of 'truth'. Dr Lvov in *Ivanov*, like Büchner's doctor in *Woyzeck*, is a meddler, a man whose personality is more important for the author's purpose than his profession, a man who is more akin to Ibsen's Gregers than the broken-down stoics who so often speak for Chekhov and Ibsen. In so far as Lvov represents something wider than his own personality, it is middle-class envy of his social superiors.

Being a novelist, with all the advantages of the narrative voice, Zola has less need of fictional spokesmen than his theatrical colleagues. His doctors, like Chekhov's, turn out to be a mixed bunch. Even so, Dr Pascal is perhaps the nearest thing to a hero that the Rougon-Macquart series produced; and it is he who comes nearest to assuming the author's mantle in his professional commentary on the family history. Such are his qualities and unprejudiced eye that Zola finds it hard to fit him into his saga of hereditary malaise and degeneration: 'He is one of those frequent cases which run counter to the laws of heredity', Zola weakly concedes. Not surprisingly, it was Dr Pascal who provoked some of Chekhov's most scathing comments. Not only was Pascal, in Chekhov's view, a travesty of the medical profession, but he was 'a grey-haired Cupid with sinewy legs like a cockerel . . . a melon caught by the autumn frost'. Not that Chekhov thought any the less of Zola as an imaginative writer. Like his compeers, he would probably have happily subscribed to Flaubert's malign accolade of 1879: 'you [Zola] are a splendid romantic. In fact, it's just for that that I like and admire you'. Nor indeed would Zola have necessarily taken it badly: 'It is true that I am a poet . . . I am up to the waist in romanticism' (1882).

14 The Dismal Science: Economic Man

If the earlier Realists had sharp noses for the formative influence of social factors, their keenest appetites generally took them off in pursuit of their prime interest, the individual. Despite Balzac's constant claim to be portraying social types, the argument and drama of his novels were sharply focused on individual types, often extraordinary, monstrous types: the arch womaniser, Baron Hulot; the embittered poor relation, Cousin Bette, with her terrifying capacity for revenge; the scheming outlaw, Vautrin, with his extraordinary powers of survival. Even as 'social' a novel as Mrs Gaskell's *Mary Barton* depicted the weavers as widely differing individuals.

With Zola and Hauptmann, however—and, much more subtly, with Ibsen, Chekhov and Fontane—the emphasis throughout was on the factors that made them similar. Ibsen's exceptional beings, who contrived to rise above the pettiness of their milieu, were shown to be exceptional, and only served to underline the point (see pp. 158–60).

For the later Realists, the most brutal of life's Procrustean beds was economic reality. Zola and Hauptmann—like Mrs Gaskell before them, presented the misery of the working classes as the misshapen offspring of an economic situation, rather than the outcome of malevolence or conscious greed on the employers' part. The employers' main crime was ignorance, and in some cases indifference, and an unquestioning assumption that they, as the owners of the means of production, had first claim to the security and comfort it engendered. Pit managers like Hennebeau in *Germinal* were working for the owners, who, based in Paris, were remote from the desperate reality of the miners' lives. Shareholders like Gregoire were largely ignorant of what the miners were enduring. When Zola shows them shouting for bread in the recession of 1867, Grégoire affably comments 'Of course, they don't mean any harm really. When they have shouted themselves hoarse, they will go home and eat their supper with all the more appetite'. The situation is later summed up by the miner's wife, Maheude, who had lost her daughter in a pit explosion and her husband in a battle between troops and strikers, 'in the long run it isn't anybody's fault . . . it's everybody's fault'.

If to some militants this might seem like moral numbness, it partly reflected the more intrusive and dramatic nature of economic change when the later Realists were writing. Although Britain, Belgium and France had experienced considerable industrial development in the early nineteenth century, the vast industrial wasteland and endless vistas of drab slum dwellings that survive today mainly date from the later half of the century. Germany did not undergo massive industrialisation until this period, while Scandinavia and Russia had to wait until the 1890s to be significantly affected. Industrial transformation was therefore a fact of life that impinged much more forcefully on the consciousness of the later Realists. Even the most introspective novelist working in the seclusion of a country property could not help but see the results as soon as he took a train to any town of consequence, while even a perfunctory glance at the newspapers showed that strikes and social unrest were a matter that could affect the order and security to which he was used, and might blemish the prosperity of the middle-class milieux in which he moved, with possible repercussions for his own royalties.

Equally intrusive was the progressively international character of the economy. In the past, when agriculture was the principal form of economic activity, and a wind-filled sail or an ambling pack-horse was the fastest means of moving freight, each region was more of an island unto itself, even if international trade was already a major fact of life. There had been bad harvests and crop diseases which had affected large stretches of Europe, but they had rarely been uniform in their incidence. With improved communications, however, and greater opportunities for regional specialisation, the economies of the various nations became increasingly interdependent. A bad harvest in the Ukraine could affect industrial profits in the Ruhr, since the fur-hatted landlords of the Dnieper, with less grain to export, could afford to buy fewer German manufactures; and in this way the misfortunes of distant peoples could impinge on the comfortably slippered existence of a novelist whose earnings happened to be invested in German steel, or, more likely, whose friends and acquaintances had similar investments.

On the whole, the middle classes had done well from the Industrial Revolution and the economic changes of the pre-1870 period. And their image in the literature of those years had largely reflected this. The bourgeois families that suffer misfortune at the hands of a hard-hearted author normally do so as the result of some particular disaster, often unexpected or partly self-inflicted, something that was individual to the family, rather than affecting their class as a whole. There had been trade recessions and depressions in particular industries, but these had been of relatively short duration, except in the case of enterprises that were either outmoded or were being edged out by newer, more efficient competitors.

The 1880s, however, brought a change which partly reflected the so-called 'Great Depression' of 1873–96. Farmers were the worst hit, their problems arising from the increasing import of cheap food and raw materials from abroad. The spread of railways across the rich plains of

Russia and America was bringing increasing quantities of grain to the coast for export to Europe, the first full force of which broke on the European farmer in the early 1870s. The next twenty years, moreover, saw shipping freight rates cut by more than two-thirds, as iron and then steel hulls permitted increasing capacity. At the same time new land was constantly being brought under the plough in America and elsewhere, with the result that food was now reaching Europe in quantities that largely outstripped the increase in population. Canning methods and refrigerated ships (1877) enabled perishables to be stored or transported for much longer periods, and the 1890s confronted the European farmer with growing cargoes of meat from the New World and Australasia. Silk growers watched with apprehension the expanding exports of China and Japan, while sheep farmers saw with equal disquiet the mounting bales of Australasian and Argentinian wool that were filling European ports. All of this undoubtedly meant cheaper food and clothing, and helped to account for the rise in real (as distinct from monetary) wages (see pp. 142−4). But it also lowered the income of farmers everywhere, even after landowners persuaded their governments to bring in protective tariffs. The overall price of food fell by two-fifths between 1873 and 1896, and that of raw materials by over a half, with the result that the total number of sheep in France and Germany was itself halved. Even with tariffs, French wheat prices fell by 43 per cent in the same period. Such a situation could only intensify the farmers' role as a battling lobby for protection, setting them yet farther apart from the urban working class with its demand for cheap food.

Governments had a hard choice. The tariffs that they imposed meant that the townsmen could only partially benefit from the fall in prices. But without such tariffs, the rural population could not have afforded to buy the industrial goods that gave the townsmen their livelihood. Food would have been cheaper, but urban wages would not have risen to the extent that they did.

The theoretical solution to such an agricultural *embarras de richesses* was for some of the producers of the surplus commodity to switch to a product in short supply. In practice, however, this was always difficult because such conversions took time and money, demand in the meantime sometimes changing. Yet where a glut or shortage was sufficiently long-term to permit remedial action, such conversions were the only real solution, the Danish and Dutch switch from grain to dairy produce being notable examples. Nevertheless farming was henceforth to be the poor relation of the European economy.

This was a period of falling prices in manufactures as well as agriculture. Although manufacturers were less hard hit than farmers, industrial prices fell by a third (see Fig. 1). At the same time Britain, France and Belgium, the pioneers of the Industrial Revolution, were acutely conscious that other countries had followed in their footsteps and were not only supplying

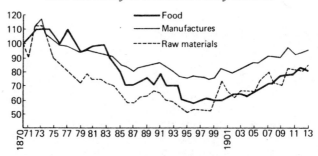

FIG. 1   The movement of world prices, 1870–1913 (1870 = 100)

their own domestic needs, but were annexing an increasing share of the international market. It was not surprising, therefore, that the older industrial nations should see these years in unhappy contrast to what had gone before.

Conversely the end of the century initiated an upswing in prices, and a remarkable rise in world industrial production, particularly by the second generation of producers, notably Germany and the United States (see Figs. 2 and 3). The excitement of these years recalled the optimism of the early

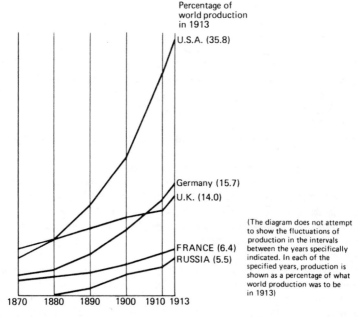

FIG. 2   The growth of industrial production in selected countries 1870–1913

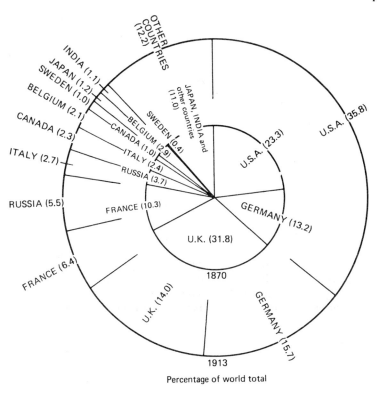

Percentage of world total

Fɪɢ. 3   The world's manufactures (percentage distribution) 1870 and 1913
Sᴏᴜʀᴄᴇ: League of Nations, *Industrialisation and World Trade* (1945).

seventies (see p. 144); so much so that it was common to think of the
intervening period as an aberration, 'the Great Depression, 1873–96',
which many saw as the product of an unlucky combination of circumstances. In more recent years, however, economic historians have tended
to see 'the depression' as a much shallower and more scattered affair than
did their predecessors, and prefer to view it as an uncomfortable stage in a
long-term trend, initiated by the Industrial Revolution. Deflation in fact
was the dominant characteristic of the greater part of the nineteenth
century, from 1817 to 1896 with a brief upward jerk from 1850 to 1873.
The fact that factory-made goods were ultimately cheaper to make than
hand-made goods was itself a deflationary element implicit in the
Industrial Revolution; while in parallel fashion the spread of railways and
steam ships was reducing the price of raw materials and food. Cheaper raw
materials, moreover, were themselves a crucial factor in reducing the cost

of manufactures, as Fig. 1 strongly suggests. Cheaper leather, wool and cotton meant cheaper shoes and clothes, for it was not only the sewing machine that was cutting costs.

In the first half of the nineteenth century, the manufacturers of Britain, Belgium and France had not been especially worried by the fall in prices, because they were continually expanding their markets and sales abroad, both in the rest of Europe and overseas. As long as there were new markets for manufacturers to tap, increased sales had more than offset the reduction in profits arising from the fall in prices. But with the rise of industry in the United States, Germany and elsewhere, the older industrial countries could no longer assume the same increase in their sales. Britain's case typified the dilemma. She had already exploited the potential of the techniques that had been the mainspring of the Industrial Revolution. And although innovations and improvements continued to expand this potential, the profit margins in these later stages were not so spectacular as in the initial breakthrough. Advances in steel manufacture in the 1870s and 80s created a certain momentum; but it was not until the expansion of the chemical, electrical and motor industries at the turn of the century that a new major impetus occurred.

Germany by contrast had not yet exhausted the élan of her initial industrial take-off. With protective tarriffs to help her, she still had a large domestic market to exploit, as well as rural neighbours to the east. Indeed when the turn of the century brought Europe new industrial opportunities, Germany was still riding high on the momentum of the old. Apart from a brief set-back in the 1870s, 'the depression' for her had been a period of rapid ascent; and the same could be said, in varying degrees, of other countries that were undergoing industrialisation.

The phenomenon that requires close examination is perhaps not so much 'the depression' as the general rise in prices and production that preceded and followed it. The price rise of 1850–73 was partly due to the expansion of credit and currency, but also to the disturbance of normal patterns of trade by brief but disruptive wars on both sides of the Atlantic. That of the post-1896 period was due, among other factors, to the increase in real wages among the manual classes, which brought more workers into the market for manufactures, and thereby expanded domestic demand. For the older industrial countries this was a major compensation for the markets they had lost through increased competition in the field of exports; though the industries that gained most in the domestic sphere were not necessarily those that had been hardest hit by foreign rivals. It also stemmed from the rapid expansion of what has been called 'the second Industrial Revolution': the development of the chemical, electrical and motor industries, which produced new categories of goods and new patterns of demand.

Even so, the so-called depression years of 1873–96 had still seen industry expanding, even in the hardest hit countries like Britain and France (see

Fig. 2). It is true that from the 1880s the United States was usurping the world leadership in industrial production that had hitherto belonged to Britain; and at last it was being realised that European primacy itself might one day be called in question. But if Europe by 1913 had only about 55 per cent of world industrial production instead of about 70 per cent as in 1870, production itself was five and a half times larger (see Fig. 3). There was also the additional consolation that much of America's industrial growth was absorbed by her own domestic needs. As an industrial exporter she occupied only fourth place in 1913, with 12.6 per cent of world exports, while Britain provided 29.6 per cent, Germany 26.4 per cent and France 13.6 per cent.

British and French writers, however, living in 'the Great Depression' of 1873–96 could only take their cue from the middle-class circles in which they lived—and this, for them was a depression. Indeed, Zola's preoccupation with it was sufficiently obsessive to colour his portrayal of the previous decade, the 1860s; and it is also arguable that Hauptmann's *The Weavers* (1892) saw the economic problems of the 1840s with too much of a nineties' eye.

In Zola's case, the problem partly sprang from his reluctance to part with the sub-title he had given to the Rougon-Macquart series: 'The Natural and Social History of a family under the Second Empire'. He had launched the project under this name in 1868, just two years before the blood-and-iron of Prussia brought an unexpected end to the Second Empire in its eighteenth year. An author less wedded to effect might have scrapped the title and struck to his plan of setting the later novels of the series in the 1870s and 80s. But Zola was determined to keep his original flag flying, even if it meant telescoping the action of the cycle into the implausibly brief span of eighteen years. Among much else, the *grande cocotte*, Nana, is obliged to conquer France with a speed scarcely emulated by Moltke's armies; while, as Zola himself admitted, 'I am in perpetual danger of anachronism'.

This danger of anachronism was nowhere more apparent than in *Germinal* (1885) and *La Terre* (1887). The hazards of the manual classes were so closely linked in Zola's mind with the current economic depression of the 1880s, that he pushed back its features to the 1860s, where his two great 'occupational' novels are set. *Germinal* treats the relatively minor crisis of 1867 as though it were the contemporary 'Great Depression' of the eighties, and wrongly blames it on American self-sufficiency in industry, with its consequent lessening of the foreign demand for French manufactures. In fact, this was as yet only a secondary factor in 1867. Of much more immediate importance to this hiccough in the French economy was the current caution of investors, who feared a Franco-Prussian confrontation in the near future that might result in their capital being at risk if it were tied up in non-moveable assets.

An analogous anachronism lies at the centre of *La Terre* where Zola wanted above all to depict what he saw as the love-hate relationship between the peasants and the earth. Moreover, he especially wished to portray it as an unrequited love, with the earth as a faithless mistress who betrays her lover, despite the labour and care he has lavished on her. He was therefore determined, come what may, to drag into his novel of the 1860s the catastrophic drop in farm prices that hit France in the 1880s. It was the type of dramatic situation that Zola's imagination relished; and it can scarcely be a coincidence that the concept of *La Terre* came to him precisely at the time that these developments were striking the French peasantry. (The original plan of the Rougon-Macquart series made no provision for a novel on peasant-life.) With characteristic licence, he hauled forward the start of American competition into the 1860s, ignoring such awkward obstacles as the refusal of French farm prices to fall significantly until a decade later (see Fig. 1), or the absence of widespread public concern until 1880. Grain prices had admittedly fluctuated in the 1860s; but official reports explained this largely in terms of more intensive domestic production.

The economic perspective of Zola, and of many of his generation, takes on a particular sharpness if one compares the Rougon-Macquart series with *La Comédie Humaine* forty years earlier. There are at first sight marked similarities between the two undertakings, which mask their fundamental differences. The Rougon-Macquart series was partly inspired by Balzac; and it was Taine who urged Zola to take Balzac as his model (see pp. 128–9). There is much that is Balzacian about his preliminary plans for it: 'I base it on a truth of the time, the hustle of ambitions and appetites'. And what he says of the Second Empire might well have been said by Balzac of the July Monarchy: 'Now that we have the Empire, everything is moving, everything is for sale' (*Le Ventre de Paris*, 1873); 'the rapidity of fortunes has singularly sharpened appetites. In the last twenty years we have witnessed the most ferocious scramble for wealth that one could ever see' (article of 1869).

Yet when it comes to depicting financial dealings, Zola was both less experienced and less interested than Balzac. Work was much more important to him as a subject than money; and significantly his better novels concerned the downtrodden Macquarts, rather than the rapacious, opportunistic Rougons.

These differences reflected on the one hand a change in awareness and preoccupations between the 1840s and 1880s; but they also corresponded to Balzac's and Zola's differing experience of life. Zola lost his father, an Italian engineer, when he was six. Unlike some other Realists who were half-orphaned in childhood, notably Stendhal and Turgenev, he was fortunate in the parent who remained to rear him; and Zola's relatively more optimistic approach to life may owe something to this. But his father's death unquestionably brought hardship to the family. When illness caused Zola to fail his *baccalauréat*, he spent two years in various menial occupations, experiencing privation of a kind that a few of the early major Realists had known. It was only when he obtained the offer of a post in Hachette's publicity department that he found himself with more congenial and tolerably paid employment.

At the same time Zola belonged to a generation that was more labour-conscious than its predecessors. The economic and social changes that engendered this awareness are familiar enough (see pp. 139–40 and 132–3); but there also sprang from them a greater attentiveness among the educated public to the broad stream of thinkers who asserted that the whole development of Man and society depended primarily on economic factors. Following on from the hard truths of Ricardo and Malthus (see p. 125), Feuerbach had reminded Europe that 'man is what he eats'. It was widely recognised that Man's aptitudes and characteristics owed their development to his search for food and warmth. And if materialists conceded that the man of feeling and intellect could not live by bread alone, they emphasised that without bread Man could not live at all—and that for the majority of men, the struggle for bread occupied by far the greater part of their conscious lives. Moreover, the dialectical element in Marxism, like Darwin's theory of evolution, emphasised the basic element of competition and conflict that characterised the human condition, already recognised by Malthus.

Yet Marxism was a symptom rather than a cause of the growing economic awareness of the educated public; and Marx's direct influence on the major figures among the later Realists remained small. It was one of the many ironies of history that Marxism should be little known outside socialist circles until after the Paris Commune of 1871. In order to win support in its suppression of the Paris Commune, the French Government had portrayed it as the work of the Internationale, which Marx had helped to found in 1864. Marx himself, remote in London, was sufficiently impressed by this propaganda to give the legend his own endorsement. Notorious overnight for the wrong reasons, Marx became a new subject of interest, which brought his work, and that of his colleagues, to the notice of many who otherwise might never have heard of it.

Its impact on the major Realists, however, was slight. At the time that he was writing *Germinal* and *La Terre*, Zola was certainly aware of the main drift of Marx's thought, even if the Marxists who feature in these novels are unattractive exponents of it. Zola was also personally acquainted with Jules Guesde, who was popularly regarded in the 1880s as one of the principal Marxists among the French socialist leaders, despite the idiosyncratic nature of his Marxism. Whether Zola knew any of Marx's writings at first hand is more doubtful. And although Zola's younger contemporary, Gerhart Hauptmann, had certainly read Marx, he was not disposed to subscribe to the bulk of the Marxist canon. Nor was it to be expected that his elder compeer, Theodor Fontane, should be more sympathetic: for him Marxism was little better than a pretext for theft. Ibsen, for his part, characteristically ignored Marx; an attitude that he truculently adopted towards many contemporary thinkers, including some who were close to his own cast of mind. Chekhov, on the other hand, periodically found his short stories on peasant and working-class life debated, and sometimes championed, by Russian Marxists. But he disliked what he regarded as their mendacity and political opportunism, and there is no evidence to suggest that he went out of his way to acquaint himself with the substance of Marxism.

Even so, Zola's generation shared Marx's awareness of the growing anonymity and uniformity of working life and, like him, recognised its erosive effects on individuality. In his preliminary plan for the Rougon-Macquart series, Zola revealingly commented 'Balzac says that he wants to paint men, women and things . . . I . . . submit both men and women to things'. Like Balzac Zola was much concerned with the moulding influence of occupation; but with him the emphasis was different. Whereas Balzac singled out the distinctive features of each occupation which made for diversity in society, Zola concentrated on the levelling aspects of work that eroded diversity of outlook between individuals. To some extent the difference stemmed from the fact that Zola was more inclined to think in class as well as occupational terms: the lot of the manual worker was constantly contrasted in his novels with that of the possessing classes, while Balzac was largely concerned with the professions as such and the effect they had on their mostly middle-class practitioners.

Yet as demonstrated in Appendix E (see pp. 184–5), Zola did not regard the levelling effect of occupation as peculiar to modern industry, even if it was the uniform drudgery of industrial life which had brought it forcefully to the attention of the writers of the time. *La Terre* was to show how the land was equally a force for uniformity among those who worked it, shaping among much else their attitudes to sex and family life (see pp. 184–5).

Chekhov

Although the delicacy of Chekhov's characterisation may tempt the reader to think otherwise, most of his figures represent social types with strong roots in economic circumstance. His landlords, academics and doctors have generally more in common with their colleagues in similar walks of life, than they have with men of broadly analogous temperaments in other occupations. According to his brother, Mikhail, Chekhov was inclined to attach more importance to environment than to heredity as a shaping influence; and the evidence of his stories and plays would seem consistent with this view, without necessarily confirming it.

Economic circumstance played an oppressive role in his early life, even more than with Zola. His father had been a Taganrog shopkeeper who had gradually drifted into severe financial difficulties. These were partly the result of the town's losing trade to Rostov on Don, a neighbouring commercial centre which had the benefit of earlier rail links with other parts of Russia. Not only did Chekhov thereby come to know material privation as a child, but he was a witness to how men's lives could be fundamentally altered by distant economic factors that were remote from their own activities or experience. Chekhov later described himself as 'terribly corrupted by being born, growing up, studying and beginning to write in a milieu where money played a grotesquely large role'. As a medical student in Moscow, he found himself having to play the role of effective head of the household, supplementing the family income by writing short stories for weekly magazines.

If his short stories reflect his understanding of the problems of the poor, his later plays display a similar insight into the difficulties of the Russian landowning classes. The friendship and hospitality of the Kiselyov family in the 1880s gave him an intimate view of the problems and preoccupations of Russian landlords, while his own eventual acquisition of a small estate in 1892 confirmed what his observations had already told him: that farming in Russia was not a paying concern, unless one was prepared to devote to it a ruthlessness and ingenuity which most Russian landowners lacked. As the steward complains in *Ivanov* (1887), 'Rationalised farming! A thousand acres of land—and not a farthing in your pocket'.

Like most European farmers, the Russian gentry were badly hit by the fall in agricultural prices between 1873 and 1896 (see pp. 140–1). Their resistance to it, moreover, had in many cases been weakened by the side effects of the Emancipation of the Serfs in 1861 (see pp. 117–18), which put them in the unfamiliar situation of having to rely more or less entirely on hired labour, over which they had no disciplinary control. Tolstory was only one of many who found the peasants were now more reluctant than ever to adopt new progressive methods of work; they knew that the landlord's only means of coercion was the threat of dismissal—which he might be unable to wield, if labour was short. Inexperience on both sides made the wage–labour relationship particularly difficult in its initial years.

At the same time the abolition of most of the landlords' judicial and administrative authority deprived them of much of their former *raison d'être*; they were no longer the virtual rulers of the neighbourhood, as their families had been before the reforms of Alexander II (1855–81). Their reaction was one of bewilderment and aimlessness. Still expecting, and still largely receiving, the traditional respect of the peasantry, they were nevertheless aware that this respect no longer had a firm functional foundation, especially when falling farm prices started to erode their remaining source of prestige, material wealth. With no clear role to play, many of them became the bored spectators of the uneventful provincial life

around them, as Chekhov's plays familiarly indicate. As Trofimov says in
The Cherry Orchard (1903),

> all your forefathers were serf-owners . . . Don't you see human beings
> gazing at you from every cherry tree in your orchard, from every leaf
> and every tree-trunk, don't you hear voices? . . . They owned living
> souls—and it has perverted you . . . so that . . . you . . . no longer
> realise that you're living in debt . . . at the expense of people you don't
> admit further than your kitchen.

Some, like Simeonov-Pishchik, seek refuge from their uncertainty in a
Micawberish optimism

> I never lose hope . . . a railway lne is built through my land, and they
> pay me for it! Something or other is sure to happen. Perhaps Dashenka
> will win 200,000 rubles. She's got a lottery ticket (*The Cherry Orchard*).

Indeed their main hope seems to lie in relinquishing the land for some non-
agricultural purpose. With industry and urban life encroaching on their
seclusion in a slight but significant way, Chekhov's Ranyevskaias, who
own the cherry orchard, are themselves invited to sell it off as plots for
holiday villas. It is moreover at this point that Chekhov gives his audience
a clear glimpse of the world of money-making and ambition that had been
much less conspicuous in earlier Russian literature (see pp. 98–9).
The speculative builder who buys the orchard represents the mentality
that triumphed in western Europe in the first half of the nineteenth
century: the mentality which Tolstoy so despised (see p. 99).

> I've bought the very estate where my father and grandfather were
> serfs . . . just you see the trees come crashing down! We're going to build
> a whole lot of new villas, and our children and great grandchildren are
> going to see a new living world growing up here.

There is nothing villainous about him; he is well-disposed to the former
owners, even to the point of initially suggesting that they implement and
profit from his scheme themselves. The future is clearly with him; and
Chekhov nowhere suggests that the future is inferior to the fading present.
Even so, he knows that every change can only be made at a price; and the
price may be a high one to pay.

If bewilderment and boredom were often the lot of a landowning gentry
that had largely lost its *raison d'être*, there were also more deeply rooted
factors that inclined men of sensibility in Russia towards a mutual
depression and despair. As Chekhov wrote in February 1888,

> an endless plain, a harsh climate, an ignorant stern people, with its

distressingly bleak history, Tartar domination, bureaucracy, poverty, ignorance, etc., Russian life weighs heavily upon the Russian; it is just as if he had to carry a rock weighing a ton on his shoulders. In Western Europe people perish because they find life cramped and stifling, in Russia because they find life too spacious. There is so much space that a little man has not got the strength to find his way about. That's what I think of Russian suicides.

15 Society versus the Individual

Most theories of progress assume that salutary change begins with the discoveries and perceptions of individuals, aided perhaps by the chance pricks of circumstance, be it Newton's falling apple or Archimedes's spilling bath-water. Few Realists disputed this. Where they differed was in their assessment of the obstacles that impeded the spread and general acceptance of these perceptions.

Chekhov, Ibsen and Fontane are cases in point. For Chekhov, living in a rural backward country, ruled by an autocracy, the initial direction that progress might take seemed clear enough; but the obstacles were enormous and disheartening. For Ibsen, moving from hotel to apartment in the democracies of western Europe, the direction was far from clear; the early obvious steps had already been taken in these countries, and the view to his eyes looked no better than before—if anything worse, since the obstacles to progress proved to be more insidious and less easy to diagnose than initial optimism had supposed. Fontane, for his part, accepted these obstacles with a gentler resignation than his compeers; yet his conclusions were in some ways the most depressing of the three, since he questioned the ability of even the enlightened individual to transcend the narrow perceptions of his milieu.

The Russian Sisyphus

Like so many members of the Russian intelligentsia, Chekhov (1860–1904) was burdened with an overwhelming sense of the enormity of the task of reform. With no central representative institutions, the only form of democratic expression in Russian public life was through the provincial and district *zemstvos* (see pp. 134–5). These were heavily weighted in favour of the landed gentry, with the result that anyone envisaging radical reform was faced with the doubly dispiriting situation of an absence of constitutional machinery on the national level and a solid wall of vested interests in the provinces. With an inert, superstitious peasantry, whose only progressive instinct was a desire for more land, and an urban working population too small to be as yet politically significant, it was hard to see how popular pressures could force the *zemstvos* and the government into a faster rate of reform. And even if the *zemstvos* were adventurous, it was always open to the government to override their decisions.

Such reform as the government had instituted (see p. 100) was largely the result of humiliation at the hands of foreigners, which taught it the bitter lesson that only modernisation could save Russia from further reverses. The substantial reforms of Alexander II (1855–81), including the emancipation of the serfs, had followed rapidly on the traumatic experience of the Crimean War, which demonstrated the helplessness of a great nation like Russia when faced with modern technology and methods, even when used as unskilfully as in the Anglo-French invasion of 1854–5. Similarly the diplomatic humiliation of Russia at the Congress of Berlin (1878) persuaded the government to envisage a further substantial programme of reform, including a measure of representation at national level. But the assassination of Alexander II (1881) put an end to these plans. Indeed the repressive rule that followed, under Alexander III (1881–94), was the period when Chekhov was taking stock of Russia and the society that surrounded him. It was therefore perhaps not surprising that he should say in 1888, 'there will never be a revolution in Russia'.

It is no reflection on Chekhov's percipience that this remark should be belied by events—and indeed was at variance with what he was later to have Toozenbach say in *Three Sisters* (1901): 'a mighty storm is coming to freshen us up ! . . . in twenty-five years or thirty years' time every man and woman will be working'. Leaving aside the question of whether Toozen-bach speaks for Chekhov, much was to happen in the thirteen years that separated these two utterances. Russia was to initiate her industrial revolution in the 1890s, with the result that both the middle classes and her embryonic industrial proletariat, still a mere 7 per cent of the nation in 1914, were to take on a significance for the future that few outside the ranks of the socialists would have predicted in the 1880s. Even so, it was to take Russia's reverses in the disastrous Russo-Japanese war of 1904–5 to panic the government into granting a national Duma in 1905–6, and Chekhov did not live to see it.

The frustration of the liberal was compounded with the boredom of Russian provincial life. As Dr Astrov says in *Uncle Vanya* (1889–97), 'I love life, but . . . the provincial dreary Russian life, I just can't bear . . .'; 'ten years of this contemptible routine . . . has . . . poisoned our blood with its putrid vapours, until now we've become just as petty as the rest.' It is in *Ivanov* (1887), however, that Chekhov comes most closely to grips with the dilemma of the would-be reformer in a static society. As he explained in a letter to the producer,

Ivanov is a gentleman, a university man . . . honest and straightforward like most people of his class . . . Russian excitability has one specific characteristic: it is quickly followed by exhaustion. A man has scarcely left the class-room before he rushes to take up a burden beyond his strength; he tackles at once the schools, the peasants, scientiic farming, and the *Vyestnik Evropi*, he makes speeches, writes to the minister, combats evil, applauds good, falls in love, not in an ordinary simple way, but selects either a blue-stocking or a neurotic or a Jewess, or even a prostitute whom he tries to save, and so on . . . By the time he is thirty, he begins to feel tired and bored . . . He is ready to reject the *zemstvo* and scientific farming, and science and love . . . He looks for the causes outside himself and fails to find them; he begins to look for them inside and finds only an indefinite feeling of guilt. It is a Russian feeling . . . add one more enemy: loneliness. Were Ivanov an official, an actor, a priest, a professor, he would have grown used to his position. But he lives on his estate . . . His neighbours are either drunkards or fond of cards . . . But life makes its legitimate demands on him, he must settle problems . . . Men like Ivanov do not solve difficulties but collapse under their weight.

That Chekhov himself escaped this kind of fate owed much to his nature, much to his circumstances. Not only was he talented and made of more resilient stuff, but, lacking inherited wealth, he had an active working life to sustain him. Even when the demands of creative writing obliged him to relinquish his medical practice, except intermittently, he retained the energy and compulsion to engage increasingly in social work and local politics. The winter of 1891−2 found him active, like Tolstoy, in promoting relief work during the Nizhny-Novgorod famine. He also subsequently played an active role in *zemstvo* politics, building schools and supervising the census of January 1897, despite increasing ill-health – and was thereby able to savour for himself the mixture of idealism and hopelessness that characterised those who saw the *zemstvos* as the potential springboard of reform in Russia.

Leviathan

When Realists felt disposed to see pale streaks of light on the horizon, a common source of hope was Man's supposed capacity for self-nurture. It was variously assumed that Man would gain increasing control over the social and economic forces that moulded him, even if he himself continued to be their product. While science and education were the hallowed bootstraps by which levitation would be achieved, it was also widely believed that democracy would be both an instrument and a guarantee of this control. Some, however, were less sure; and one of these was Ibsen. For him, Man's hope of bettering society was continually frustrated by the close grip of society on the individual, blinkering his perceptions and stifling any inspiration that was out of the ordinary.

The individual in conflict with society is an ancient theme; but it acquired growing force during the nineteenth century as the state grew more powerful, and came increasingly to regard itself as the embodiment of society. In previous centuries governments had neither the technological wherewithal nor the inclination to be a constant adjudicating presence in the everyday lives of the mass of the population. Even in the early nineteenth century, the individual's *rapports* with the state were largely confined to matters of taxation, public order and military protection. His conflicts with 'society' were far more likely to be with private employers, landlords and uncongenial neighbours—elements which loomed far larger in his life than a distant government which rarely impinged on his existence except in the shape of the tax collector, the policeman and the recruiting sergeant. Unless he was a misanthrope or an outlaw, he was unlikely to be at odds with 'society' as a whole: merely with individuals within it.

The state, on the other hand, was seen as the ruler, not the embodiment, of society; and conflict with it was only exceptionally a protest against society as such. With the growth of representative institutions, however, and the spread of the franchise, the state increasingly claimed to embody, as well as rule, society. As indicated in Table 3, the later nineteenth century was a period when universal male suffrage was making rapid

TABLE 3   Political and social reform before 1914

	Universal male suffrage	Accident insurance or employer's liability	Sickness insurance	Old-age pensions	Un-employment insurance
Germany	1867	1884	1883	1889	
France	1848	1898		1910	
Russia	1906 (qual.)	1903	1912		
Austria	1907	1887	1888	1906*	
Italy	1912	1898		1898*	
Spain	1890	1900			
Portugal	1901	1913			
Belgium	1893	1903		1903	
Holland		1901	1913	1913	
Denmark		1897		1891	
Norway	1898	1894	1909		
Sweden		1901		1913	
Switzerland	1874	1911	1911		
Bulgaria	1879				
Romania		1912		1912	
Greece	1864	1901			
Britain		1897	1911	1908	1911

*Voluntary scheme.
(Dates of developments after 1914 are omitted.)

headway in Europe; and superficially it might have been expected that this would entail greater public control over government, especially in view of the growing constitutional checks on the powers of the central and east European monarchies. But the fact that electoral power was slipping from 'the notables' to the masses did not mean that the new electorate could exercise greater control than the old. Indeed a good case may be made out for arguing the reverse, since a mass electorate is less able to provide the continuous informed criticism of government that had characterised the vigilance of 'the notables'. As men of property and education, 'the notables' were better equipped for this role. The mass electorate on the other hand tended to give a blank cheque for a limited duration to the party or man of its choice; and it is only when government policies touched its pocket or its pride that there was an outcry.

A more important factor in strengthening the executive was the growing complexity of the task of governing greater numbers in an age of increasing speed and technology. The electric telegraph had already linked both sides of the Atlantic as early as the 1860s, while the next decade saw Europe linked with the Pacific and the Far East. Nearer to home, the invention of the telephone by Graham Bell in 1876 gradually increased the whole tempo of life by replacing the to-ing and fro-ing of messenger boys with a virtually instantaneous *tête à tête* between correspondents, thereby enabling industry and commerce to respond immediately to the demands and changes of the market. And only two decades later, the development of wireless by Guglielmo Marconi in 1896 was to enable merchants to give instructions to ships at sea, as well as vastly increase the knowledge and power of governments. These developments made public life move many times faster and multiplied the number of decisions a minister had to make in a day. If government was to be carried on at all, vast discretionary power had to be given to him. Diplomatic negotiations that used to take months now took only days; and wars that had taken decades were now merely a matter of several years at most. Yet paradoxically a debate in parliament on government policy took more time to arrange than before, not less. And the vast increase in parliamentary business meant that an extraordinary debate on government policy could only be secured on major issues. Accordingly a government's critics found it progressively more difficult to comment on the conduct of day-to-day affairs. Politicians thus had to turn increasingly to the Press and non-parliamentary speeches as a means of criticism, this itself giving greater power to the Press and creating a new force with which governments had to reckon. But the Press was not the electorate; and it could be argued that in its attempts, both to influence the electorate and to speak in its name, the growing power of the Press confused rather than helped the attempts of the public to control government. At the same time, the power of the Press, as it was to emerge in the inter-war years, must not be predated. As late as 1898 General Kitchener could walk through a waiting group of journalists, and say: 'Get out of my way, you drunken swabs'.

In these circumstances even the old-style liberals had to revise their ideas of what constituted a tolerable level of government power. Not only were governments obliged to act more quickly, but they were also better informed than formerly. Intelligence services and various instruments of enquiry enabled a government to know more about most matters than the majority of critics. This knowledge and power progressively inclined the public to accept the idea that the government was more competent than other bodies to deal with the problems of society. At the same time the very complexity of modern civilisation demanded increased regulation of life, otherwise collisions of interest would have created chaos. Both on a national and a local level public authority had to assert itself, if advantage was to be taken of the potential improvements in living standards offered by modern technology. This made for an alarmingly powerful state; but it certainly made for better living conditions.

Although the politicians and the general public were coming to accept the power of the state, some writers accepted it less willingly: Ibsen, for instance, condemned the state as 'the curse of the individual'. In this he differed markedly from Zola, and indeed from his devoted admirer, George Bernard Shaw, who as a Fabian Socialist shared Zola's faith in the ability of the state to regenerate society. For them, it was not the state that was alarming but rather society itself when left to its own devices. Modern technology not only increased the power of the state, but also increased the ability of the owners of factories and large estates to exploit the labouring masses, even if this was offset by the growth of workers' organisations. Given the increasing size and expense of modern equipment, no worker could afford to compete independently with the owners, and therefore had no option but to work for them. Zola's *Germinal* and Shaw's *Widowers' Houses* (1893) depict a society where the state left the poor unprotected against the self-interest of the owners of the means of production and the propertied classes in general. For Ibsen, by contrast, society and the state were no more to be trusted than the oppressors who composed it.

The truculent oracle

Born in the same year as Tolstoy, and dying only four years before him, Ibsen (1828–1906) was a giant in his own country, and like Tolstoy had a vision that spread much wider than the customary concerns of Realism. A painter and poet, as well as a playwright, he was to explore the wilder shores of subjective experience, and develop a form of symbolism that was far removed from Realist literature, his own included. Even so, he always retained a materialist view of Man, which underlay his various excursions into the sphere of poetic imagination. And, unlike Tolstoy, he did not seek to escape the implications of this view by resorting to a religious or non-rational *modus vivendi*.

As with others of his generation, the characters in Ibsen's so-called 'problem plays' of 1877–84 tend to exemplify social phenomena rather than types of personality, despite their careful delineation as individuals. If the economic foundations of their attitudes are less obtrusive than in Zola, they are none the less there. He knew them well enough from his own childhood. His father had run a general store in a small timber port in eastern Norway; and, after initial prosperity, he had run into financial difficulties, like Chekhov's father. Thereafter he became morose and unsociable: characteristics which left their mark on his young son. Ibsen's early literary successes, however, were far removed from social issues. That they turned in this direction was partly due to the influence of Georg Brandes, a Scandinavian equivalent of George Lewes (see pp. 91–3) and Hippolyte Taine (see pp. 128–30), who among much else had helped to spread the influence of Taine and John Stuart Mill in northern Europe. It was he who challenged Ibsen in 1871–2 to address his talents to contemporary problems.

His challenge bore fruit some six years later in *Pillars of Society* (1877), Ibsen's indictment of mercantile greed and dishonesty—more particularly of the large-scale variety that had been familiar enough in France for half a century, but which was relatively new in Norway. The expansion of railways in the 1870s gave this small rural maritime country a taste of the hard-edged competition that Balzac had known forty years earlier. Norwegian society, however, had not yet learnt to accept openly the merciless ethos of the nineteenth-century business world. The mercantile communities of the seaboard towns were too small for businessmen to be able to view their competitors quite so easily as faceless entities, to be demolished like material obstacles, without regard to the human reality that lay behind them. Moreover social conventions still had a strong Lutheran basis, which discouraged naked self-interest from openly admitting its identity. Therefore, although greed and dishonesty played a significant role in Norway's years of modernisation, more effort was made to conceal it than in countries whose society no longer laid claim to strict traditional standards of morality. Self-interest was therefore often compounded with hypocrisy. And, as the title of the play indicated, *Pillars of Society* was as much directed against hypocrisy as against unscrupulous gain.

What Ibsen saw as the self-interest and hypocrisy of Norwegian provincial life came under further attack in *Ghosts* (1881, see Appendix F) and *An Enemy of the People* (1882). In *Ghosts* the suffocating nature of small-town society is symbolised by syphilis (see p. 186), whereas in *An Enemy of the People* it is expressed by the fact that the town's water supply is polluted from the local tanneries. Since the town's prosperity depends on its reputation as a spa, the bulk of its inhabitants are in favour of concealing the matter.

Ibsen's target in this play, however, is much wider than provincial society: it is society as a whole, and the assumptions that underlie western liberal democracy. Dr Stockmann is not only 'an enemy of the people' by virtue of being the discoverer of an inconvenient truth; but the very fact of his training and perception is enough to put him at odds with the ill-informed self-interest of most of the population. Until science and education have transformed society, enlightenment and democracy are bound to be at odds. As Stockmann says,

> The majority *never* has right on its side . . . the stupid people are in an absolutely overwhelming majority all the world over . . . The minority is always in the right . . . the scattered few among us who have absorbed new . . . truths . . . stand . . . so far ahead that the compact majority has not yet been able to come up with them; and there they are fighting for truths that are too newly-born into the world of consciousness to have any considerable number of people on their side as yet.

Nor is truth a static corpus of knowledge that the majority could eventually assimilate in time. Not only are its frontiers always moving, but it is itself undergoing constant change. In Stockmann's words:

> A normally constituted truth lives . . . at most twenty years . . . it is only then that the majority recognises them . . . These 'majority truths' are like last year's cured meat—like rancid tainted ham; and they are the origin of the moral scurvy that is rampant in our communities.

In sum, 'The most dangerous enemy of truth and freedom amongst us is the compact majority—yes, the damned compact liberal majority.' As for the party-politics that produce the compact majorities, 'A party is like a sausage-machine; it mashes up all sorts of heads together into the same mincemeat—fatheads and blockheads.' 'Party programmes strangle every young and vigorous truth'.

That Stockmann is speaking for Ibsen is amply clear from Ibsen's letters; and his remarks are all the more interesting when seen in the context of Ibsen's political development. As a young man of nineteen, Ibsen had responded enthusiastically to the February revolution of 1848 in Paris; and he had subsequently contributed various unsigned articles to a Norwegian radical newspaper. In fact he came very near to having to expiate his radicalism in prison, when the editor was arrested in July 1851. But fortunately for Ibsen, the editor kept a courageous silence on the identity of his contributors, despite a heavy prison sentence. Thereafter Ibsen was to became disillusioned with revolutionary activity. Like Büchner, he had seen fellow radicals imprisoned, with no tangible achievement to show for their labours; and he came increasingly to regard any form of violent change as premature and barren. Education was the only effective change-maker. Moreover, and to a degree that was untypical of most Realists, he adopted an attitude of sceptical aloofness to what he regarded as the pettiness of politics and its continual obligation to compromise with ideals. As he wrote to a friend in 1884, 'I do not believe in the emancipatory power of political measures'. Indeed, until the public were educated, there was every danger that democracy could be as tyrannical as autocracy: the ignorant self-interest of the many swamping the clear-sightedness of the enlightened few. For Ibsen sanity lay in keeping state authority to a minimum. Like John Stuart Mill, on whom Ibsen largely kept a grudging silence, he feared for the truth when it was faced with vested interests and the power of the state.

At the same time, however, Ibsen's castigation of 'the compact liberal majority' must not be mistaken for a condemnation of liberalism as such. Ibsen's target is the assumption that majorities are always right, and that liberal majorities are especially right. His fear was that democracy ran the risk of letting people take liberty for granted; whereas liberty was always at risk even from those who most sincerely professed to defend it. As he said, with Shavian gusto:

> the liberals are the worst enemies of Freedom. Spiritual and intellectual freedom flourish best under absolutism. (1872)
>
> Russia is a splendid country. Think of all the grand oppression they have . . . Only think of the glorious love of liberty it engenders. Russia is one of the few countries in the world where men still love liberty and make sacrifices for it . . . Remember that they possess a writer such as Turgenev (1874)

Theodor Fontane

Ibsen's strongest individuals defy the constraints of society; Fontane's ultimately accept them. The protagonists in *Effi Briest* (1894) recognise, or unconsciously concede, the impossibility of escaping the attitudes engendered by society. And even those who try to escape ultimately capitulate. To some extent this reflects the unexceptional nature of Fontane's characters: they are not of a calibre, or a sufficiently cheerful insouciance, to transcend their environment, like Dr Stockmann, nor do they undergo the bitter experience that teaches Mrs Alving in *Ghosts* or Nora in *A Doll's House* to see beyond the conventional assumptions of their milieu.

The distinction may also reflect, however, Ibsen's and Fontane's differing experience of society and the attitudes they derived from it. Ibsen escaped early in life from the narrow confines of Norwegian provincial life, which he so despised. Once a student in Christiania (Oslo), he never went back to it, except as an occasional visitor; and his subsequent literary attacks on it were mostly composed in the exuberant sunlight and bustle of Rome and Munich. Fontane's life, by contrast, was largely spent in the Prussian locales that provide the setting for most of his novels. He was part of the society he describes; and if he is critical of many of its attitudes, he understood and felt sympathy for those who professed them. His family, though middle-class, had close connections with the Prussian aristocracy, and there was much that he admired in it. Its strongest virtue in his eyes was its sense of commitment to a collective national interest; an attitude that was in marked contrast with the self-interest of many of the more successful members of the bourgeoisie. It was an extension of the military virtues into civilian public life, and it had its limiting provisos. A man might give himself entirely to the service of the state, sacrificing health and leisure; but in return he would expect his estates and family property to be protected and respected. In Fontane's view, the quintessence of this attitude was to be found in Frederick-William I (1713–40), the 'Sergeant King' who sacrificed the remnants of his son's affection in the interests of what he saw as the public good. When the crown prince made an unsuccessful attempt to escape from Potsdam, Frederick-William forced him to witness the execution of the friend who had helped him—his verdict being that 'it is better that he should die than that justice should vanish from the world'. For Fontane, this verdict was 'profoundly moving'; it represented 'the *moral* force on which this land, this equally hateable and lovable Prussia, is based'.

On leaving pharmacology for journalism, Fontane was for a time on the editorial staff of the conservative *Kreuzzeitung* during the crucial decade of German unification. But its 'with God for King and Fatherland' ethos became too much for him; and 1870 found him transferring his talents to the liberal *Vossische Zeitung*—which also had the advantage of a fairly liberal pension scheme. While conceding that 'they are better than their reputation, these much maligned *Junkers*', his instincts rejoiced

> that we still have a non-Prussian Germany. Oberammergau, Munich, Weimar—those are the places that make one happy. Faced with standing-at-attention, fingers to the trouser-seam . . . I get sick. And I am a dyed-in-the-wool Prussian.

While *Effi Briest* displays an Ibsenesque perception of how accepted social attitudes may destroy individual happiness, it also shows how individuals who depart from what society expects of them risk disaster. This is not of itself an endorsement of society's expectations, nor is it necessarily a condemnation of those who transgress them. It is merely a statement of what is likely to happen if they do. This follows from the fact that all members of society are in varying degrees conditioned by society's attitudes. Effi's adultery with Major Crampas ultimately results in death for both of them; not because Effi's husband desires it, but because his training and milieu make him feel duty bound to demand satisfaction of Crampas and live apart from Effi, despite his personal disinclination to do either. Effi and Crampas, for their part, accept their retribution as just. Crampas, dying on the duelling ground, gives a smile of acquiescence, while Effi and her parents feel no bitterness, only sorrow, in the life of solitary seclusion that her husband's course of action forces on her. He, on his side, stoically accepts the lonely middle age that awaits him. The author blames no one; each ultimately behaves as society would have him behave, and if society is implicitly criticised, it is only indirectly.

The most disturbing feature of the book is its suggestion that even the most enlightened critic of society's attitudes cannot in the last analysis cut loose from them. Effi's husband, Innstetten, and his close friend, Wüllersdorf, share the author's awareness of the unhappiness that will almost certainly result from a strict observance of society's prescriptions in this case. They are able to envisage alternative courses of action. Indeed Innstetten's personal inclination is to forgive Effi; and Wüllersdorf points out that since only the four of them know what she has done, to forgive and forget would entail no affront to society's expectations. Yet Innstetten feels compelled to reject this congenial solution. As he explains to Wüllersdorf, even

> if you . . . are discretion itself towards others, . . . *you* know about it and . . . every word that you hear me exchange with my wife will be checked by you, whether you want to or not, and if my wife talks about being faithful or, as women do, sits in judgement on another woman, then I shan't know where to look.

Wüllersdorf's reply is equally revelatory, coming, as it does, from the most intelligent and perceptive character in the book. 'It's terrifying to think that you are right, but you *are* right . . . our own cult of honour . . . is idolatry. But we must submit to it, as long as the idol stands.' It is not a mere question of duty: the individual's interior attitudes and requisites for peace of mind have already been determined.

Ibsen would have dismissed this conclusion as a tame capitulation—inescapable, perhaps, for the bulk of men who know no better, but unworthy of a perceptive man like Wüllersdorf who recognises the cult of honour as 'idolatry'. As Ibsen said in 1872: 'my own conviction is that the strongest man is he who stands most alone': an assertion that he repeated ten years later as the closing line to *An Enemy of the People*.

16 Hope and Despair

Compared with their predecessors, the later Realists impart a somewhat comfortless air. Zola, who was more optimistic than most, speaks of 'the profound melancholy that lies at the end of all philosophy' (*La Terre*). Chekhov likewise concluded, in the words of one of his characters, that 'thoughts of the transitoriness of life, its lack of meaning and aim, of the inevitability of death' are 'the highest and final stage in the realm of thought' (*Lights*, 1888). Even Fontane, with all his affection for humanity and the living world, has Wüllersdorf say of Major Crampas in *Effi Briest* 'He's fond of life and at the same time indifferent to it. He takes everything that comes, while realising that it's not worth much'. Ibsen's pessimism is characteristically more forthright: 'The development of the human race took the wrong turn from the start'. And, bristling like a furious owl, he would conclude that it would have been better for mankind if the Ark had been torpedoed.

To some extent, this reflected the greater distance of these writers from what earlier generations had regarded as the secular liberation (see p. 55). Viewed with the jaundiced eyes of the 1880s, Secular Man did not seem significantly happier than his more credulous antecedents, and many suspected that he was less so. The pursuit and contemplation of 'truth', scientific or otherwise, did not of itself guarantee happiness, except perhaps for the dedicated scientist and scholar. Similarly the material promise of the Industrial Revolution, although surpassing all expectation in its quantity and extent, had been uneven in its growth and incidence. Production and living standards were higher at the end of the century than anyone would have dared to predict at the beginning. Yet the so-called 'Great Depression' (see pp. 140–6) had raised fears in the older industrial powers that the limitless possibilities that had seemed to shine in earlier decades were either illusory or would be largely usurped by the new industrial giants of America and Germany. And even those who remained confident that production would wax ever larger and brighter, had occasionally to admit that the better nourished, better educated urban masses of the *fin de siècle* were not necessarily a better advertisement for humanity than the ignorant peasants of earlier centuries. Human nature seemed to be much as it had always been, while the incentives to altruism had arguably grown less; with the removal of rewards in the hereafter, and the growing conviction that self-interest was the key to success. Even the great benefactors of society, the founders of philanthropic trusts, whose millions promoted art, science and learning, had initially made their pile in the naked cut-and-thrust of the business world. For every hospital bed or university scholarship there was someone who had earlier been driven to the wall or forced to live on a lower level of expectation: or so it seemed to the more *désabusé* surveyors of what the nineteenth century had achieved.

Social Darwinism

This disillusionment proceeded not only from the fading of earlier, overoptimistic hopes, but also from the current vogue of social Darwinism. Ambivalent in the emotions it aroused, social Darwinism seemed to promise progress on the one hand, but at the price of the gospel virtues on the other. Both Marx and Darwin had emphasised the element of struggle in human development. But unlike Marx, Darwin did not predict a time when the struggle would ultimately cease; it was so basic to the functioning of nature that life was inconceivable without it. Life in all its forms was a continuing process of elimination, a perpetual conflict in which the weakest would always be pushed under. Chekhov, for all his admiration for Darwin (see p. 127), was appalled at the implications of his work.

Herbert Spencer (1820–1903) was the most remarkable of the thinkers who attempted to apply Darwinian principles to human society. His *Social Statics* (1850), *Principles of Psychology* (1853–5) and *Principles of Biology* (1864) were in fact just part of a much larger edifice, seeking to present a comprehensive view of the universe, with formulas that were applicable at all levels of existence: from basic molecular theory to the workings of the most complex civilised societies. An intimate friend of George Eliot and George Lewes (see pp. 91–2), Spencer resembled Lewes in having an assimilative mind and a readiness to perceive links and common factors. His work in some respects pre-dated Darwin in its evolutionary vision of life; and Darwin readily acknowledged Spencer as a man whose thinking was travelling on a parallel course to his own.

With a remorseless logic, Spencer condemned what he called 'the artificial preservation of those least able to take care of themselves', be they individuals or business enterprises. No good could come of protecting people against their own ignorance or weakness.

> Partly by weeding out those of lowest development and partly by subjecting those who remain to the never-ceasing discipline of experience, nature secures the growth of a race who shall both understand the conditions of existence and be able to act up to them . . . If to be ignorant were as safe as to be wise, no-one would become wise.

Spencer nevertheless still saw a role for the protective forces of the law and the medical profession, since the potential victims of malefactors, or disease and injury, were not necessarily the weaker members of the community: a bullet or an outbreak of cholera could wipe out a Pasteur or a Bismarck as swiftly and irrevocably as it could rid society of its defectives and degenerates. Darwin, however, saw problems even here:

> there is reason to believe that vaccination has preserved thousands who from a weak constitution would formerly have succumbed to small-pox. Thus the weak members of civilised societies propagate their kind. No-one who has attended to the breeding of domestic animals will doubt that this must be highly injurious to the race of man (*The Descent of Man*, 1871).

An increasing suspicion that progress and philanthropy were fundamentally incompatible was a major source of Ibsen's pessimism, and that of many of his contemporaries. As Dr Rank concludes, in *A Doll's House* (1879): 'sentiment is turning society into a sick-home', in which the feeble shall inherit the earth. And yet, threatened as Rank is by congenital syphilis, he knows that his own survival is dependent on this sentiment. Darwin, for his part, attempted to resolve the dilemma by saying that although philanthropy could have specific deleterious consequences for humanity, it was nevertheless a form of co-operative self-preservation that was part of Man's secret of success.

The problem, as always, was drawing the line is specific cases; and once again the main hope seemed to lie with science and education.

Science
Zola put it at its most absolute in Dr Pascal's famous lines:

> I believe that the future of humanity lies in the progress of reason through science . . . I believe that the sum of [acquired] truths, always growing, will ultimately give Man an incalculable power and security . . . I believe in the final triumph of life.

Or again, as Bertheroy says in Zola's *Paris* (1897–8):

> science alone is revolutionary, the only force which, high above the puny events of politics and the empty bustle of factions and ambitious men, is working for the humanity of the future and is preparing truth, justice and peace!

Even so, Zola was not insensitive to what neo-Christian intellectuals, misquoting Brunetière, called 'the bankruptcy of science'. Catholic writers challenged the belief that science of itself could ever improve human nature, and claimed that morals had, if anything, deteriorated in the course of the nineteenth century. Moreover the precepts of science seemed to suggest that self-interest was the *sine qua non* of progress, thereby directly challenging everything that experience had shown to be most conducive to human happiness. For this, and for other reasons, Zola became increasingly interested in socialist ideas, albeit of a mildly Fabian character, since they appeared to offer a means of protecting the weak, while still linking humanitarian aims with the unimpeded progress of science (see pp. 169–70).

At the same time, Zola continued to find consolation in the more modest potentialities of science. Its direct capacity for improving human nature might be limited; but it could at least improve Man's material milieu. Sheltered by science from the more abrasive pressures of a hostile environment, human nature might more often show its better side, in that the anxieties and *sauve-qui-peut* ethos of a subsistence existence would be less in evidence.

Gerhart Hauptmann saw salvation in patient observation. Taking the Zurich psychiatric clinics as his model, he believed that it was the duty of the writer and the sociologist to observe society, and establish criteria of healthy normality, against which the deficiencies of society could be measured. He regarded the incursion of industry into rural society as a traumatic experience, creating psychological disturbances in society that only knowledge and patience could cure. He hated industrialisation, while recognising its necessity and inevitability. He saw the invasion of the countryside by industry as a perversion of rural life, several of his early works portraying the advent of the railway as a harbinger of misery, like the ravens which the Vikings released from their ships to ascertain where land lay—and whose dark approaching shapes were recognised by the invaded peoples as the vanguard of death and destruction.

Chekhov's faith in science and education was more self-effacing than Zola's, but none the less real. It stemmed partly from professional training and conviction, partly from the progressive elimination of other sources of hope. In his early manhood in the 1880s he had felt drawn to Tolstoyan idealism: not in its specifically religious form, but rather on account of its respect for values that experience had shown to be fundamental to human happiness. He also shared its distrust of untried intellectual solutions, as well as feeling some sympathy for its principle of non-resistance. His encounter, however, with the appalling life of the convict settlement on Sakhalin (see pp. 135–6) destroyed this sympathy. Chain gangs, floggings and corruption among the prison staff patently brutalised both convicts and warders, leading Chekhov to conclude that non-resistance would merely perpetuate this brutalisation, without sublimating the suffering. As he wrote in March 1894,

Tolstoy's philosophy . . . took possession of me for six or seven years . . . Now something in me protests, reason and justice tell me that in electricity and steam there is more humanity than in chastity and vegetarianism.

Education

Like virtually every Realist who ever wrote, Chekhov believed that 'the mother of all evil is gross ignorance'. The problem was how to dispel it, since this ignorance 'is equally characteristic of all our parties and movements' (1888). Moreover, until Russia had representative institutions at a national level, there was little that liberal political activity could do. He participated energetically in the improving activities of the *zemstvo* at local level (see p. 135), and was active in providing schools (see p. 154). But this limited progress to the slow gradual pace of personal example.

The intellectuals and other spokesmen of reform inspired no more confidence in him than the political parties. As he wrote in 1899, 'I don't believe in our intelligentsia. It is . . . false . . . lazy'. Professor Serebryakov in *Uncle Vanya* is the archetype of the parasitical intellectual who is able to live on the labour of other people because, in their innocence and admiration, his benefactors imagine that they are serving science and humanity in providing for his material wants. As in George Eliot's Casaubon (see p. 179), the reader detects the element of self-loathing which every successful writer of conscience feels when he compares his own congenial lot with the labours of those ordinary mortals whose admiration gives him a living. Chekhov not only distrusted the element of pose involved in literary and other forms of intellectual work, but he feared its propensity for introspection, resulting from its lack of daily contact with the everyday world of ordinary people. The same was true of the leisure of the liberal gentry. As Ivanov laments, 'I, a healthy, strong man, have somehow got transformed into a sort of Hamlet or Manfred, or one of those "superfluous" people, the devil knows which ! . . . to me, it's a disgrace!' The answer is to 'build your . . . life according to an ordinary pattern . . . don't go fighting windmills . . . do your small job, the job God gave you . . . It's more human and honest and healthy.' And, as the engineer concludes in *Lights* (1888), 'It would be all right if, with our pessimism, we went to live in a cave, or made haste to die, but as it is, we live, feel, love women, bring up children, construct railways.'

Work and other people are what make life bearable. The theme runs like a litany through all the later plays. 'We must work . . . The reason we feel depressed and take such a gloomy view of life is that we've never known what it is to make a real effort. We're the children of parents who despised work' (*Three Sisters*). Zola, similarly, believed that hard work gave a semblance of meaning to life—and lessened the time available for debilitating meditation on the human lot: *L'Oeuvre* (1885–6) significantly concludes with the exhortation 'Allons travailler.'

In the final analysis, Chekhov's hopes for humanity rested with the individual: 'I see salvation in individual personalities, scattered here and there all over Russia, whether they are educated men or peasants . . . They are a power that counts' (letter of 1899). Like George Eliot, Chekhov believed in the diffusive influence of individual lives: a faith he enunciated in *Uncle Vanya* (1889–97) and *Three Sisters* (1901). Dr Astrov in *Uncle Vanya* stoically follows his calling of country doctor in a small unappreciative community. Although he knows that whatever he achieves is infinitesimal compared to the enormity of the ignorance, poverty and ill-health that surrounds him, he finds sustenance in the thought that he is contributing something to what may be a better future. 'I'm conscious of the fact . . . that if mankind is happy in a thousand years time, I'll be responsible for it even though only to a very minute extent'. The mechanics of this influence become clear in *Three Sisters*; but they are already implicit in Astrov's assumption that his example and opinions will make some impact, however slight, on those around him. And these in turn will convey them, albeit in diluted or imperfect form, to those with whom they come in contact. The idea is expressed symbolically in the trees that Astrov plants. These will influence the climate and the soil, and make life better for later generations, thereby perpetuating his influence. As the battery commander, Vershinin, wistfully speculates in *Three Sisters*,

> In two or three hundred years, or maybe in a thousand years . . . life will be different. It will be happy. Of course, we shan't be able to enjoy that future life, but all the same, what we're living for now is to create it . . . you might say that's the only happiness we shall ever achieve.

And like Astrov, Vershinin sees individual effort and opinion as the leavening force.

> Obviously, you can't hope to triumph over all the mass of ignorance around you; as your life goes by, you'll have to keep giving in little by little until you get lost in the crowd, in the hundred thousand. Life will swallow you up, but you'll not quite disappear, you'll make some impression on it. After you've gone, perhaps six more people like you will turn up, then twelve, and so on, until in the end most people will have become like you.

His lieutenant, Baron Toozenbach, is less confident.

> After we're dead, people will fly about in balloons . . . the sixth sense will be discovered, and possibly even developed and used, for all I know . . . But I believe life itself will remain the same . . . people will still be sighing and complaining: 'How hard this business of living is!'—and yet they'll still be scared of death . . . not merely in a couple of hundred years' time, but in a million years. Life . . . always goes on the same; it follows its own laws, which don't concern us, which we can't discover anyway.

Dr Astrov is in some ways the sort of doctor that Turgenev's Bazarov might have become—albeit gentler and less abrasive in his opinions and attitudes (see pp. 108–9). Despising the rhetoric and ineffectiveness of political protest, in a country where autocracy reduced such protest to mere gesture, he believes in example and conversation as the instrument of change. Yet, like George Eliot's 'number who lived faithfully a hidden life, and rest in unvisited tombs', Astrov anticipates no particular gratitude from later generations.

> I wondered whether the people who come after us in a hundred years' time, the people for whom we are now blasting a trial . . . would they remember us and speak kindly of us? No . . . I wager they won't! [They will] despise us for having lived in so stupid and tasteless a fashion.

As with Ibsen's Dr Relling, the force of Astrov's observations are the stronger for being uttered by a man who is far from perfect. Weighed down by misunderstanding and the boredom of provincial life, he drinks heavily, and like Relling epitomises truth speaking through the shell of human weakness.

Politics

Zola lived in a country where universal male suffrage theoretically called the tune; he could therefore think in shorter spans of time than Chekhov. Yet he recognised that universal suffrage might be an obstacle, as well as an inducement, to social reform. It was, for example, a patent fact of French politics that until the industrial working class became a majority of the nation—which did not happen until the middle decades of the next century—their needs would continue to be frustrated by the combined interests and electoral strength of the peasantry and the middle classes. If time was ultimately on the side of the industrial workers, it might need pressures of a different sort to make life more tolerable for them in the meantime. Mrs Gaskell in the 1840s implied that public knowledge of industrial conditions would of itself lead to improvement; but Zola in the 1880s and 90s was less sanguine. It was not just a question of his *scepticisme de libre penseur* against Mrs Gaskell's Christian optimism. Conditions had undoubtedly improved, and public awareness had been a helping factor, but experience showed all too clearly that conscience alone would not bring about a juster society.

As with nearly all Realists, however, violent solutions found no brief in any of his novels: despite the gusto with which he portrayed the drama of social violence. In *Germinal*, strikes and violence bring no advantage to the miners—just as in Hauptmann's *The Weavers* (1892), the rebellion merely leads to the death of Hilse, the old weaver, arguably the most sympathetic character in the play. In *Germinal's* closing pages, when Etienne strides off to make contact with the Internationale in Paris, he began to wonder whether violence really helped things on at all . . . what a waste of energy! It was dawning on him that some day legal methods would be much more terrible . . . that would be the big day, when they could legally band together . . . through their unions . . . millions of workers against a few thousand idlers, they would take over power and be the masters.

The fact that Zola was composing *Germinal* in the year the unions became fully legalised in France may or may not have inspired these words; perhaps happily for Zola, he did not foresee the sad story of disunity and indecision that was to prevent the unions being a more effective instrument of pressure.

In any case, Zola's socialism was of a very mild Fabian character; and it is significant that Marxists and anarchists make a poor showing in his novels. *Germinal* reveals extreme socialists of all persuasions only too ready to sacrifice the miners to long-term ends. The anarchist, Souvarine, blows up the mine, killing dozens, while Pluchart, the representative of the Internationale, persuades the miners to engage in a hopeless strike, so that they would exhaust their provident fund and become dependent on the Internationale for finance.

Commitment to life

If there were times when Zola had doubts as to whether socialism and science would ever significantly temper the competitive self-interest that characterised human society, his enthusiasm for life, its enormity and complexity, was there to sustain him. When Jean Macquart, in the concluding pages of *La Terre*, meditates on the cruelty and futility of life, he finds himself unconsciously admiring its inscrutable grandeur:

> it might be that blood and tears were needed to make the world move on. What does our happiness count in the great system of the stars and the sun? . . . Only the earth remains immortal . . . She uses even our crimes and our miseries to make life and more life for her hidden ends.

Similarly, when Macquart is spreading manure in the fields, Zola characteristically describes him as 'breathing it in with a virile delight as if it were the very odour of the earth's coitus.'

If, in Zola's view, an exuberant commitment to life was in the final analysis the only salvation open to humanity, Chekhov, for his part, was more circumspect in his allegiance:

> My holy of holies is the human body, health, intelligence, talent, inspiration, love and the most absolute freedom—freedom from violence and lying, whatever forms they may take (letter of 1889).

As for Hauptmann, what he saw as the inadequacies of social solutions gradually led him to seek an interior answer, his increasing introspection taking him far from the characteristic concerns and preoccupations of Realism.

Ibsen and the necessity of illusion

A temperament like Ibsen's was not of a sort to respond cheerfully to the implications of determinism. His acceptance of determinism as an unpalatable but inescapable fact was at odds with his instinctive admiration for self-assertion and independence of mind, qualities which the poet in him saw as an emanation of free will. This was a dichotomy that George Eliot had learnt to resolve by separating the contenders onto different levels of consciousness: objective and subjective (see pp. 94–5). She was also more fortunate than Ibsen in that a warmer disposition had inclined her to find emotional compensations in the concept that all humanity, past, present and future, were united in one common web of casuality; an idea that offered little comfort to Ibsen, who did not especially relish being linked with the fools and undesirables who, in his opinion, made up the bulk of mankind.

Nor did he find much joy in the particular concepts that gave Zola and Chekhov the courage to keep on hoping. In so far as he found consolation in anything, it was in what he called 'the revolution of the spirit': 'politicians . . . only want individual revolutions, external revolutions, political, etc. But all that is just small change. What matters is the revolution of the spirit'. By this he meant something akin to the interior revolution, proclaimed by Bazarov in Turgenev's *Fathers and Sons* (see pp. 108–9): the revolution that was dependent on education, the revolution that Büchner had likewise proclaimed in the last months of his short life (see pp. 64–5).

Education, however, was a long-term process; and it posed the formidable question that if society itself was corrupt, who were to be the educators? Ibsen's answer, like Chekhov's, was 'the enlightened few' (even if his faith in their diffusive influence was less sustained than Chekhov's). The conclusion of *An Enemy of the People* is a case in point. Stoned and driven from his house by the population, Stockmann announces his intention to devote himself to educating street urchins—boys as yet uncorrupted by the money-making ethos of the town. 'I am going to experiment with curs, just for once; there may be some exceptional heads among them.' To which his son asks, 'And what are we going to do when you have made liberal-minded and high-minded men of us?' 'Then you shall drive all wolves out of the country'.

The exuberance of Stockmann was a far remove from the morose brooding quality that often characterised Ibsen's darker hours of reflection. As he wrote to Brandes in 1871, 'There are times when the whole history of the world seems to me but a mighty shipwreck, and the only sane course is to save oneself. I hope for nothing from isolated reforms. The whole human race is on the wrong tack'. And again, the following year, 'every historical development has been but a lurch from one delusion to another'. Yet, even at Ibsen's most destructive, the individual and the interior revolution remained for him the starting point of hope. A visitor described him at a drinking session in 1883–4:

> Late at night—some where around the sixth glass—Ibsen really started talking . . . wants to wipe everything out . . . mankind must start from the foundations to rebuild the world—and they must begin with the individual!

Yet the problem remained as to what Man was to do in the meantime. Part of the answer—a chilling answer—was given in *The Wild Duck* (1834).

Ibsen's so-called 'problem plays' advance in a dialectical fashion, each presenting a challenging antithesis to the conclusions of its predecessor. *An Enemy of the People* exalted the courageous man of vision who is prepared to defy the ill-informed assumptions of the herd, while *The Wild Duck* would appear to condemn such boldness as destructive and self-defeating; the confidence of the first seems to be swallowed up in the scepticism and tragedy of the second. On the face of it, Gregers is another Stockmann: a man leading a brave campaign against falsehood, a man trying to rescue people from self-delusion and force them to face reality, as he sees it. Gregers likens himself to a clever dog that retrieves wounded duck that are hiding in the muddy depths of a river, and brings them into the clear light of truth and self-realisation. But, as events demonstrate, not everyone can face reality; the blinding light at the surface may be too much for them. The murky river bottom may be the only environment in which they can survive. Gregers destroys the Ekdal family by trying to make them come to terms with the doubtful paternity of their daughter. Imagining that they will be able to embark on a new life based on truth and mutual forgiveness, he is astonished to find that his revelations lead to estrangement and suicide. As their neighbour, Dr Relling, points out, one cannot expect moral magnanimity of a family that has nothing to give. It is all very well 'coming to a workman's cottage to present your "demands of the ideal"; but the people in this home are all insolvent.' It is a moral parallel to Woyzeck's assertion that 'we poor can't afford to have morals': in this case, only the morally strong can sustain ideals. Men can only respond within the limitations of their own personalities. Some have the strength to accept the truth unadorned; others would be destroyed, if forced to do so.

Dr Relling knows Hjalmar Ekdal's limitations. When the reality of these limitations began to dawn on Ekdal himself, Relling sustained his flagging self-confidence by encouraging him in his more harmless illusions. 'If you take away make-believe from the average man, you take away his happiness'. 'All the world is sick, pretty nearly . . . make-believe . . . is the stimulating principal of life'.

Ibsen is also insistent that in the last analysis only the individual can save himself. Nora in *A Doll's House* finds salvation, albeit of a desperate kind, when she defies conventions and family claims, and sets off to 'educate myself'. Gregers seeks to instil the same resolution in the Ekdal family; but coming from without, with no corresponding inner drive, it destroys instead of saving. As Ibsen himself wrote in his preliminary notes for the play, 'Liberation consists in securing for individuals the right to free themselves, each according to his particular need.'

The long-term implications for humanity are therefore bleak. *An Enemy of the People* offered hope in the shape of Stockmann's open-minded urchins, who, under his tutorship, would grow into adults who would leaven the lump of the society they entered. *The Wild Duck*, on the other hand, suggests that the leaven will not work unless the dough is already of a quality and a disposition to rise, which is only true of a minority of men. How then can the educator educate, without destroying? Must he be content, like Relling, to sustain illusions? The conclusion would seem to be that the bulk of humanity is caught in the vicious circle of its own limitations, which the sharp light of Truth cannot enter without withering its happiness and will to live.

The final blow that drives home the ineluctability of human limitations is Gregers's reaction to the tragedy he has caused. Despite his shock, he has learnt nothing from it. When Ibsen, like George Eliot, shows Ekdal and his wife being drawn closer together in their grief at the death of their daughter, Gregers can only exclaim 'Hedwig has not died in vain. You saw how his grief called out the best that was in him'. Relling's rejoinder might well chill the hearts of those who find comfort in George Eliot.

> In eight or nine months, little Hedwig will be no more to him than a beautiful theme to declaim on . . . you will see him wallowing in emotional fits of self-admiration and self-compassion.

Life before death?
Despite everything, even the grimmest-eyed Realists preferred life to death. Compared to Romanticism, Realism had few suicides among its leaders. They admittedly had the advantage of facing life with fewer illusions. But their will to live was ultimately sustained by three principal factors.

Like most thinking people, they were impelled by a certain curiosity as to what would happen. Life might be a bad play, but they stayed to the end, largely out of curiosity. Life likewise retained a certain attractiveness when they remembered that they had an eternity of death before them. There were aeons of time in which to be dead, just as there had been millions of years in which they had been unborn; a few brief decades of life, however unhappy, were more bearable when recognised as the only respite from an eternity of nothingness.

This, however, was to view the matter merely from the perspective of personal consciousness. There remained the great causal web of existing matter, which inclined most Realists to a feeling of belonging and responsibility to humanity as a whole. One's own death, through suicide or normal causes, was not the end of things; not did it solve anything, other than terminate one's own unhappiness. It left it to others to clear up the mess, literally as well as metaphorically, and savoured too much of selfishness.

Looking to the collective future, Realists continued to burn incense before the twin deities of science and education, in the expectation that these forces would gradually improve the quality of life: for some at least, if not for all. This was a goal that seemed worth living for. And if, none the less, there were times when the future of humanity did not seem worth this effort—given the ignoble selfish nature of most men—the Realist, like all of us, could take a paradoxical satisfaction in comparing his own shortcomings with the best of men around him. There were such a reassuring number of people who were better and less egotistical than himself—to say nothing of those in the future, as yet unborn—that his own efforts on humanity's behalf no longer seemed misplaced; they merely seemed inadequate.

Nor was the unhappiest of lives entirely devoid of precious moments. As Wüllersdorf tells Innstetten in *Effi Briest*:

> The best thing is to hold the fort until you drop. But first of all, to get as much as you can out of the small things, the very small things of life, and to have an eye for violets in bloom or the Luise Monument decked out with flowers or little girls skipping in long lace-up boots. Or . . . go into the Friedenskirche where Kaiser Friedrich is buried . . . And while you're standing there, just think what *his* life was like, and if that doesn't reassure you, then you're beyond all help.

A The Determinist Case

As indicated in Chapter 1, most nineteenth-century determinists understood 'heredity' and 'environment' as including everything that made a man what he was. Conception was generally recognised as the dividing line between the respective dominions of these two groups of factors, although meticulous demarcation experts still tussled over borderland issues such as congenital syphilis and the other hazards that the unsuspecting foetus could encounter during gestation.

Nineteenth-century determinism was largely based on the assumption that matter could neither be created nor destroyed: an assumption that was implicit, if not always stated. No phenomenon, be it a person, a thought or an event, could have an autonomous existence that owed nothing to its antecedents and surroundings. Everything was the outcome of the interaction of pre-existing factors, which were themselves the product of earlier factors: each object or occurrence was a link in a mesh of causal chains, stretching back to 'the beginning of things' (in a world still joyously uncomplicated by Einstein). The word 'chance' had no place in this scheme of existence, except to designate something that was unexpected by the participants or observers of a particular situation. Philosophical text-books were rich in illustrative examples of why 'chance' should be banished from academic speech: the many written by Scottish professors showing an understandable predilection for unhappy incidents involving falling roof slates—the influence of environment being nowhere more evident than in a philosopher's choice of illustration. (These would demonstrate how the lethal impact of a falling slate on a passer-by was the nodal point of many causal chains; and they would similarly explain how in principle an omniscient being could trace back each chain to the dim beginnings of existence.)

The contemplation of such examples confirmed determinists in the sobering if familiar view that all things—acts, thoughts and states of being—were shaped by the interplay of their antecedents and surroundings and could not be otherwise than what they were. For things to be different, there would need to be extraneous, formative influences that were not part of the sum total of existing matter; it would require autonomous 'spiritual' elements that existed independently of the material world. On such an analysis, only the believer in supernatural forces, such as God and the non-corporeal soul, could envisage a logical alternative to determinism.

Between determinists and their opponents, a great deal of misunderstanding surrounded the phrase, 'free will'. Most determinists saw the individual as having a specific identity, and recognised that he made active choices between alternative courses of action. Yet, in conceding this, they stressed that his identity and predilections were themselves the product of inherited characteristics, upbringing and surrounding pressures, past and present. Moreover the choices open to him were likewise dependent on circumstances that lay beyond his power to control. The chooser might be 'free' to follow his own inclinations, but fundamentally his inclinations were not of his own choosing. Even if he sought to assert his freedom by opting for the alternative he liked less, that too would be a product of his prevailing state of mind—and this in reality would be the only alternative open to him. On this showing, the phrase 'free will' seemed to determinists to be a misnomer.

And yet they were faced with the singular fact that there were atheists and materialists who rejected determinism and professed their faith in free will. In some cases, this attitude sprang from misconceptions concerning determinist claims. They erroneously supposed that there was no place for the unexpected in a determinist view of human behaviour, and accused determinists of naïvely imagining that prediction lay within their grasp. In fact determinists were at pains to point out that mankind would always lack sufficient data to make prediction a reality, except in simple cases.

Other critics who attacked them belonged to what would now be called the trolley-bus school of thought. They represented an articulate expression of what a large section of the thinking public still believes today. Upholding the golden mean of moderation, they eschewed the extremes of determinism and free will: represented in the twentieth-century garage of concepts by the tram and the motor bus. They denied that Man was a tram, perpetually condemned to run along the rails of heredity and environment. They would have equally denied, however, that Man has the freedom of movement of the motor bus, able to go where it likes, as long as it is fed with petrol and succeeds in avoiding sizeable obstacles. For them, the true analogy of Man would have been the trolley bus, a vehicle that cannot stray further than the length of its trolley masts from the wires of heredity and environment, and yet enjoying a considerable latitude of movement.

Attractive though this qualified view might be, it presented the same problem as the more absolute type of free-will concept: it presupposed a degree of autonomy that has to be accounted for. Like the driver of the trolley bus, the particular will is an entity with origins; it cannot materialise out of nothing. To do so would require either self-generation or supernatural intervention: possibilities that were both discounted by the materialist opponents of determinism. Rejecting both God and the non-corporeal soul, they confined the will's existence to the brief span between conception and death—and yet still claimed for it an autonomy that was only partially conditioned by heredity and environment. How this could be, they failed to make clear.

In practice, however, they and other nineteenth-century voluntarists largely based their faith on subjective experience. As Dr Johnson had said before them, 'Sir, we *know* our will is free, and there's an end on't'. But, as Flaubert and other Realists discovered (see p. 67), once the intellect accepted determinism, subjective experience tended increasingly to follow suit. The individual who analysed his own decisions became progressively aware of his identity as an accumulation of needs and attitudes, constantly if imperceptibly modified by its successive encounters with the outside world.

His sense of personal responsibility nevertheless remained a reality on the level of subjective experience; and George Eliot, among others, was at pains to show how determinism and a concept of morality could be reconciled (see pp. 94—7). It was arguable, moreover, that the determinist was intellectually more disposed to regard the attitudes and shortcomings of others with understanding and sympathy; even if his generosity did not always keep pace with his intellect. He was also more compellingly aware that men were dependent on each other for such improvement as they could achieve; each was part of the other's environment. Admittedly the individual's readiness to respond to others' needs was itself a determined response—or so the logic of determinism would demand. But helping others could still bring him satisfaction and self-fulfilment on the level of subjectivity; and this too was an issue that George Eliot considered closely (see pp. 94–7).

It followed that determinists also had a reply to the many critics who rejected determinism on the grounds that it impoverished the quality of life by eliminating the ennobling functions of choice and responsibility. It goes without saying that objections of this sort were not themselves arguments; one might as well deny the proposition that old men grow feeble, on the grounds that it affronts human dignity. Yet there remained in these objections, based on human self-esteem, an assumption that many determinists wished to challenge, notably George Eliot. For her, life was positively enriched by the web of causality that linked all men: the dead, the living and the yet-unborn (see pp. 96–7). And, in her view, what seemed lost on the level of objective reality, 'responsible choice' and the like, was fully retained on the level of subjective experience (see pp. 94–7).

Not all determinists, however, were so easily reconciled to the implications of their professed beliefs. Many took a more sombre view of its consequences for human self-respect; and writers such as Büchner, Flaubert and Ibsen accepted the voluntarists' verdict that determinism emptied life of meaning. Yet they were equally insistent that to deny determinism was no solution. For them, Man's only claim to some surviving shred of dignity was to face up to the unpalatable truths of life, with stoicism and courage.

B *Tristram Shandy*, Determinism and Prediction

Among much else, *The Life and Opinions of Tristram Shandy* (1759–67) was an exuberant monument to the anarchic possibilities of determinism. Although many of the architects of determinist thought had refrained from suggesting that life had a specific purpose, they had nevertheless tacitly assumed that it had a certain unity of direction. Calvinism had envisaged a divine plan, as indeed did many of the Deists. Even the materialists, such as Hobbes, had seen the human struggle as having discernible and comprehensible characteristics: if unedifying, it at least conformed to rational expectation. Similarly the evolutionists of the late eighteenth and early nineteenth centuries saw life evolving in what seemed to them a progressive and desirable direction (see pp. 32–5). Sterne, however, saw determinism as rich in the unexpected.

> Pray, Sir, in all the reading which you have ever read, did you ever read such a book as Locke's Essay upon the Human Understanding? . . . It is a history-book, Sir, . . . of what passes in a man's own mind . . .

Sterne had learned from Locke, among much else, that the mind at times may associate sense impressions that have no rational connection, other than a coincidental link in time or circumstance. And Locke had notably instanced a dancer who could never perform well except in the presence of an old trunk that happened to be in the room where he first learned to dance. Associations of this kind are the stuff of *Tristram Shandy*. Each character lives in his own world of accumulated associations, with the result that each responds differently to the same words or happenings. Uncle Toby lives in a world dominated by his interest in military fortifications; Walter Shandy's reactions are conditioned by his reading; and the others all respond to given situations in such a variety of ways that only an omniscient being could predict them. The reader, too, shares in this diversity of mind, so that the author is at continual pains to assure himself that the reader has taken his statements in the sense he intended them.

> By the word *Nose* . . . and in every part of my work, where the word *Nose* occurs—I declare, by that word, I mean a Nose, and nothing more, or less.

The book is a devastating reminder that an awareness of determinism solves nothing. Without an omniscience of all things past, the future is as inscrutable as ever—and the past and the present equally beyond our comprehension.

C Eliot's Moral Dialectic

In the view of Bernard Paris (*Experiments in Life*), Eliot saw moral development as a three-staged affair, akin to a dialectic. The initial primitive stage was one of self-centredness, in which the individual saw life as revolving around his own needs and problems: as in the case of Rosamond Vincy in *Middlemarch*, whose perceptions go no further than her own interests and inclinations. Lacking the imagination and intelligence to see beyond the conventional material values of her socially-aspirant mother and of her genteel school upbringing, she remains confined to this initial stage, unable to comprehend or sympathise with the difficulties and concerns of her husband, the talented doctor, Lydgate. Egoism, of a subtler kind, underlies the attitudes of Dorothea Brook, as she appears at the beginning of the novel. Like so many of the principal figures in Realist literature—Julien Sorel, Emma Bovary, Frédéric Moreau, and all the other spiritual descendants of Don Quixote—she is the victim of the discrepancy between the high expectations that her reading has aroused, and the prosaic realities of the milieu in which she finds herself. A strong determination and a deep sensibility combine to make her something of a religious militant; yet Middlemarch does not seem to her to offer the scope for the sort of high-purposed activity that she craves. Seeking spiritual and intellectual enrichment, she marries a local ecclesiastic with scholarly pretensions and a comfortable income, whom she mistakenly assumes to be a man of academic distinction. While her aims are high-minded, Eliot indicates that they are fundamentally self-centred, since, although she may not be aware of it, self-fulfilment is her prime objective.

The second stage of Eliot's moral dialectic is characterised by growing self-criticism and an increased awareness of the needs of others: a development that is often the product of a deeply felt emotional experience, be it suffering, pity or love. Dorothea is drawn out of her spiritual egoism by pity for her husband—despite the exasperated resentment he frequently arouses in her. She sees the worthlessness of his academic undertaking, and realises that he himself has secret doubts that make him inwardly miserable. This concern in fact is her first deep experience of feeling genuine selfless compassion: selfless, in that it offers no hope of reward in the shape of intellectual enrichment.

Love, too, can be a decisive catalyst, as when Fred Vincy is inspired by Mary Garth to be less self-centred. But whatever the initiatory impulse, this second stage runs the risk of a new and different danger: that of self-depreciation and despair. Fred Vincy is periodically overcome by a numbing sense of his own unworthiness, when he contemplates the moral strength of Mary Garth. And Dorothea, ashamed of her wealth as a well-provided widow, embarks on a life of systematic self-denial, which brings little consolation to herself and only limited benefit to those she seeks to help; mainly because it is a self-appointed discipline, rather than a response to other's needs.

Salvation, when it comes, is largely the outcome of a closer fellow feeling with those around her: pity and love both playing a vital role in establishing this relationship. This in fact represents the third and final stage of Eliot's dialectic, a reconciliation between the preceding stages, but in which the individual recognises that, despite his limitations, he has something to offer to other people. In Fred Vincy's case, the recognition of his love creates a new self-respect, shorn of egotistical vanity. With Dorothea, the transition is more complex. Will Ladislaw's love for her is a primary factor; but it is also influenced by her courageous attempts to rescue the Lydgates' marriage, attempts which both teach her the virtues of practical sympathy and make her aware of the limitations of high-minded idealism when it is divorced from direct contact with others' problems. Her marriage to Will Ladislaw, on the other hand, enables her to reconcile the subjective demands of her nature with the objective demands of the world around her. As a political reformer's wife, she can both fill a useful role in society and achieve interior fulfilment through her love for her husband.

The ultimate lesson is that no-one can effectively help others, if he does it to the exclusion of his own subjective needs. To be of service, one must learn to receive as well as to give. Felix Holt is a case in point. In living for others, he has neglected his own emotional needs. He is determined to avoid the kind of fate that befalls Lydgate in *Middlemarch*.

> I'll never look back and say, 'I had a fine purpose once—I meant to keep my hands clean, and my soul upright, and to look truth in the face; but pray excuse me, I have a wife and children . . .'

It is Esther Lyon who enables him to reconcile living for others and personal self-fulfilment: '[she] made a man's passion for her rush in one current with all the great aims of his life'.

What is sobering, however, about these successful examples of moral development is their dependence on extraneous factors, especially the influence of other people. Even such a morally strong character as Mary Garth is very much the product of circumstance. Unlike the other major characters in the book, she has already largely traversed the first two stages of Eliot's moral dialectic before the novel opens. She has the advantage of the inherited characteristics and family influence of her father, while her somewhat plain features and limited financial resources have reconciled her to a fairly modest expectation from life. Even so,

> Her shrewdness had a streak of satiric bitterness continually renewed and never carried utterly out of sight, except by a strong current of gratitude towards those who, instead of telling her that she ought to be contented, did something to make her so . . .

What eventually enables her to achieve fulfilment is the realisation of her hopes in Fred Vincy.

The prospect is clearly much less hopeful for those who are less fortunate in their emotional encounters, such as Lydgate, or fail to have any at all. Even the abject Bulstrode eventually reaches a certain moral equilibrium through the healing sympathy of his wife; although disgrace and suffering are arguably the principal catalyst in his development. But Eliot does not pretend that there is hope for everyone. Unlike Mrs Gaskell, her determinism is not tempered by ultimate faith in God's mercy; things are what they are. And in so far as she hoped that the examples of moral development in her novels might succeed in inspiring some of her readers to take stock of themselves, this too she recognises as part of a predetermined pattern, as ineluctable and unpredictable in its incidence as everything else in the world.

D Zola, Heredity and Environment— Gervaise and her sons

Zola's easy-going manipulation of the hereditary factors in the Rougon-Macquart series is exemplified by his treatment of Gervaise and her sons. She is classified in the 1878 genealogy as taking after her hard-working mother; and much of *L'Assommoir* (1876–7) is consistent with this. Yet in the second genealogy of 1893, she is classified as '*élection du père*', and a great deal is made of the alcoholism of both her father and grandfather. This scarcely accords with the text of the novel itself. Not only was Gervaise careful during most of her life not to acquire a taste for drink; but when she finally succumbs, it is long after her husband has brought ruin on the family. He, for his part, only took to drink when an accident deprived him of work, albeit temporarily, and undermined his self-respect. In both cases, their misfortune is precipitated by environmental factors; and it is the environmental factor of jealous neighbours which speeds their decline. In so far as Gervaise is the victim of heredity, it is largely her tolerant easy-going nature, which prevents her being sufficiently firm with her husband when he starts slipping into self-indulgent habits.

The interrelation of heredity and environment in her destiny is perhaps most clearly stated at the beginning of the novel:

> she had let herself be pushed into things because she didn't dare hurt someone's feelings. Her one hope now was to live among decent people . . . She thought of herself as a coin flipped into the air to come up heads or tails, according to the hazards of landing on a rough pavement.

Although her son, Jacques, the homicidal engine-driver in *La Bête Humaine*, is perhaps the one principal figure in the series whose career clearly fulfils Zola's assertions concerning heredity, it is significant that he was only an afterthought in Zola's plan. He is completely absent from *L'Assommoir*; and according to the first genealogy of 1878 Zola originally intended Etienne Lantier, the future hero of *Germinal* (1885), to embody the hereditary nemesis that haunts the Macquart family. He is classified there as '*Election de la mère* . . . *Hérédité de l'ivrognerie se tournant en folie homicide. Etat de crime.*' When it came to writing *Germinal*, however, Etienne's development took a different course, despite flickering glimpses of Zola's original concept; and Zola subsequently felt obliged to transfer his homicidal tendencies to a newly created elder brother, a *frater ex machina*, Jacques Lantier, who was to be the subject of *La Bête Humaine* (1889–90). In the 1893 genealogy, Etienne merely becomes '*mélange dissémination*', with no mention of hereditary alcoholism, or homicidal and criminal tendencies. Etienne's killing of his rival at the end of

Germinal might seem to vindicate Zola's initial description of him; but it happens as the result of extreme provocation, and is not central to his general development. Even so, Zola's sense of obligation to his original plan betrays itself in *Germinal*'s occasional awkward asides on Etienne's violent temper, in which the author pays alimony to his initial concept.

E Zola and the Manual Classes

Zola boldly asserted in his preface to *L'Assommoir* (1877) that it was 'the first novel about the people that does not lie, that has the smell of the people'. This was something of a snub to other authors, including the Goncourts, who had already attempted to write working-class novels; but it perhaps partly reflected the resentment of a man who had known short commons for those who had not. But, while the tenement life of *L'Assommoir* was familiar enough to Zola, the preparation of *Germinal* was a different matter; and Zola could here claim no more knowledge than the Goncourts of the mining conditions he wanted to portray. He therefore paid a brief visit to a mining area near the Belgian border, Valenciennes; and as he was later to remark, 'A fortnight is usually enough for me; I prefer a short striking impression'. This might seem a cynical refutation of all the principles of clinical observation that Zola professed. But, as a well-known foreign ocrrespondent was to claim sixty years later, to write well about a place arguably requires either a fortnight or at least six months—anything in between is useless: initial impressions are lost, and the additional information one gains merely poses problems without there being sufficient time to find the answers. The visit, though brief, was busy, as was reflected in his copious notes. It was also preceded by a considerable amount of preparatory reading, of a technical and topographical nature. In much the same way, the composition of *La Terre* (1887) involved a brief week of rapid note-taking in La Beauce.

Germinal's details of wages and working conditions in the mines are reasonably accurate; and although Zola deliberately dwelled on what was sensational and exceptional, his picture of the hazards and miseries of working underground accorded with what was technically possible, if not historically typical. His main departures from fact lay in his account and explanation of the vagaries of the international economy in the later sixties (see pp. 145–6): misrepresentations that he compounded in *La Terre*, where factual accuracy was much more frequently sacrificed to symbolism and dramatic effect.

Even so, both novels remain powerful assertions of how environment moulds men.

> The flat fertile lands of La Beauce, easy to plough but demanding ceaseless effort, have made its men reserved and reflective, capable of passion only for the earth.

Respect and land tenure are synonymous. Old Fouan's decline in *La Terre* dates from the moment he divides his land among his children; and significantly his last energies are spent in a pathetic scheme to lay claim to a plot of one and a half acres: a scheme which significantly restores some of the respect that he had relinquished with his land.

Zola also shows how land tenure profoundly affected married life and family size. The splitting-up of farms among heirs, in accordance with the Revolutionary and Napoleonic inheritance laws, was a strong inducement to family limitation. And in *La Terre* and *Germinal* Zola demonstrates how the attitudes of the agricultural and industrial classes to birth control differed fundamentally, on account of this factor. While in every family an extra child meant an extra mouth to feed, the industrial worker could at least look forward to sending his children out to work at the age of eleven or so. And until they got married and moved out of the household, they were a source of income. As Maheude remarks in *Germinal*, concerning her seven children: 'you didn't give it a thought and then they just came along naturally. But when they grew up, they brought in money and kept the home going.' For the land-holding peasant, however, the situation was markedly different, in that although more children meant a larger number of breadwinners, they were working the family land; and the bread they won came from their own family resources, not from an alien employer. Surplus children could admittedly be sent elsewhere to work as wage labourers; and their income could be used to augment the family holding. But marriage would terminate this contribution; and yet they would still be entitled to an equal share of the family land when their parents died or became too old to work it. With the passing of each generation, farms became smaller and more numerous, thereby putting the peasant under strong pressure to keep his family small, if his children's holdings were to be economically viable. Consequently the second half of the century saw a dramatic decline in the peasant birth rate—especially in regions where Church influence was weak. Clergy and patriotic Nationalists alike shook their heads as they compared this situation with the proliferation of the peasant in Germany, where the inheritance laws were less egalitarian and the influence of the churches stronger. Available evidence indicates that peasant birth control in France mainly took the form of interrupted intercourse: what the Dutch peasantry called 'leaving church before the singing'. As Buteau says of himself in *La Terre*, he 'ploughed hard without sowing seed'; and, symptomatically, when his wife and his cow are both about to give birth, it is the vet, not the doctor, who is sent for.

When it comes to politics, Zola's peasants have much in common with George Eliot's in *Middlemarch*. The villagers of Frick (see p. 88) would certainly have sympathised with Old Fouan when he says:

> Take this universal suffrage, it doesn't put any meat in the stew, does it? The land-tax pulls us down and they're always taking our children for wars. And, as for their revolutions, they can keep them, six of one and half a dozen of the other, and still the peasant stays a peasant.

Yet Napoleon III could be relied on to protect the tax-paying peasant against the architects of expensive schemes of social reform; and Zola, once again, shows the marked difference in attitude between the peasants in *La Terre*, who are favourably disposed towards the Emperor, and the miners in *Germinal* who would have preferred a government with more of a social conscience.

F Ibsen, the Individual and Environment
Ghosts and *A Doll's House*

Although heredity and congenital syphilis hang like a Greek curse over Oswald Alving in *Ghosts* (1881), the play is fundamentally concerned with environment and, more particularly, the debilitating grip of society on the individual. Pastor Manders and Oswald's mother are shown in their very different ways as products of a narrow, repressive community where conventional piety masks the less savoury aspects of a Norwegian seaport; indeed it is the deadening chill of this society that has driven Oswald's father to a dissolute life, with terrible consequences for Oswald. In strict physiological terms, congenital syphilis is not an inherited disease, but a disease contracted during gestation from the mother's infected womb. The prime characteristic that Oswald has inherited from his father is his 'joy of life', which is not of itself an evil thing; it becomes so only through the influence and constraints of society.

> Over there [in Paris] the mere fact of being alive is thought to be a matter of exultant happiness . . . I am afraid that all these feelings that are so strong in me would degenerate into something ugly here.

Ibsen's dramatic use of congenital syphilis is primarily as a symptom and a symbol of the insidious influence of provincial hypocrisy and narrow mindedness, just as Gerhart Hauptmann in *Before Dawn* (1889) uses hereditary alcoholism as a symptom of a rural society disrupted by sudden industrial change. Although Hauptmann was sufficiently impressed by the chilling tales of his Zurich medical friends to become a total abstainer at the time he was writing *Before Dawn*, his concern in the play was primarily environmental.

Ibsen saw the individual frustrated at all levels of society, including the narrow intimacy of the family. Nora's desperate efforts to find self-fulfilment in *A Doll's House* (1879) reflect the predicament of most women in a man-made society. Yet the play is not primarily concerned with women's emancipation as such: it is a study of the individual as victim of society's assumptions. When Nora's husband tells her 'Before all else, you are a wife and a mother', she replies 'I don't believe that any longer. I believe that before all else I am a reasonable human being'. Her complaint is that both her father and her husband have treated her as a child, discouraging the serious side of her nature by allowing her no initiative: 'I have existed merely to perform tricks for you . . . It is your fault that I have made nothing of my life'. And, significantly, when she decides to leave her husband and family, it is to 'try and educate myself'.

Even so, the position of women in Norway in the 1870s was arguably a particularly relevant case for Ibsen. The very recent growth of a Norwegian urban bourgeoisie removed its women from the active responsible role of a farmer's or landowner's wife, and immured them in a town home, where the housework was the responsibility of servants. Time hung heavy on their hands, giving them more than ample opportunity for reading and reflection on the frustrating nature of their lot. Yet, although Ibsen had been on friendly terms since 1870 with one of the leading feminist protagonists in Norway, he was at pains to avoid involvement in the various campaigns for votes and equal opportunities for women. In the last analysis, his views on the role of women were not so very different from George Eliot's (see p. 92). As he told the Norwegian Society for the Woman's Cause in 1898:

> I must reject the honour of having consciously worked for the woman's cause . . . For me it has been an affair of humanity . . . It is the women who shall solve the problem of humanity. As mothers they are to do it. And only *so* can they do it;
> it rests with the *mothers* by means of strenuous and protracted exertions to rouse a conscious sense of *culture* and *discipline*.

If this was not the sort of talk that the society members were hoping to hear, they could perhaps take some small consolation from Ibsen's earlier campaigns in Rome to get women given equal voting rights in the Scandanavian Club, to rescue it from 'men with . . . little thoughts . . . achieving certain little advantages for their own little and subservient selves': a Stockmannesque speech that provoked a captain of marines to consider challenging Ibsen to a duel.

Some books

The following suggestions are restricted to books that were found useful in compiling these chapters. Given the breadth of the subject, the list doubtless omits many that both specialists and non-specialists would regard as essential. Readers requiring a general bibliography of accessible books on Realism should turn to F. W. J. Hemmings (ed.), *The Age of Realism* (Penguin, 1974), pp. 387–401, or to those in the larger works listed below. (The editions listed are those used in the preparation of this book.)

Chapter 1 Beating the Bounds
(a) On the general issues posed by Realism, see Erich Auerbach, *Mimesis* (Princeton U.P., 1968), especially pp. 454–92; F. W. J. Hemmings (ed.), *The Age of Realism* (Penguin, 1974): a succinct survey that omits Britain and Realist drama; Damian Grant, *Realism* (Methuen, 1970): a brief discussion of the connotations of the term; Harry Levin, *The Gates of Horn: a study of five French Realists* (O.U.P., 1966).
(b) Readers interested in the antecedents to the Realist novel should look at Ian Watt, *The Rise of the Novel: studies in Defoe, Richardson and Fielding* (Chatto and Windus, 1957); Hemmings, *The Age of Realism* (Penguin, 1974), Ch. 1; Maximillian E. Novak, *Defoe and the Nature of Man* (O.U.P., 1963); Mark Kinkead-Weekes, 'Defoe and Richardson' in R. Lonsdale, *Dryden to Johnson* (Barrie and Jenkins, 1971); Henri Fluchère, *Laurence Sterne: from Tristram to Yorick. An interpretation of Tristram Shandy*, tr. Barbara Bray (O.U.P., 1965); Vivienne Mylne, *The Eighteenth-Century French Novel: techniques of illusion* (Manchester U.P., 1965); English Showalter, *The Evolution of the French Novel, 1641–1782* (Princeton U.P., 1972).

Chapter 2 The Shaping Forces of Society
(a) On society in Revolutionary Europe, see E. J. Hobsbawm, *The Age of Revolution, 1789–1848* (Mentor Books, 1964); Norman Hampson, *The First European Revolution 1776–1815* (Thames and Hudson, 1969); Alan Milward and S. B. Saul, *The Economic Development of Continental Europe 1780–1870* (Allen and Unwin, 1973); Norman Hampson, *A Social History of the French Revolution* (Routledge and Kegan Paul, 1966), especially Chs. 5 and 10; Alfred Cobban, *The Social Interpretation of the French Revolution* (C.U.P., 1964): an interesting critique which overstates its case; Jacques Godechot, *La Grande Nation*, 2 vols. (Aubier, 1956); André Fugier, *La Révolution Française et l'Empire napoléonien* (Hachette, 1954); F. M. H. Markham, *Napoleon* (Mentor Books, 1966).
(b) Relevant aspects of seventeenth- and eighteenth-century fiction are treated in the works listed under Section (b) of Chapter 1.
(c) On Stendhal, general studies include F. W. J. Hemmings, *Stendhal: a study of his novels* (O.U.P., 1964); Geoffrey Strickland, *Stendhal: the education of a novelist* (C.U.P., 1974); Levin, *The Gates of Horn* (O.U.P., 1966), Ch. 3; Auerbach, *Mimesis*

(Princeton U.P., 1968) pp. 454–92. See also the books listed under Section (c) of Chapter 3, notably the invaluable Francine Marill Albérès, *Le Naturel chez Stendhal*. On Stendhal's political views, see in particular his *Journal (1811–1823)*, Vol. V (Le Divan, 1937) and *Mémoires d'un Touriste*, 3 vols (Le Divan, 1929).

Chapter 3 Determinist Thought
(a) An invaluable reference work on individual thinkers is the *Dictionary of Scientific Biography* (ed. C. C. Gillespie), of which thirteen volumes have so far appeared (Scribner, 1970–6). There are many general surveys of seventeenth- and eighteenth-century thought; two of the more accessible are Peter Gay, *The Enlightenment: an interpretation*, Vol. II: *The Science of Freedom* (Knopf, 1969), and John H. Randall, *The Career of Philosophy*, Vol I: *From the Middle Ages to the Enlightenment* (Columbia U.P., 1962); see also the widely ranging chapter by A. V. Judges, 'Educational ideas, practice and institutions', *New Cambridge Modern History*, VIII, pp. 143–73. *Brett's History of Psychology*, edited and abridged by R. S. Peters (Allen and Unwin, 1953) is still useful.
(b) On individuals, see Aram Vartanian, *La Mettrie's L'Homme Machine. A study in the origins of an idea* (Princeton U.P., 1960); Georges Le Roy, *La Psychologic de Condillac* (Boivin, 1937); R. Lefèvre, *Condillac, ou la joie de vivre* (Seghers, 1966); D. W. Smith, *Helvétius. A Study in Persecution* (Clarendon P., 1965). The best study of the Idéologues, *faute de mieux*, remains the vintage Fr. Picavet, *Les Idéologues* (1891, repr., Franklin, 1971).
(c) Stendhal's intellectual formation may be followed in Francine Marill Albérès's admirable *Le Naturel chez Stendhal* (Nizet, 1956) and V. del Litto's *La vie intellectuelle de Stendhal. Genèse et évolution de ses idés (1802–1821)* (P.U.F., 1962). Particular aspects of his thought are dealt with in Francine Marill Albérès, *Stendhal et le sentiment religieux* (Nizet, 1956), Fernand Rude, *Stendhal et la pensée sociale de son temps* (Plon. 1967), and Jean Théodorides, *Stendhal du côté de la science* (Aran, Switzerland, Editions du Grande Chêne, 1972).
(d) The repercussions of determinist thought on earlier writers are examined notably in E. Novak, *Defoe and the Nature of Man* (O.U.P., 1963) and Henri Fluchère, *Laurence Sterne* (O.U.P., 1965). The series, *Diderot Studies* (Syracuse U.P., and Droz: ed. Otis Fellows) contains a number of articles relevant to Diderot's determinism and *Jacques le Fataliste*.

Chapter 4 Man and Beast
(a) On evolutionary thought, the *Dictionary of Scientific Biography* (Scribner, 1970–6) is always useful. See also Bentley Glass *et al.*, *Forerunners of Darwin, 1745–1859* (J. Hopkins P., 1959) and Théophile Cahn, *La Vie et l'oeuvre d' Etienne Geoffroy Saint-Hilaire* (P.U.F., 1962).
(b) On phrenology and physiognomy, the *Dictionary of Scientific Biography* (Scribner, 1970–6) is a painless source of information.
(c) The most readable substantial biography of Balzac is André Maurois, *Prometheus: the life of Balzac*, tr. Norman Denny (Penguin, 1971). For Balzac's work, see F. W. J. Hemmings, *Balzac: an interpretation of 'La Comédie humaine'* (Random House, 1967); Levin, *The Gates of Horn* (O.U.P., 1966), Ch. 4; Herbert J. Hunt, *Balzac's Comédie Humaine* (Athlone P., 1959); Bernard Guyon, *La Pensée politique et sociale de Balzac* (Armand Colin, 2nd edn., 1967): an especially useful study of the evolution of his ideas; Jean-Hervé Donnard, *Balzac. Les realités économiques et sociales*

dans la Comédie Humaine (Armand Colin, 1961); René Bouvier, *Balzac. Homme d'affaires* (Champion, 1930). Detail on particular issues may be gleaned from the articles in the various numbers of *Les Etudes balzaciennes* (1951–60) and in *L'Année balzacienne* (1960–   ).

Chapter 5   *Úne Société Embourgeoisée?*
(a) A useful introduction to nineteenth-century France is provided in J. P. T. Bury, *France 1814–1940* (Methuen, 1959). More specific studies include D. H. Pinkney, 'The Myth of the French Revolution of 1830', *A Festschrift for Frederick B. Artz*, eds. D. H. Pinkney and T. Rupp (Duke U.P., 1964), pp. 52–71; D. H. Pinkney, *The French Revolution of 1830* (Princeton U.P., 1972); and particular points of interest are discussed in Douglas Johnson, *Guizot* (Routledge and Kegan Paul, 1963), Chs. 1, 4 and 5.
(b) On other countries, see Hobsbawm, *The Age of Revolution* (Mentor Books, 1964); Milward and Saul, *The Economic Development of Continental Europe* (Allen and Unwin, 1973); Robert Schnerb, *Le XIX Siècle: l'apogée de l'expansion européenne* (P.U.F., 1955); F. B. Artz, *Reaction and Revolution, 1814–32* (Harper, 1963); T. S. Hamerow, *Restoration, Revolution and Reaction: economics and politics in Germany, 1815–1871* (Princeton U.P., 1958).
(c) On Balzac, see Section (c) of Chapter 4

Chapter 6   *Pessimism*
(a) There are many books on the repercussions of secularisation. Among the more readable are Owen Chadwick, *The Secularization of the European Mind in the Nineteenth Century* (C.U.P., 1975) and D. G. Charlton, *Secular Religions in France, 1815–1870* (O.U.P., 1963).
(b) On Büchner, see Maurice B. Benn, *The Drama of Revolt. A Critical Study of Georg Büchner* (C.U.P., 1976); Herbert Lindenberger, *Georg Büchner* (S. Illinois P., 1964); A. H. J. Knight, *Georg Büchner* (Blackwell, 1951); J. P. Stern, 'A world of suffering: Georg Büchner', *Reinterpretations. Seven Studies in Nineteenth-Century German Literature* (Thames and Hudson, 1964), pp. 78–155.
(c) On Germany in Büchner's time, see Hamerow, *Restoration, Revolution and Reaction* (Princeton U.P., 1958), Milward and Saul, *The Economic Development of Continental Europe* (Allen and Unwin, 1973.), Ch. 6.

Chapter 7   *More Pessimism*
(a) The most accessible and enjoyable biography of Flaubert is Enid Starkie's *Flaubert. The Making of the Master* (Penguin, 1971) and *Flaubert, the Master* (Weidenfeld and Nicolson, 1971). On his intellectual formation there remains René Dumesnil's ageing *Flaubert. Son hérédité, son milieu, sa méthode* (1906, repr. Slatkine, 1969) and *Gustave Flaubert. L'Homme et l'oeuvre* (Brouwer, 1932). Much can be learned from perusing his letters, *Oeuvres complètes de Gustave Flaubert. Correspondance*, 13 vols (Conard, 1926–54), with the help of Charles Carlut, *La correspondance de Flaubert. Etude et repertoire critique* (Nizet, 1968). See also Pierre Castex, *Flaubert: L'Education Sentimentale* (Centre de Documentation Universitaire, 1965); Levin, *The Gates of Horn* (O.U.P., 1966), Ch. 5.
(b) On France in Flaubert's time, see Theodore Zeldin, *France, 1848–1945*, Vol. 1 (Clarendon P., 1973); Roger Price, *The French Second Republic. A Social History* (Batsford, 1972); Bury, *France, 1814–1940* (Methuen, 1959) and Johnson, *Guizot*

(Routledge and Kegan Paul, 1963); F. W. J. Hemmings, *Culture and Society in France, 1848–1898. Dissidents and Philistines* (Batsford, 1971).

(c) An attractive, well-illustrated survey of Europe in these years is W. E. Mosse, *Liberal Europe. The Age of Bourgeois Realism 1848–1875* (Thames and Hudson, 1974). The significance of the 1848 revolutions in Europe as a whole is succinctly summarised in Charles Pouthas, 'The Revolutions of 1848', in *The New Cambridge Modern History*, Vol. X (C.U.P., 1960), pp. 389–415.

Chapter 8 *The Industrial Revolution*

(a) Among the innumerable books on the Industrial Revolution, the reader might look at *The Fontana Economic History of Europe*, Vol. 3: *The Industrial Revolution* and Vol. 4: *The Emergence of Industrial Societies* (Collins, 1973); David Landes, *The Unbound Prometheus. Technological Change in Western Europe from 1750 to the present* (C.U.P., 1969); E. J. Hobsbawm, *Industry and Empire* (Penguin, 1969); Phyllis Deane, *The First Industrial Revolution* (C.U.P., 1965); Milward and Saul, *The Economic Development of Continental Europe* (Allen and Unwin, 1973). The social consequences in Britain are examined in G. D. H. Cole and Raymond Postgate, *The Common People, 1746–1946* (Methuen, 1961).

(b) The literary reflection of industrialisation is briefly surveyed in Raymond Williams, *Culture and Society 1780–1950* (Penguin, 1963), notably Pt. I, Ch. 5.

(c) On Mrs Gaskell, see J. G. Sharpe, *Mrs Gaskell's Observation and Invention. A Study of her Non-Biographic Works* (Linden P., 1970); Arthur Pollard, *Mrs Gaskell. Novelist and Biographer* (Manchester U.P., 1965); Edgar Wright, *Mrs Gaskell. The Basis for Reassessment* (O.U.P., 1965).

(d) On George Eliot, see the books listed under Chapter 9.

Chapter 9 *A Modus Vivendi?*

The most perceptive and stimulating book on Eliot's thought is Bernard Paris, *Experiments in life: George Eliot's quest for values* (Wayne State U.P., 1965). The best biography is Gordon S. Haight, *George Eliot* (O.U.P., 1968), who has also edited the well-indexed *The George Eliot Letters*, 7 vols (O.U.P., 1954–6). Eliot's determinism is ably summarised in Neil Roberts, *George Eliot. Her beliefs and her art* (Elek, 1975). See also David Daiches, *George Eliot: Middlemarch* (Arnold, 1973); Thomas Pinney, 'More leaves from George Eliot's Notebook', *Huntingdon Library Quarterly*, xxiv (August 1966); Peter Jones, *Philosophy and the Novel* (Clarendon P., 1965), Ch. 1 ('Imagination and Egoism in *Middlemarch*').

Chapter 10 *Russia and the Realist Response*

(a) Brief surveys of Russian history can be found in Lionel Kochan, *The Making of Modern Russia* (Penguin, 1963) and Nicholas Riasonovsky, *A History of Russia* (O.U.P., 1963). The best detailed account is Hugh Seton-Watson, *The Russian Empire 1801–1917* (O.U.P., 1967). See also the invaluable collection of essays contained in C. E. Black, *The Transformation of Russian Society: aspects of social change since 1861* (Harvard U.P., 1967). Protest in Russia is examined in E. Lampert, *Sons against Fathers. Studies in Russian Radicalism and Revolution* (O.U.P., 1965) and Franco Venturi, *The Roots of Revolution. A History of the Populist and Socialist Movements in 19th Century Russia* (Weidenfeld and Nicolson, 1960).

(b) Turgenev's ideas are examined in Henri Granjard, *Ivan Tourguénev et les courants politiques et sociaux* (Institut d'Etudes Slaves de l'Université de Paris, 1966) and

Isaiah Berlin's evocative lecture, *Fathers and Children. Turgenev and the liberal predicament* (Clarendon P., 1972). Readable biographies include David Magarshack. *Turgenev* (Faber, 1954) and Avrahm Yarmolinsky, *Turgenev. The man, his art and his age* (Collier, 1961).

Chapter 11 Experience versus the Intellect
(a) The fullest biography in English is Henri Troyat, *Tolstoy*, tr. Nancy Amphoux (Penguin, 1970). On Tolstoy's ideas, see the following works by Edward B. Greenwood, *Tolstoy: the Comprehensive Vision* (Dent, 1975); 'The Unity of *Anna Karenina*', Landfall, No. 58 (June 1961); 'Tolstoy, Wittgenstein, Schopenhauer. Some connections,' *Encounter* xxxvi, No. 4 (April 1971). See also Peter Jones, *Philosophy and the Novel* (Clarendon P., 1965) Ch. 2 ('Action and Passion in *Anna Karenina*') and Tolstoy's *A Confession* tr. Aylmer Maude (World's Classics, 1921).
(b) On Tolstoy's Russia, see the books listed in section (a) of Chapter 10; and Edward C. Thaden, *Conservative Nationalism in 19th century Russia* (U. Washington P., 1964).

Chapter 12 La Bête Humaine
(a) On evolutionary thought, see the *Dictionary of Scientific Biography* (Scribner, 1970–6); Jay M. Savage, *Evolution* (Holt, Rinehart, 1963); D. J. Merrell, *Evolution and Genetics* (Holt, Rinehart, 1962). See also R. L. Schoenwald, *Nineteenth-Century Thought: the discovery of change* (Prentice-Hall, 1965).
(b) General outlines of Naturalism include Pierre Cogny, *Le Naturalisme* (P.U.F., 1968); René Dumesnil, *Le Réalisme et le Naturalisme* (del Duca, 1962); Lilian Furst and Peter Skrine, *Naturalism* (Methuen, 1971).
(c) On Zola, see F. W. J. Hemmings, *Emile Zola* (O.U.P., 2nd edn. 1966), and Levin, *The Gates of Horn* (O.U.P., 1966), Ch. 6. Zola's view of Man is examined in Henri Martineau, *Le Roman scientifique d'Emile Zola* (Baillière, 1907). See also Section (b) of Chapter 14.
(d) For Chekhov, see Section (a) of Chapter 13.
(e) On Ibsen, see Section (b) of Chapter 15.

Chapter 13 The Ubiquitous Doctor
(a) The most useful survey of Chekhov's Realism remains W. H. Bruford, *Chekhov and his Russia. A sociological study* (Routledge, 1948). Biographies include Ronald Hingley, *A New Life of Anton Chekhov* (O.U.P., 1976), and David Magarshack, *Chekhov. A life* (Faber, 1952). See also R. L. Jackson (ed.), *Chekhov. A collection of critical essays* (Prentice-Hall, 1967).
(b) On Chekhov's Russia, see the books listed under Section (a) of Chapter 10.
(c) Gerhart Hauptmann is the subject of Leroy R. Shaw's *Witness of Deceit. Gerhart Hauptmann as critic of society* (U. California P., 1958).
(d) On Ibsen, see Section (b) of Chapter 15.

Chapter 14 The Dismal Science
(a) Economic changes are surveyed in *The Fontana Economic History of Europe*, Vols 3 and 4 (Collins, 1973); Landes, *The Unbound Prometheus* (C.U.P., 1969); *New Cambridge Modern History*, Vol. XI (C.U.P., 1962), Ch. 2 ('Economic Conditions'); Christian Ambrosi and M. Tacel, *Histoire économique des grandes puissances à l'époque contemporaine* (Delagrave, 1963).

(b) Zola's response to economic issues is examined in Guy Robert, *La Terre d'Emile Zola. Etude historique et critique* (Société d'Editions Les Belles Lettres, 1952); Richard H. Zakarian, *Zola's 'Germinal'. A critical study of its primary sources* (Droz, 1972); Ida Frandon, *Autour de 'Germinal': le mine et les mineurs*(Droz, 1955); Elliott Grant, *Zola's 'Germinal': a critical and historical study* (Leicester U.P., 1962); Colin Smethurst, *Emile Zola: Germinal* (Arnold, 1974). See also the books listed in Section (c) of Chapter 12.

(c) On economic and social conditions in Russia see the books listed in Section (a) of Chapter 10.

(d) For Chekhov's response to economic issues, see the books listed in Section (a) of Chapter 13.

Chapter 15 *Society versus the Individual*

(a) On the increase of government control in society, see the following chapters in the *New Cambridge Modern History*, Vol. XI (C.U.P., 1962): Ch. 1 ('Introduction') Ch. 4 ('Social and political thought'), Ch. 7 ('Education'), Ch. 8 ('The armed services'), Ch. 9 ('Political and Social Developments in Europe'), Ch. X ('The German Empire'), Ch. XI ('The French Republic'), Ch. XX ('International relations'). See also Landes, *The Unbound Prometheus* (C.U.P., 1969).

(b) Ibsen's reactions to these issues are discussed in Brian W. Downs, *Ibsen—The intellectual background* (C.U.P., 1946). The best biography is Michael Meyer, *Ibsen. A Biography* (Penguin, 1974). See also Halvdan Koht, *Life of Ibsen* (Blom, 1971); Janko Lavrin, *Ibsen* (Methuen, 1950).

(c) On Fontane, see Joachim Remak, *The Gentle Critic. Theodor Fontane and German Politics, 1848–1898* (Syracuse U.P., 1964); J. Dresch, *Le Roman social en Allemagne (1850–1900)* (Alcan, 1913); J. P. Stern, 'Realism and Tolerance: Theodor Fontane' in *Re-interpretations. Seven studies in Nineteenth-Century German Literature* (Thames and Hudson, 1964).

(d) On Fontane's Germany, see Gordon Craig, *The Politics of the Prussian Army, 1640–1945* (O.U.P., 1964); Pierre Bertaux, *La vie quotidienne en Allemagne au temps de Guillaume II* (Hachette, 1962); A. J. P. Taylor, *Bismarck* (New English Library, 1968); A. J. P. Taylor, *The Course of German History* (Methuen, 1961); Michael Balfour, *The Kaiser and his times* (Penguin, 1975).

Chapter 16 *Hope and Despair*

(a) On Social Darwinism, see Schoenwald, *Nineteenth-Century Thought* (Prentice-Hall, 1965) and *The New Cambridge Modern History*, Vol. XI, Ch. 4 (C.U.P., 1962).

(b) On Zola, see the books listed in Section (c) of Chapter 12 and Section (b) of Chapter 14.

(c) On Hauptmann, see Shaw, *Witness of Deceipt* (U. California P., 1958.)

(d) On Ibsen, see Section (b) of Chapter 15.

Index